FINANCING AND MANAGEMENT OF HIGHER EDUCATION IN INDIA

FINANCING AND MANAGEMENT OF HIGHER EDUCATION IN INDIA

The Role of the Private Sector

Prof. J.L. AZAD
(Collabration with Ramesh Chandra)

GYAN PUBLISHING HOUSE
NEW DELHI-110002

Financing and Management of Higher Education : The Role of the Private Sector-An In-depth Study

ISBN: 978-81-212-1067-6

Published in 2010 in India by
Gyan Publishing House
23, Main Ansari Road, Darya Ganj,
New Delhi-110002
Phones : 23282060, 23261060
Fax : 011-23285914
E-mail: books@gyanbooks.com
Website: www.gyanbooks.com

Laser Type Setting by: Rudra Computer Graphics, Delhi
Printed at : Gian Ridhi Offset Printers, Delhi

Contents

Appendix

Acknowledgements

The authors express their profound gratitude to Professor B.P. Khandelwal, Director, NUEPA, who not only agreed to provide infrastructural and other academic facilities at the National Institute of Educational Planning and Administration (now University), but also provided guidance at various stages of the study. Our thanks are also due to Professor M. Mukhopadhyay for his help and encouragement to the research team. We are indebted to Professor G.D. Sharma for allowing us to use his papers/notes, particularly relating to WTO and GATS. Professors J.B.G. Tilak and Sudha Rao gave their suggestions/views about the various aspects of the study, for which we are extremely grateful.

We express our sincerest thanks to Prof. Furqan Qamar of the Jamia Millia Islamia, Dr. Manju Narula and Dr. Geetha Rani of NUEPA for providing very competent and ungrudging academic support which involved analysis and interpretation of huge financial and other data as also preparing drafts of the relevant chapters relating to the study.

We are beholden to Dr. T.N. Dhar and Dr. K.L. Gandhi, who offered us unstinted help at all stages of the study. They gave very useful comments/suggestions about the contents of the Report. But for their help, we would not have been able to finalise the Report within the time frame given to us.

We are also thankful to the eminent respondents – vice chancellors, academics, educational administrators and representatives of the industry, who gave us their well considered views/suggestions about the variegated problems of private participation in higher education and other related issues.

We are extremely grateful to Professor K. Venkatasubarmanian, former Member, Planning Commission, Professor Satya Bhushan, Professor K.B. Powar, Shri M.K. Kaw, and distinguished members of the NUEPA Faculty, who participated in the Seminar to consider the draft Report of the Study and offered useful suggestions relating to various issues raised in the Report.

The authors are obliged to NUEPA staff particularly, Miss Nirmal Malhotra, who ungrudgingly provided the relevant literature, Reports and Journals relating to the study. We are also beholden to Mrs. Deepak Makol, Shri N.D. Khandpal, and Shri Parshuram, who gave us access to the Reports and other relevant documents concerning this study.

We express our gratitude to various officers in the Administration and Finance Departments of NUEPA for facilitating our work at the University.

We are also grateful to Shri Soumen Panja, Shri Shankar Singh and Shri Mohan Lal for offering us very competent computer assistance as also drawing up graphs, diagrams and figures relating to the study.

We shall be failing in our duty if we do not offer our sincerest thanks to Shri Sudhir Dagar of NUEPA for providing very efficient, competent and ungrudging assistance in redrafting and updating the Report. He single handedly completed the task of redrawing the figures and graphs in the light of the updated data. His contribution to the finalisation of the study is monumental and it is difficult to find appropriate words to express our gratitude to him.

1

Introduction

The system of higher education in India, as also in other countries of the world, is subjected to an inexplicable ambivalence on the part of the government as well as the society. It is extolled as a crucial factor for survival; for it provides people with "an opportunity to reflect on the critical, social, economic, cultural, moral and spiritual issues facing humanity" (National Policy on Education, 1986). It is also considered as a potent instrument for producing scientific and technical manpower of the highest calibre. The Punnayya Committee (1994) has rightly said that for India, to attain the cutting edge of technology, it is institutions of higher learning that offer hope. Further, they provide an excellent opportunity of vertical mobility to the deprived sections of society.

Higher education has also been facing sharp criticism for its apparent inability to provide education relevant to the needs and aspirations of the ever-escalating numbers of seekers of knowledge. It has also been castigated as the exclusive preserve of the elitist groups who are, generally, alienated from the socio-cultural mores of the country of their origin. It is quite often contended that the system of higher education has developed an in-built process of metabolic degeneration in that quite a large number of students entering the portals of university institutions are thrown by the way side resulting in a huge loss of human and financial resources. The phenomenon of ever escalating unemployment and under-employment of educated youth in the developing countries has further aggravated the situation, giving rise to its outright, but undeserved, condemnation in these words: "the whole process of higher education has become warped, dysfunctional, producing a number of unemployable young men and women". (The Challenge of Education, 1985).

In the welter of denunciations, it is conveniently forgotten that institutions of higher education have been inundated by never-ending streams of young men and women aspiring to get university degrees, quite a few of whom are ill-prepared, on account of poor schooling facilities, to benefit from higher education. It is also not appreciated that a number of universities have become hot-beds of political intrigues, which have severely undermined their autonomous character and sapped their capacity for free and unfettered intellectual inquiry. Further, these institutions have been subjected to an unprecedented financial squeeze, which has afflicted the system since the early seventies and does not yet seem to be loosening its stranglehold.

Higher education in the erstwhile British Colonies, particularly India, is facing a 'crisis of identity' in that it has become heterogeneous in complexion, size and quality. The quality could not be maintained because of the absence of proper planning and adequate academic and physical facilities. In spite of concerted efforts at structural reorganisation, it has not developed a personality of its own. The institutional pattern is marked by a sort of academic stratification: a few financially viable institutions co-existing with the vast multitude of what may be called academic "ghettos" perennially afflicted by paucity of resoruces. The bulk of affiliated colleges. (which are responsbile for a sizeable proportion of student enrolment on the Indian sub-continent) do not appear to be of much concern to the governments and hence do not seem to be a significant part of the academic configuration. Even the University Grants Commission (UGC) has abandoned about half of these colleges by describing them as academically non-viable institutions and ineligible for its assistance. This underlines the pathetic academic condition of these colleges mainly affiliated to some of the state universitites. It is worth-while to mention that India still needs more expansion in higher education because, out of over one billion people in the country, only 6 per cent of the relevant age group study in colleges and universities. Further expansion, however, would have to proceed in a systematic and planned manner, keeping in view the availability of physical and academic facilities.

The causes of educational morass are complex and varied. The unregulated institutional expansion, the lack of a firm policy about student admissions, particularly in general education courses, the some-what irrelevance of university curriculum to socio-economic milieu of the country, the antiquated methods of teaching, the stifling strangle-hold of examination system and continuing paucity of physical and financial resoruces could be mentioned as the main causative factors of the malady afflicting the university education system. Any improvement of higher education would, therefore, call for a multi-dimensional approach.

Resource Crisis – A World Wide Phenomenon

The severe resource crunch in education as also in higher education is not peculiar to the developing countries. It is a worldwide phenomenon of escalating enrolments chasing shrinking resources. As reported in a World Bank Study (1992) : "Through the 1970s, enrolments consistently expanded at a fast rate than public resources devoted to higher education.

While in African countries enrolments expanded at an average rate of 13.5 per cent and real resources expanded 4.1 per cent per year; in Latin America, enrolments grew 12.9 per cent per year, resources increased by 5.2 per cent. Similar trend occurred in Asia, France and Middle East. Indeed separate data on Asia alone show that while enrolments continued growing 6.8 per cent per year, real resources contracted by 4.8 per cent per year." There is, therefore, need for the governments to allocate larger resources for this sector. It is also necessary for institutions of higher education to take steps for mobilizing additional resources from other than government sources. It is in this context that, among others, contribution from private bodies assumes significance.

Commonwealth Countries

An analytical study of the budgetary position of education and higher education in some Commonwealth countries reveals a depressing scenario. For example, Pakistan and Bangladesh are facing a severe resource crisis, which has adversely affected their capacity to provide adequate finances for institutions of higher education. The position of Sri Lanka, Britain and Canada is equally disturbing. A synoptic review of two countries; one 'developing' and the other 'developed', follows:

Sri Lanka

There has been a marked diminution in the budgetary resources available for education in Sri Lanka. From 4.3 per cent of the G.N.P. in 1966, the total resources for education plummeted to slightly more than 3 per cent of G.N.P. in 1984-85. Further, in spite of increase in the budgetary allocations for higher education from 12 per cent to 20 per cent during the period under review, the universities are facing a serious resource crisis. As pointed out by Clark & Neave (1992): "The greatest constraint for higher education planning is the inadequacy of financial resources. Therefore, both public and private sectors have to be included in the planning process. The private sector has not only to supplement the limited resources of the public sector, but also to establish links between the employers and the higher education institutions, making higher education planning socially and economically more meaningful and purposive .....".

Britain

British universities have faced a serious financial squeeze since 1980s. According to Gareth Williams (1994) : "Continued stringency in public funding of higher education is as near certain as it is possible to be in any prediction of the future. There has been a fall of over 30% in public funding per student since 1980. Higher education institutions will continue to be faced with a choice between quality decline, increase in teaching input per member of staff, organizational improvement, the use of cost-reducing technology or increasing income from sources other than the Funding Councils. Persuading government to change its mind is not a plausible alternative."

The imbalance between escalating enrolments and the quantum of resources being provided for higher education has been succinctly brought out by Shattock (1995): "In Britain, the number of students (in universities) increased by two thirds (68 per cent) between 1982 and 1992. Numbers rose by 11 per cent between 1991 and 1992 and by a further 6 per cent between 1992 and 1993. But since 1980, public expenditure per home student has fallen by 30 per cent...."

The Fall Out

The world wide resource crisis and the improbability of the governments being in a position to provide adequate resources has forced governments to think of alternative methods of financing of higher education. In India, the

University Grants Commission and the All India Council for Technical Education appointed two committees, (1993, 1994) which, among other things, made suggestions about mobilization of additional resources. The New Economic Policy launched in 1990 with its accent on economic liberalization, decentralization, decontrol, foreign equity participation and privatization has, put the seal of acceptability on, among other things, pro-active participation of private bodies in the management and financing of higher education.

An extreme, though illogical, corollary of the new economic policy could be the dismantling of the state machinery for administration, financing and regulation of educational institutions, particularly those providing higher education. To be specific, it would allow market forces to determine the size of student enrolment, establishment of new institutions and expansion of existing institutions, determining the curricula and methods of teaching and laying down the amount of cost recovery from students besides tapping other sources of revenue. In fact, it would mean leaving the field primarily to private sector. That the government is ostensibly considering involving private bodies in higher education is substantiated by the fact that a bill for setting up of private universities has been introduced in the Indian Parliament. Further, one of the newly constituted states in India has allowed the establishment of a number of private universities without adequate infrastructure.

Private financing of higher education, imposing user charges or permitting the establishment of fee charging private institutions, has been suggested in a World Bank Study (1992). The reasons advanced for this suggestion are:

i) "It will resolve financial problems (of universities) and will ensure that resources are proportional to number;
ii) Its potentially adverse effect on equity within the sub-sector is blunted by the fact that most students at this level came from relatively advantaged social background;

iii) It will encourage efficiency in the use of resources as providers become accountable to students; and

iv) In a market oriented economy, tuition income will give institutions important signals about employment demand..."

We do not intend to enter, at this stage, into an argument with the World Bank study except stating that not all the points made by the Bank would stand the test of critical scrutiny.

British Response

The British response to the continuing resource crisis has been a shift from producer domination to consumer sovereignty. According to Williams (1994): "The transformation has been dramatic. Within ten years, the students have been metamorphosed from apprentices to customers and their teachers from master craftsmen to merchants. Funding formulae were developed between 1988 and 1993, which expressly linked finance to student numbers and research output. Very few resources are available to individuals and groups that do not contribute to saleable output in this sense."

The financial management structure has been drastically overhauled. The ageing University Grants Committee was unceremoniously replaced by the Universities Funding Council (UFC) on the basis of the recommendations of the Croham Committee (1987). For a couple of years, the U.F.C. co-existed with the Polytechnics and Colleges Funding Council (P.C.F.C.). The method of funding evolved by the U.F.C. through 'bid system' and 'guide prices' met with a storm of protests from the academic community. As a result, the U.F.C. was replaced in 1993 by three Higher Education Funding Councils (H.E.F.Cs.); one each for England, Scotland and Wales. The Councils have evolved elaborate formulae to provide grants for teaching and research. It is also the statutory responsibility of the Councils to ensure that quality of higher education is assessed in all institutions it funds through Quality Assessment Committee (QAC). In the case of research, the quality is assessed by a Research Assessment Exercise (RAE) by peer review and the quantum of funds determined on that basis.

Another aspect of the Economic Policy is the accent on Globalisation with its concomitant emphasis on, among other things, the unrestricted entry of foreign universities in the developing countries including India. Under the present WTO regime, it is difficult to come out of the emerging socio-economic and educational scenario that is fast developing all over the World. It is, however, necessary to study the impact of 'internationalisation' of higher education and to identify steps needed to mitigate its adverse effects.

Need for the Study

The preceding analysis has brought to focus the serious resource crunch, which has overtaken the system of higher education in most of the developing and developed countries. It is also apparent that the financial squeeze has come to stay for quite sometime and therefore it has impelled the various countries to think of finding alternate sources of funding institutions of higher education. An easy escape route is the privatization and marketisation of higher education. "Underlying the proposal for a market oriented approach and the privatization of educational provision is the reality of a reduced funding base for education. This is particularly evident in case of countries in which relative economic standing and programmes have deteriorated steadily." (International Encyclopaedia of Education, 1994).

It is, therefore, necessary that the nature and extent of involvement of private sector in establishing, funding and managing institutions of higher education should be critically examined. It would also be necessary to find out the likely impact of privatization on institutions of higher education, particularly with reference to the twin objectives of equity and excellence. It will give us an insight into the manner and extent to which private participation could be promoted, keeping in view the continuing financial crunch that the university system is facing. The likely effects of globalisation and its corrollary of internationalization of higher education will also need to be examined.

The Conceptual Framework

Education has been recognized as a unique investment in man. It is instrumental in accelerating the process of socio-economic and cultural development. Higher education, being at the apex of the educational system, is an essential input for meeting the manpower requirements of the highest calibre in crucial areas of national development. It is also an important contributory factor for ensuring social justice by providing vertical mobility to deprived sections of society by making higher levels of knowledge accessible to them and, in the process, improving the quality of life of the nation as a whole.

The crucial role of higher education, as enunciated above, underlines the importance of providing adequate resources for its maintenance and development. With this end in view, the governments have been providing financial support to the university system. This system of funding has taken a variety of forms in a number of countries. The predominant system has been termed as 'negotiated funding' in which allocations are made on the previous years' expenditure with some incremental additions based on a formula. In some countries 'input funding' has been introduced under which a relationship is sought to be established between costs and efficiency. This entails cost consciousness and accountability. A supplementary system is 'project funding', through which finances are provided for specific research programmes.

In the recent past, the governments are moving towards involving private bodies in the financing and management of higher education. As already stated, an extreme formulation of privatization could mean complete dissociation of state with the management and financing of higher education and allowing the market forces to determine the establishment and expansion of institutions, appointment of faculty, development of curriculum, laying down costs of education and determining sources of financing of educational institutions.

This is based on the assumption that it will enhance efficiency of the system when the government buys academic services from producers or subsidizes students to buy them. Further, to the extent the private sector takes up the responsibility of managing higher education, the government will be relieved of its responsibility. It has also been claimed that higher education enhances the earning capabilities of students and, therefore, it is, unnecessary for the government to subsidize their education.

Complete privatization of higher education is still at the conceptual stage. In most of the countries, there is co-existence of public and private sectors. In some countries, like Japan, Republic of Korea, Philippines and Latin American Countries, mass private and restricted private sectors have developed, while in most countries of South Asia, including India, Africa and Western Europe, mixed system dominated by public sector exists. In some countries, like the Netherlands and Belgium, both co-exist under public funding. Countries with limited private sector involvement are Sweden, United Kingdom, France, Spain, Thailand etc. In very few countries, universities have been established as corporate bodies, with shares being bought and sold over the stock exchanges.

In actual fact, it is difficult to categorize the institutions of higher education into watertight compartments of public and private sectors. A "private" institution may be receiving substantial funds from government, while a "public" institution may be generating large resources for its sustenance. Similarly, both government and private bodies may participate, in varying degrees, in the management of institutions.

There are two significant issues, which permeate the university education system regardless of the patterns and procedures of its funding. An important, but seemingly contradictory phenomenon, relates to accountability vs. autonomy of the system. The accountability aspect has assumed considerable significance since mid-seventies, when the universities had to undergo prolonged periods of financial squeeze. The questions that merit deeper probing are: whether public accountability of university institutions will erode their autonomy? Whether it will stultify freedom of thought, which is important for the flowering of intellect? What are the parameters of accountability, which will not dilute the academic freedom of the universities?

Another related issue is equity-excellence syndrome. To what extent can the concept of equity be applied without devaluing excellence. In an era when equality of opportunity is the guiding principle of the democratic polity, how can it co-exist with excellence, which implies nurturing the intellect of the top few?

It would be too optimistic to claim that a study of the type contemplated will find answers to these questions, which are of fundamental significance to university education system. There is, however, need for an in-depth study of the system of financing and management of higher education in order to see the effectiveness of various systems evolved by different countries and to suggest a system most suited to university institutions.

Review of Literature

During 1970s and 1980s, several studies have been completed on problems and prospects of university finances.

These studies have highlighted the problems of finances arising mainly due to expansion and growth. Raj (1970), Malik (1971), Bose (1971), Mukherji (1971), Naqvi (1971), Gautam (1972), Deshmukh (1972), Sharma (1977) focused on the problems emanating from the growth in enrolment for higher education. Shah (1967), Singh (1974), Jayaraman (1974), Kaul (1974) probed the role of the state government in the context of deteriorating conditions of quality of higher education. Kamath and Panchamukhi in their various contributions have discussed some aspects of higher education during the post-independence period and also highlighted the deepening financial crises facing higher education in India, and referred to the unplanned growth of higher education. The financial position of the universities in India during 1970s and 1980s itself, is characterized as one of shrinking resource base, leading to a crisis or near-crisis situation. (Tilak, 1988).

The studies conducted during 1990s generally relating to funding of and mobilization of additional resources for higher education system. Azad (1975, 1982, 1989) examined the system of financing of higher education with particular reference to the system of grant-in-aid by the state governments. He suggested the adoption of effective measures for the development of system of government support based on the principles of equity, specificity, adequacy, elasticity, promotional, efficiency and academic freedom. Azad (1999) laid emphasis again on the increasing need for the same in the changing economic conditions. Tilak (1993) examined several policy alternatives, including student fees, student loans, graduate tax and privatization. Nanjundappa (1994) suggested universities to mobilise resources from philanthropists and also stressed the need of linkages with industries to raise resources for universities. He also emphasised the need for giving recoverable loans rather than outright grants to students. Sharma and Qamar (1990) highlighted the factors responsible for inefficiency because of under-utilization of resources in higher education system. According to Garg (1994) raising resources by university from its own sources (student fees and other receipts) will not go beyond a certain limit. The present arrangement of grant-in-aid system needs drastic changes in terms of activities and programmes to fine-tune autonomy and accountability as complementary and mutually reinforcing processes and not as management devices.

Bray (1998) mentioned that many higher education institutions now solicit donations from alumni; many encourage professors to undertake consultancy services; and some are moving into direct business ventures. Further he added that Vietnam is among the countries in which higher education institutions have been forced by escalating costs and inadequacy of revenues from the government to earn independent incomes. On the contrary, Singapore has a strong economy and has had continued government budgetary support to higher education. Even in Singapore, however, the 1990s underlined a philosophy that higher education institutions should develop their own sources of revenue and reduce dependence on the government. Azad and Dhar (1994) analysed the budgetary position of central universities, deemed to be universities and Delhi colleges in the aftermath of the report of UGC Committee under Justice Punnayya (1993). Tilak et. al (2000) brought out a study on the resources and expenditure pattern of selected universities in India, particularly depicting the changing pattern of finances, after the economic reforms policies were introduced.

Raghena Thaw (2000) suggested that financial requirements to upgrade the infrastructure of the institution of higher education can be met by setting up Higher Education Finance Corporation (HEFCI) of India. Its role would be to promote and aid the growth of institutions in the fields of science, engineering, technology, medicine and management. He suggested that HEFCI be capitalized with a corpus fund of about

Rs.500 crore, leveraged suitably with long-term credit in the form of educational bonds. These bonds would enjoy tax free status i.e. 100 per cent tax exemption for donations to academic institutions of national standing. It would be an alternate mechanism of government's commitment to higher education without direct involvement.

Some studies in India indicate that universities and colleges are not suffering from want of funds but from resource mismanagement. Singh (1971), Sharma (1978), UGC (1979-80), Sharma and Qamar (1990), Narula (2000) highlighted the factors responsible for inefficiency because of under-utilization of resources in higher education system.

Objectives of the Study

The basic objectives of the study are:

1. To examine the contribution made by the private sector including industrial and commercial houses, in establishing, financing and management of institutions of higher education,
2. To suggest measures for promoting larger partnership of private bodies in higher education without diluting the autonomy of the universities as also ensuring equity and excellence in the system.

The study addresses the following questions:

1. What are the sources of finance available to university institutions and the relative contribution by government, local bodies, fees and other charges etc. ?
2. What techniques are adopted to raise additional resources? In this context, to discuss the methods of introducing an efficient and equitable system of cost recovery as also the extent to which outright grants may be replaced by repayable loans.

3. What is the role of government, specialized bodies, non-government organizations and private sector in the financing and management of higher education?
4. What is the impact of globalisation on education, particularly with reference to internationalization of higher education?
5. How to ensure equity without sacrificing excellence?
6. What will be the impact of privatization and marketisation of higher education on access, efficiency and equity in higher education?
7. What changes should be brought about in the policies of funding and management of higher education in order to ensure an integrated development of the institutions of higher education?

Methodology

(i) Questionnaires

(a) A structured questionnaire was drawn up to elicit the views of a select body of academicians, scholars and administrators about the various aspects of private participation in higher education. Another questionnaire aimed at soliciting the views of representatives of industrial houses. The issues about which the opinions/views were solicited included:

(i) The nature and level of privatization of higher education.
(ii) Industry-university relationships.
(iii) Corporatisation of university education.
(iv) Marketisation of higher education.
(v) Self-financing colleges; and
(vi) Internationlisation of higher education in the context of globalisation of economy.

A copy each of the Questionnaires is placed in the appendices. It may be mentioned that out of about 200 academics and administrators, who were approached, only 41 condescended to respond.

(b) Data Schedule : The data about university finances were sought to be obtained from the universities. For this purpose, a detailed data schedule was sent to universities i.e., central, state and deemed to be universities. The information asked for was in respect of year of establishment, teaching and non-teaching staff, income; recurring and non-recurring; expenditure; break up of salaries of teaching and non-teaching staff; student welfare services etc. for the years 1996-97 and 2001-02. The universities were also requested to indicate whether any effort to mobilize additional resources has been made during the years under study. The information received from the universities was as follows:

In all 29 universities responded. Besides Aligarh Muslim University (AMU) which is a Central University, three Deemed to be Universities and 25 State Universities' responses were analysed. Among the State Universities, the region-wise position was: Central-7, Northern-3, North-Eastern-4, Western 4 and Southern-7. Eastern-Nil. In quite a few universities, information on various items was neither accurate nor internally consistent. Further, information received from some universities was incomplete. For such universities, annual reports and budgets of the particular year were consulted and the information was analyzed and interpreted meaningfully. Attempt was made to analyse the pattern of financing of universities of different types in India, with particular reference to various sources of income and expenditure.

The sources of income were classified into:

- Government Grants: Central Government, UGC, AICTE, etc., State Governments and Local Bodies.
- Tuition fees.
- Internal sources.

- Other sources.

The pattern of expenditure of universities was analyzed by classifying the expenditure into:

- Direct Teaching Costs,
- Indirect Teaching Costs,
- Student's Welfare Schemes,
- Examinations, etc.

The direct teaching costs consist of teaching, non-teaching inputs. The indirect teaching costs consist of library, laboratory, publications etc. Student welfare activities consist of hostel, scholarships, students' support/welfare. The pattern and procedures of university finances have been analyzed to examine sources of finances in terms of per student cost. Also overall surplus or deficit budget is calculated to examine the financial health of universities.

Non-Government Sources of income:

- Student fees of various types,
- Endowments/donations;
- Income from schemes like fellowships, project grants, consultancy services etc.

Secondary Sources

These sources include mainly the annual budgets, annual statements of income and expenditure and the annual reports of universities under study. The other sources of data used in this study are various documents and reports of the Government, published by the Ministry of Human Resource Development, Planning Commission, University Grants Commission etc. In addition to published books, research papers and articles, and studies about economics and financing of higher education have also been looked into.

Delimitations

1. It is largely a macro-level and primarily library-based study. The financial position of universities has, however, been examined in depth.

2. Time series data about higher education finance for the last 5 years have been subjected to a critical review.
3. The study relates mainly to general education.

Problems Encountered

The main problem encountered in carrying out this study was the reluctance of some of the high and mighty of the academic and industrial world to give a written response to the various questions posed to them. They were willing to enter into a dialogue with the research team, but to put their views in black and white was not acceptable to them. Even some of those, who were gracious enough to accept our request to give their views in writing, seemed to have lost their patience in between and either did not respond to some questions or responded to them partially. At times, the response was in 'telegraphic' language, which could not be precisely deciphered. The response from the representatives of the industrial and commercial houses was equally disappointing. Out of 25 who were approached, only 5 responded. Out of 5, only two responses were of use to us.

The responses from the universities were also not very encouraging. The total number of university institutions that supplied information is only 29, with Eastern Region choosing to be blacked out. An analysis of the responses revealed inconsistent and incomplete data. It was therefore decided to supplement the data with the information available in their annual reports/ budgetary documents, which most of the universities made available on our request. In quite a few cases, however, even that information was not complete.

In spite of all these problems, which generally characterize questionnaire based studies, an attempt has been made to analyse and interpret the data and to draw meaningful conclusions.

2

Financing of Higher Education

The system of higher education in India as also in other countries of the world is facing a serious resource crisis, which does not appear to show any sign of abatement in the foreseeable future. This is evident from an inexplicable, but seemingly calculated, indifference on the part of the government to provide adequate financial support for the system. The rapidly dwindling financial outlays made available for this otherwise much acclaimed sector since early seventies are an eloquent testimony to the implicit indifference on the part of central and state governments. The nadir was reached in early nineties, when higher education was described as a 'non-merit' good for which the government had little responsibility of funding. 'Self financing' and 'privatisation' became important components of government policy towards higher education. This view found an echo in a Report (2000) of the PMs' Task Force consisting of representatives of two industrial houses, who recommended, among other things, limiting UGC's role to liberal and performing arts, privatisation of higher education and market orientation of the existing educational institutions. The underlying idea of this *volte-face* was that the government should gradually withdraw from financing of higher education and leave its funding and management to private bodies or to the universities themselves.

In the back drop of this grim scenario confronting higher education, it is proposed to make a critical analysis of financing of higher education in the post-independence period in order to identify changes that have occurred in the patterns and procedures of its financing as also to suggest measures for augmenting resources for this important sector. The analysis will be undertaken in three parts:

Part I – The Behaviour of Educational Finance: Centre and States

Part II – Financing of Higher Education

Part III – Mobilising Resources

Part I – The Behaviour of Educational Finance

(1) All India

There has been a rapid growth in educational expenditure in India since independence. In 1950-51, an amount of Rs.114 crore was spent on education. According to the latest estimates, the total government expenditure on education was Rs. 97,547 crores in 2005-2006. If the expenditure incurred on education by departments other than the departments of education (central and states) is also included, the total budgeted expenditure on education and training would amount to Rs. 1,20,347 crores. This works out to about 3.9 per cent of the Gross National Product (GNP).

1.1 Expenditure on Education by Centre and States

Table 2.1 (p. 31) indicates the break-up of expenditure incurred by central and state governments:

It would be seen that while there has been about 11 times increase in over all expenditure on education by education departments, the expenditure by the central government increased about 28 times as against about 10 times by state governments It may also be stated that while the percentage expenditure incurred by the central and state governments was in the ratio of about 7:93 in 1970-71, the central share of

Table 2.1: Expenditure on education by education departments and other departments

(Rs. Crores)

	Centre		States		Total	
	Education Depts.	*Total expenditure by all Depts.*	*Education Depts.*	*Total expenditure by all Depts.*	*Education Depts.*	*Total expenditure by all Depts.*
1970-71	659.40	659.40	8,284.10	9,048.90	8,943.50	9,708.30
1975-76	1,261.00	1,730.70	16,830.00	19,121.40	18,091.00	20,852.10
1980-81	2,239.00	3,128.50	31,503.00	36,924.10	33,742.00	40,052.60
1985-86	5,285.00	9,151.80	69,284.70	81,591.60	74,569.70	90,743.40
1990-91	1,644.21	2,420.45	15,819.62	18,340.88	17,463.83	20,761.33
1995-96	3,317.53	5,551.02	28,789.66	33,217.67	32,107.19	38,768.69
1996-97	3,672.61	6,314.83	33,018.69	37,901.31	36,691.30	44,216.14
1997-98	4,716.65	7,860.16	38,023.96	44,444.85	42,740.61	52,305.01
1998-99	6324.30	9676.52	45341.55	52342.98	51665.85	62019.50
1999-00	7318.66	11145.81	57812.01	66399.97	65130.67	77545.78
2000-01	8385.96	12817.30	56898.68	65419.24	65284.64	78236.54
2003-04	10177.47	17100.77	63519.84	72630.67	73697.31	89731.63
2004-05	13228.74	21139.04	73358.84	84319.84	79210.62	91418.06
2005-06	18337.04	26998.77	79210.62	91418.06	97547.66	120346.83

Source: Trends of Expenditure on Education and Analysis of Budgeted Expenditure on Education, MHRD for various years.

Table 2.2: Expenditure on Education by Centre and States

(Rs. Crores)

	1984-85 (Actuals)	*Percentage of Edn. Exp. to Total Budget*	*1995-96 (Actuals)*	*Percentage of Edn. Exp. to Total Budget*	*2005-2006 (Budgeted)*	*Percentage of Edu. Exp. to Total Budget*
Centre						
Revenue	445.32	1.60	5550.52	3.97	28928.75	6.48
Capital	0.07	0.00	0.02	0.00	0.00	0.0
Loans and Advances	0.35	0.00	0.50	0.00	0.00	0.0
Total	**445.74**	**1.60**	**5551.07**	**3.05**	**28928.75**	**5.62**
States/ Union Territories						
Revenue	5908.46	20.20	32627.57	22.30	90101.12	19.58
Capital	60.21	1.40	379.06	2.01	1300.49	0.19
Loans and Advances	8.74	0.30	211.04	2.56	16.47	0.12
Total	**5977.41**	**16.40**	**33217.67**	**19.15**	**103118.08**	**8.48**
Total: Centre and States/UTs						
Revenue	6353.78	11.00	38178.09	13.40	119029.88	13.13
Capital	60.28	0.50	379.06	1.04	1300.49	0.17
Loans and Advances	9.09	0.10	211.54	0.64	16.47	0.10
Total	**6423.15**	**7.80**	**38768.69**	**10.90**	**120346.84**	**7.19**

Source: Analysis of Budgeted Expenditure on Education for 1984-85, 1995-96 and 2005-2006.

expenditure rose to about 22 per cent of the total expenditure in 2005-06. This shows increasing investment on the part of the central government in education over the years. Much of the central government expenditure in 2005-06 is on account of the Sarva Shiksha Abhiyan (SSA)

1.2 Expenditure on Revenue and Capital Account

Table 2.2 (p. 32) indicates the break-up of expenditure under Revenue and Capital account incurred by the central and state governments:

As is obvious from the table, bulk of expenditure on education is on revenue account in case of both union and state governments. There was slight increase in the percentage of expenditure on capital account; from 0.5 per cent to a little over one per cent during the period 1984-85 and 1995-96. In 2005-2006, however, the percentage of expenditure on capital account came down to an all time low of about 0.17 per cent. There was sizeable reduction in the percentage expenditure on loans and advances.

(2) States

2.1 Although education has been included in the Concurrent List of the Seventh Schedule of the Indian Constitution, state governments remain the main agencies for administration and financing of educational programmes, particularly at the school stage. While the overall proportion of revenue budget being spent on education was 13.13 per cent, (except for Sikkim) most states were spending more than the average percentage indicated above of their revenue budget on education. There were, however, sizeable variations among the states. Table 2.3 (p. 34) indicates state-wise position.

Jammu and Kashmir, having spent 12.98 per cent of its revenue budget on education, had the dubious distinction of being the lowest among the major states in terms of educational expenditure. In contrast, Maharashtra was spending over 25 per cent of its revenue budget on education. Curiously enough, Punjab, among the economically advanced states was spending a lowly 13.25 per cent of its budget on education.

Table 2.3: Percentage of Expenditure on Education to Total Revenue Budget – State-wise – 2004-05

Below 10	*10-15*	*15-20*	*20-25*	*25 & above*
Sikkim (9.18)	Arunchal Pradesh (12.43)	Orissa (15.63)	Gujarat (20.66)	Maharashtra (25.33)
	J & K (12.98)	Himachal Pradesh (17.28)	Jharkhand (20.90)	
	Punjab (13.25)	Goa (17.38)	Kerala (20.96)	
	Nagaland (14.18)	Mizoram (17.98)	Rajasthan (21.08)	
	Andhra Pradesh (14.30)	Karnataka (17.99)	Delhi (24.42)	
	Pondicherry (14.46)	West Bengal (18.52)	Uttaranchal (24.73)	
		Meghalaya (18.53)	Chhatisgarh (25.01)	
		Assam (18.82)		
		Tamil Nadu (19.16)		
		Manipur (19.19)		
		Uttar Pradesh (19.45)		
		Madhya Pradesh (19.46)		
		Bihar (19.82)		

(Figures in parentheses indicate percentages).

The figures for different states relate to 2004-05 except for Goa, Orissa Maharashtra, Manipur, Mizoram, Nagaland, Tripura, U.P., Uttaranchal, West Bengal, Delhi which relate to 2003-04)..

Source: Analysis of Budgeted Expenditure on Education, 2003-04 to 2005-2006; Ministry of Human Resource Development (MHRD), 2006.

2.2 *States' Investment in Education*

In order to find out the position of states' investment in education in relation to their economic capacity to spend on education, as reflected in the State Domestic Product, the State Governments were classified in terms of these two variables. Table 2.4 sums up the position:

Table 2.4 : Percentage Total Budget on Education and Training (Rev.) to States Net Domestic Product

Below 2	*2-5*	*5-10*	*10 and above*
Delhi (1.61)	Andhra Pradesh (2.61)	Bihar (7.64)	Mizoram (10.03)
	Haryana (2.73)	Assam (8.0)	Sikkim (17.90)
	West Bengal (2.75)	Arunachal Pradesh (8.78)	
	Punjab (3.06)		
	Gujarat (3.18)		
	Goa (3.64)		
	Maharashtra (3.68)		
	Tamil Nadu (3.79)		
	Madhya Pradesh (3.89)		
	Orissa (4.28)		
	Uttar Pradesh (4.32)		
	Chhatisgarh (4.37)		
	Rajasthan (4.45)		
	Jharkhand (4.74)		
	Nagaland (4.79)		

Source: Analysis of Budgeted Expenditure on Education, 2005-2006; Ministry of Human Resource Development (MHRD), 2006.

It would be seen that most of the states spent between 2-5 per cent of their Net Domestic Product on Education. In this connection, it may be stated that the Education Commission (19064-66) had proposed that the centre and states may provide about 6 per cent of their Net Domestic Product on Education. This has not been achieved so far even after over 40 years of the recommendation made by the Commission.

Relationship Between States' Investment in Education and State Domestic Production (SDP)

The relationship between the per capita expenditure on education, overall and sectoral, and per capita state domestic product (SDP), was sought to be examined statistically by

Table 2.5 : Rank Coefficients of Correlation (r) between per capita SDP of States and the per capita Expenditures on Education - Total Education, Elementary, Secondary and Higher Education

Year	*SDP & Total Education*	*SDP & Elementary Education*	*SDP & Secondary Education*	*SDP & Higher Education*
1960-61	0.78	0.50	0.63	0.74
1965-66	0.63	0.39	0.71	0.58
1970-71	0.65	0.42	0.73	0.43
1975-76	0.71	0.42	0.82	0.37
1980-81	0.56	0.30	0.54	0.19
1990-91	0.81	0.41	0.83	0.84
1996-97	0.62	0.26	0.72	0.64

Source: For 1960-61 to 1980-81, see J. L. Azad: Government Support for Higher education and Research, (1984). For Subsequent Years, Calculations were made on the basis of data taken from Selected Educational Statistics for the relevant years. For SDP, data were collected from Government's Economic Surveys for various years.

working out Rank Co-efficients of Correlation between the two variables. The underlying assumption was that there would be a positive relationship between the two variables. Table 2.5 explains.

It would be seen that:

(i) there is a significant correlation between per capita expenditure on education as a whole and per capita State Domestic Product, although the relationship has fluctuated over the years;

(ii) the relationship between the two variables in regard to elementary education appears to be less significant, apart from the fact that the coefficient has declined substantially over the years, contradicting the current assumption that states are giving high priority to elementary education;

(iii) there is significant relationship between the two variables so far as secondary education is concerned; and

(iv) although the coefficient in respect of higher education has been quite significant, there has been a steep decline in the relationship between the two variables between 1961 and 1981.

To sum up, it could be stated that there is an overall positive relationship between states' economic capacity and expenditure on education in spite of some states not providing financial inputs consistent with their economic development. The dwindling relationship between these two variables in regard to elementary education should be a cause for concern and needs further investigation.

2.3 Extent of Variation

The extent of variation among the variables indicated by coefficients of variations is indicated page 38:

It would be evident that:

1. The variation in the per capita SDP increased during the years 1980-81 and 1990-91. Thereafter, it has declined substantially.

Table 2.6: Coefficients of Variation between per capita SDP and the per capita Expenditure on Education as well as its components

Year	*Per Capita SDP*	*Per Capita Expenditure on Education*	*Per capita Expenditure on*		
			Elementary Education	*Secondary Education*	*Higher Education*
1960-61	19.22	32.07	42.69	50.10	48.00
1965-66	29.48	24.40	30.50	37.50	28.52
1970-71	24.62	27.26	46.52	45.97	31.09
1975-76	22.20	33.67	39.00	46.33	34.38
1980-81	32.31	34.48	38.93	47.33	30.97
1990-91	34.00	46.00	31.00	73.00	60.00
1996-97	23.00	40.00	33.00	63.00	43.00

2. The largest variation was in case of secondary education: 50 per cent in 1960-61, increasing to 63 per cent in 1996-97. Similar increase occurred in the case of education as a whole.
3. In case of higher education, position has been quite irregular. The coefficients of variation declined from 48 per cent in 1960-61 to an all time low of about 29 per cent in 1965-66. Thereafter, there has been a steady increase, with 1990-91 recording a high of 60 per cent. This plummeted to 43 per cent in 1996-97.

The preceding analysis indicates that while state SDP is a major determinant (or should be) of the quantum of its investment in education as a whole, it has very little influence on sectoral allocations. Further, no definite trend is discernible in the provision of intra-sectoral resources over the years. There are wide variations among the states in this regard.

Distribution of Expenditure by Levels of Education

The table below indicate the distribution of educational expenditure by levels of education for the period extending from 1990-91 to 2005-06.

Table 2.7 : Distribution of Expenditure of Various Levels of Education: State and Union Territories (Percentages)

	Elementary			*Secondary*			*Higher*		
	1990-91	*1999-2000*	*2005-06*	*1990-91*	*1999-2000*	*2005-06*	*1990-91*	*1999-2000*	*2005-06*
Direction Inspection and Administration	2.4	2.4	3.08	2.30	1.38	2.63	0.8	1.1	1.19
Assistance to Govt. Schools or Colleges	37.5	49.5	41.40	32.9	32.46	34.72	22.2	25.1	22.65
Assistance to Private Schools or Colleges	25.9	21.4	21.10	51.7	53.45	46.05	45.0	47.3	44.58
Assistant to Local Bodies	22.7	22.2	26.94	7.5	7.37	8.8	-	-	-
Assistance to Universities	-	-	-	-	-	-	29.2	25.5	30.14
Teacher Training	6.5	0.3	0.22	0.8	0.43	0.43	-	-	-
Non-Formal Education	0.5	0.1	0.98	0.7	0.17	0.51	-	-	-
Scholarships	-	0.2	0.10	0.2	0.12	0.21	0.6	0.15	0.27
Text Books	-	0.3	0.30	0.8	0.34	0.37	-	-	-
Others	4.5	3.6	5.88	3.6	4.28	6.78	2.1	0.89	1.17
Total (Rs. In Lakhs)	7729	27905	3973224	5154	20844	2611748	1836	8248	106851

Source : Analysis of Budgeted Expenditure on Education for Various Years.

It would be noted that bulk of government expenditure on various sectors of education is for the establishment and maintenance of educational institutions. There is very little expenditure on qualitative development i.e. for Teacher Education, Scholarships, Text Books etc. This is a cause of concern and needs to be looked into.

World wide Disparities in Educational Investment

The disparities observed in the quantum of investment in education in different states is not peculiar to India; it seems to be a world-wide phenomenon. This is indicated, among other things, by a comparison of percentages of educational expenditure in different continents to the total world expenditure with corresponding percentages of enrolment to the total world enrolments and per capita and per student expenditures.

Table in **Appendix I** indicates per capita, per student public expenditure on education (in US dollars), and the percentage expenditure and percentage enrolment in various continents as also for the world as a whole. The following points need highlighting:

1. In terms of per capita and per student expenditure, African Continent occupies the lowest position; the range being $41 for Africa and $982 for Europe in 1994. Africa is also the lowest in per student expenditure ($231.42) and Oceania the highest: ($3631.78).
2. There are wide disparities in expenditure on education in terms of student enrolment in different countries of the world. In 1994, the developing countries accounted for 77.18 per cent of the world enrolment, while the percentage of world expenditure was as low as 15.54 per cent. Asian countries accounted for 58.28 per cent of world enrolment, while the percentage of world expenditure incurred by these countries was as low as 22.72.
3. Over the years, there has been down-sliding of expenditure in the developing countries. In 1980, the percentages of world enrolment and expenditure in these countries stood at 73.05 and 19.67 respectively. By 1994, while the

developing countries accounted for 77.18 per cent of the world enrolment, their share of world expenditure declined to 15.54 per cent.

It would be unfair to be critical of developed countries for the large disparity that exists between developing and developed countries of the world in terms of educational expenditure. Investment in education is determined largely by the state of economic development, which signifies the capacity of countries to spare funds for education and priority that they give to education. The fact that developing countries are faced with unenviable situation of accelerating enrolments chasing dwindling resources is, however, a cause of major concern for these countries.

Part II – Financing of Higher Education

It is proposed to examine the financing of higher education:

(a) in successive five years plans, and

(b) in terms of overall sectoral expenditures.

(a) Expenditure in Plans

An analysis of financial outlays for various sectors underscores their changing fortunes. Table 2.8 (p. 42) sums up the position.

The following may be noted:

1. There has been decline in overall percentage of outlays provided for education upto the Seventh Plan. Thereafter, the position has improved somewhat. In the First Plan (1951-56), 7.9 per cent of total plan outlay was provided for education. Thereafter, after a continuous downslide, the position started improving with Ninth Plan registering a percentage of 6.22; still far short of the position in the First Plan.
2. Elementary education stated with a formidable percentage of 56 in the First Plan. Thereafter, there was a sharp downward trend with the so-called Plan-holiday (1966-69) registering an all time low of 23 per cent. Thereafter,

Table 2.8: Plan Expenditure on different Sectors of Education (Percentages)

(Rs. in million)

	First Plan	*Second Plan*	*Third Plan*	*Plan Holi-day*	*Fourth Plan*	*Fifth Plan*	*Sixth Plan*	*Seventh Plan*	*Plan Holi-day*	*Eighth Plan*	*Ninth Plan* (Outlay)*
	1951-56	*1956-61*	*1961-66*	*1966-69*	*1969-74*	*1974-89*	*1980-85*	*1985-90*	*1990-92*	*1992-97*	*1997-2002*
Elementary Education	**56**	**35**	**34**	**23**	**30**	**36**	**33**	**37**	**37**	**49**	**51**
In million rupees	850	950	2010	750	2390	3170	8360	28490	17290	124237	273630
Secondary Education	**13**	**19**	**17**	**16**	**18**	**18**	**21**	**24**	**22**	**23**	**19**
In million rupees	200	510	1030	530	1400	1560	5300	18320	10530	57889	100167
Adult Education	**NA**	**NA**	**NA**	**NA**	**NA**	**NA**	**9**	**6**	**9**	**6**	**2**
In million rupees	NA	NA	NA	NA	NA	NA	2240	4700	4160	14144	11075
Higher Education	**9**	**18**	**15**	**24**	**25**	**23**	**22**	**16**	**12**	**9**	**8**
In million rupees	140	480	870	770	1950	2050	5590	12010	5880	23614	44807

(Contd.)

(Contd. Table 2.8)

	First Plan	*Second Plan*	*Third Plan*	*Plan Holi-day*	*Fourth Plan*	*Fifth Plan*	*Sixth Plan*	*Seventh Plan*	*Plan Holi-day*	*Eighth Plan*	*Ninth Plan* (Outlay)*
	1951-56	*1956-61*	*1961-66*	*1966-69*	*1969-74*	*1974-89*	*1980-85*	*1985-90*	*1990-92*	*1992-97*	*1997-2002*
Others	**9**	**11**	**12**	**11**	**13**	**12**	**4**	**3**	**2**	**4**	**11**
In million rupees	140	300	730	370	1060	1060	1080	1980	1180	9081	57783
Technical Education	**13**	**18**	**21**	**25**	**13**	**12**	**11**	**14**	**17**	**10**	**9**
In million rupees	200	490	1250	810	1060	1070	2730	10830	8230	25174	47786
Total	**100**	**100**	**100**	**100**	**100**	**100**	**100**	**100**	**100**	**100**	**100**
In million rupees	**1530**	**2730**	**5890**	**3230**	**7860**	**8910**	**25300**	**76330**	**47270**	**254139**	**535248**
% of Total Plan Outlay	7.86	3.83	6.87	4.84	5.17	3.27	2.70	3.50	4.20	4.90	6.20

Source: Government of India Plan Documents and Union Budget Documents for various years. Figures for Ninth Plan obtained from Planning Commission.

** Information about the approved outlay for various sectors (except elementary education) in the states is not available. The figures have been extrapolated on the basis of the outlays proposed by the state governments for various sectors.*

there has been a gradual rise culminating into 51 per cent of the Plan allocations being earmarked for this sector in the Ninth Plan.

3. Secondary education, starting with a modest percentage of 13 in the First Plan, reached an all time high of 24 per cent in the Seventh Plan. Thereafter, however, there has been a steep decline with Ninth Plan recording a modest percentage of 19.
4. Higher education also started with an insignificant 9 per cent in the First Plan. The Fourth Plan recorded an all time high of 25 per cent, whereafter, there has been a continuous downward trend, culminating into a lowly percentage of 9 in the Eighth Plan. In the Ninth Plan, the percentage outlay plummeted to an all time low of 8 per cent.
5. The case of technical education is no different. From 13 per cent of the outlay provided for this sector in the First Plan, the percentage went up to 21 in the Third Plan, (which corresponded to the post Chinese incursions period). Thereafter, however, there has been a steep downward trend with Ninth Plan registering only 9 per cent for this sector.

(b) Over all Sectoral Expenditure

The same picture emerges, when sectoral expenditures are considered for selected years. Table 2.9 (p. 45) indicates the plan and non-plan expenditure during the period 1986-87 to 2006.

Table 2.9 there has been sizeable increase in percentage of expenditure in respect of elementary education. From an overall percentage of 43.3 in 1986-87, the percentage escalated to about 53 in 2005-2006. This is because of substantial increase in the plan outlays i.e., from 35.3 per cent in 1986-87 to about 69 per cent in 2005-2006. There was marginal reduction in the percentage outlay provided for secondary education i.e., from 31.5 per cent, it came down by about 2.0 percentage point to 29.28 in 2005-2006. There has, however, been substantial reduction in Plan outlays provided for university education,

Table 2.9 : Plan and Non-Plan Outlays/ Expenditure: Centre and States

(Figure in percentages)

	1986-87 (Actual)			*1991-92 (Actual)*			*2005-06 (Budgeted)*		
	Plan	*Non-Plan*	*Total*	*Plan*	*Non-Plan*	*Total*	*Plan*	*Non-Plan*	*Total*
Elementary Edn.	35.3	44.5	43.3	37.1	44.9	43.8	68.93	47.52	52.95
Secondary Edn.	20.2	33.3	31.5	25.1	32.2	31.2	11.46	35.40	29.28
Adult Edn.	3.4	0.2	0.6	8.7	0.3	1.5	1.35	0.11	0.42
University Edn.	15.2	14.2	14.3	10.3	13.7	13.2	5.52	13.01	11.11
Physical Edn, Sports and Youth Welfare	2.3	1.2	1.3	0.3	0.1	0.1	0.04	0.06	0.05
Other Programmes/ Language Edn.	11.9	3.1	4.4	4.9	5 4	5.4	6.51	0.90	2.32
Total (General Education)	88.3	96.5	95.4	86.4	96.6	3.2	93.81	97.00	96.13
Technical Education	11.7	3.5	4.6	13.6	3.4	4.8	6.19	3.00	3.87
Total Education	**100.00**	**100.00**	**100.00**	**100.00**	**100.00**	**100.00**	**100.00**	**100.00**	**100.00**

Note: *Outlays for 'Languages' have been merged with Secondary Education.*

which was reduced from 15.2 per cent in 1986-87 to 5.2 per cent in 2005-2006.

The non-plan expenditure on secondary education has remained almost stable - i.e., in the realm of about 33-35 per cent. In case of university education, there has been a reduction of about 1 percentage points during the period under review. In case of technical education, there has been substantial reduction in the percentages under plans. There was some reduction in the percentage expenditure under the non-plan head also. Physical education, sports etc. also got reduced outlays during the period under study.

(c) Share of Public Expenditure on Higher Education in GDP and Overall Expenditure

The following table indicates the share of expenditure on higher education in the GDP as well as the overall expenditure on education:

Table 2.10: Share of Public Expenditure on Higher Education in GDP and Education Expenditure

Year	*Expenditure (Revenue) as percentage of GDP*	*Expenditure on Higher Education as Percentage Expenditure on all Sector*	*Expenditure on Higher Education Percentage of GDP*
1	2	3	4
1990-91	3.84	2.70	0.77
1991-92	3.80	2.58	0.75
1992-93	3.72	2.59	0.73
1993-94	3.62	2.54	0.71
1994-95	3.56	2.50	0.69
1995-96	3.56	2.43	0.65
1996-97	3.53	2.42	0.64
1997-98	3.49	2.32	0.62
1998-1999	3.85	2.52	0.69
1999-2000	4.25	2.95	0.86

Year	*Expenditure (Revenue) as percentage of GDP*	*Expenditure on Higher Education as Percentage Expenditure on all Sector*	*Expenditure on Higher Education Percentage of GDP*
1	2	3	4
2000-01	4.33	2.96	0.89
2001-02	3.84	2.31	0.69
2002-03	3.79	2.34	0.70
2003-04	3.50	2.13	0.62
2004-05 (RE)	3.68	2.30	0.66

Source: Selected Educational Statistics, 2005-06, Ministry of HRD, New Delhi (P.105).

It would be noted that there has been diminution in the percentage of educational expenditure in relation to Gross Domestic Product during 1990-2005. Similar diminution has also occurred in the expenditure on higher education as percentage of over all expenditure as also of the Gorss Domestic Product. It is notworthy that the period under study corresponded to the post Reforms period. This substantiates the view that the government has not been very enthusiastic about providing adequately for education as also for higher education. It has already been stated that this negates the recommendation made by the Education Commission (1964-66) to provide 6 per cent of the GDP for education.

The Impact of Inflation

It has also been noticed that there has been erosion of the real expenditure on higher education because of the ever increasing inflationary tendencies. The following table indicates the down slide in the real expenditure on higher education as indicated in the per student expenditure.

It would be seen that during the 12 year period between 1991 and 2003, the real per student expenditure was reduced by about 26 per cent. This, along with the dwindling proportion of expenditure for education over the years, particularly after the Fourth Plan period, should be a cause of concern.

Table 2.11: Public Expenditure on Higher Education

Year	*In Current Prices*	*In 1993-94 Prices*	*Index*
1990-91	5652	7676	100.00
1994-95	7329	6687	87.12
1997-98	7793	5692	74.15
2000-01	10543	6367	82.95
2002-03	9692	5666	73.81

Source: Based on Analysis of Budgeted Expenditure on Education for various years.

(Adapted for J.B.G. Tilaks' Report of the CABE Committee on Financing Higher and Technical Education, 2005).

Part III – Mobilizing Resources

Inadequate Investment

In the preceding analysis, problems relating to financing of higher education and the role of the central and state governments has been briefly discussed. In the context of providing financial support to university institutions, it has been pointed out that the total investment in education, though sizeable, is inadequate to meet the ever-rising needs of education, including higher education. Further, there has been a continuous erosion in the real value of investment in education because of the spiralling inflation, which has overtaken Indian economy.

The governments' priorities have also undergone significant changes with higher education no longer being high on its agenda despite its crucial role in national development, particularly, at a time when scientific and technological research and development determines the pace of growth.

In this none-too-comfortable situation, there is need for augmenting resources for education as also for higher education.

Before making suggestions in this regard, it would be pertinent to examine the quantum of investment in education as a whole in terms of two variables: (i) educational expenditure as a percentage of the GDP and (ii) educational expenditure as a percentage of overall expenditure on all sectors.

Educational Expenditure as Percentage of GDP

It has been contended that one of the important factors responsible for the inadequacy of resources for education as also for higher education is the inability or unwillingness of the government – both central and states – to provide an adequate share of GDP for educational development. The share of expenditure on education as percentage of GDP has not even reached four much less six as recommended by the Education Commission more than four decades ago.

Table in Appendix-II indicates the percentage of GDP spent on education during the period 1961-62 to 2004-05. It would be seen that the percentage remained less than 2 during the first decade i.e. 1961-62 to 1969-70, signifying that the Education Commission's recommendation that 6 per cent of the GDP should be spent on education did not make any tangible impact on the allocation of resources. Even in the next decade, during 1970-71 and 1980-81, it remained in the realm of 3 per cent. Thereafter, it has remained less than four percent except for the years 1999-2000 and 2000-2001 when it touched a figure of four percent. This, is however, inadequate to meet the burgeoning requirements of an ever-rising enrolment at different levels of education and the urgent need to enhance quality and relevance of education. This is cited as the root cause of the sluggish rate of educational development and also lack of quality in education. Ironically, the Education Commission's recommendation has been accepted by the Government of India and reiterated in the National Policies on Education and in successive five years plans. The issue under consideration is of national significance and deserves to be examined in depth.

It is an indisputable fact that, inspite of spending large amounts on education, year after year, the quality of education has been deteriorating. The large drop-out rates at the elementary education stage, the continuing wastage at the secondary and higher education stages in terms of about 50 per cent of students failing to make the grade, are indicative of the deep malaise that afflicts the educational system. Further, the successive educational surveys conducted by National Council of Educational Research and Training (NCERT) have highlighted the deteriorating physical and academic infrastructural facilities available with educational institutions.

While we would welcome a larger percentage of GDP being spent on education, we would like to examine the question in a wider context, that is the appropriateness of earmarking a *specified* proportion of GDP for a particular sector. While not going into the merits of the case, it does not appear to be prudent to insist on providing a specified percentage of GDP even for an important sector like education without assessing the needs of other sectors, which are equally starved of resources. It also does not appear to be an economically viable proposition to provide a large quantum of resources without having undertaken an objective assessment of needs and the spending capacity of the education sector. In case, earmarking of specific proportion of GDP for various sectors becomes an accepted method of resource allocation, we may end up in an economically unenviable position of piercing through the ceiling of 100 per cent!

It would be logical not to insist upon an ad hoc percentage of GDP being earmarked for education. The allocations of resources should be based on realistically assessed needs of education in the context of requirements of other sectors, the capacity of the system to effectively and meaningfully utilise the amounts provided and the ability of the economy to provide resources of that order. Further, it would also be necessary to mobilise community support for education.

International Experience

The experience of the international community is an indicator of the validity of the above argument. **Appendix III**

Table 2.12: Educational Expenditures in Selected Countries

Country	*Year*	*Educational Expenditure as percentage of GNP*	*As percentage of Total Government Expenditure*
South Africa	1986	6.0	15.8
	1996	8.6	14.9
	2005	5.3	NA
Canada	1970	8.6	17.8 (1975)
	1994	6.9	12.9
USA	1985	4.9	15.3
	1994	5.4	14.4
	2005	5.6	15.5
China	1970	1.3	4.3
	1996	2.3	12.2 (1993)
	2005	NA	NA
India	1970	2.6	10.7
	1998-99	3.7	11.6
	2005	3.8	NA
Israel	1970	5.7	8.1
	1994	4.9	12.3 (1993)
	2005	NA	NA
France	1970	4.8	24.9
	1996	6.0	10.9
	2005	5.4	NA
Russia	1970	3.9	NA
	1996	3.0	NA
	2005	3.8	11.5
Australia	1970	4.1	13.3
	1995	5.5	13.5
	2005	4.9	NA

(Figures in parentheses indicate the years)

Source: UNESCO, Statistical Year Book, Various Year.

indicates the quantum of educational expenditure as percentage of GNP for some selected countries. It would appear that it is difficult to discern any consistent trend. The following Table 2.12 is illustrative:

It would appear that, barring South Africa, no country was spending more than 6 per cent of their GNP on education. Even the USA, one of the most advanced countries of the world, was spending 5.6 per cent of its GNP on education.

The following points need emphasis:

1. Educational expenditure should be determined by felt needs and not on the basis of a pre-determined percentage of GNP
2. Utilisation of resources, is also important in this regard, because it determines the capacity of the system to gainfully utilise the investment.
3. Community should be encouraged to provide resources for education. Absolute dependence on the state would not be conducive to the proper development of education.
4. Costs of education should be partly shared by the beneficiaries/utilisers of educated manpower.

(ii) Educational Expenditure as a Percentage of Overall Expenditure

Appendix II indicates the percentage of expenditure on education as a whole in terms of the overall expenditure. It would appear that, in spite of yearly fluctuations, there has been overall increase in the percentage of educational expenditure in terms of the overall expenditure. From a percentage of 10 in the first decade 1961-71, with minor fluctuation for some years, the percentage oscillated between 12 and 13 in the decade ending 2005-06. In the intervening years, 1998-99 to 2000-01, it reached a figure of a little over 14 per cent.

It could be concluded that no set pattern is discernible in the percentages over the four decades under study, signifying that the allocation of resources for education depends more on the availability of resources for each year rather than on fixed percentage of allocation of resources.

Dwindling Private Resources

The problem of inadequacy of government funding of higher education has been accentuated by the fast dwindling private contribution to investment in education in the post independence period. In 1950-51, government, including local bodies, contributed about 68 per cent of total resources for education. By 1992-93 (for which authentic information is available) the government contribution had increased to over 94 per cent of the total expenditure. Perceptible decline has occurred in the case of income from tuition fees (from about 20 per cent to about 3 per cent) and endowments and other sources (from 11.6 per cent to about 3 per cent). It is quite apparent that unless some special measures are taken, these two sources can virtually be written off even as modest contributors to funding of education as also of higher education.

Measures for Raising Resources

Some of the measures, which could be adopted for raising additional resource for education, are discussed below:

Student Fees

At the outset, it is proposed to examine the recommendations of the various committees set up by the UGC on resource generation through revision of fees, so that income from them becomes an important source of financing higher education. There are a variety of views for promoting student funding (through fees) as a method of financing higher education. The arguments in favour of a hike in fees include:

- When nation needs to achieve universal elementary education and total literacy and lacks funds for education, it becomes imperative to provide adequate resources for that sector even by diverting resources from higher to primary levels of education. Higher education should be financed largely by student funding through fees. Thus, increase in fees may augment the required funds for the cash-starved institutions of higher education, as government does not have adequate resources to finance higher education.

- Expenditure on higher education will have to be borne by the society. The affluent sections should bear reasonable cost of higher education in the form, among other things, of fees which reflects both ability of, and willingness to, pay for education.
- Since private rates of return to higher education are said to be high, an individual needs to finance his or her own education either from his present or future income. Further, it is argued that subsidies to higher education are regressive in nature, redistributing the income from the poor to the rich. This requires that subsidies to higher education should be reduced and eliminated in the long run.
- Higher fees would improve internal efficiency of the system as fees are adequately and regularly realised and therefore students inevitably pursue their academic goals more seriously. An increase in fees would be viewed as a mark of respectability to the system in so far as higher fees give prominence to an institution and is also helpful in making institutions and their personnel and clientele accountable.
- It is generally perceived that fees are extremely low and have not been revised for decades and need to be revised and adjusted to inflation and also revised periodically in accordance with the rise in costs of higher education.
- Differential fee has the merits of enhancing recovery of expenditure, removing subsidy from those who are in a position to pay and enabling the financially weaker students to undertake professional and higher studies.

The arguments against hike in fees include:

- While 'Education For All' goals provide the foundations of a nation, higher education determines the nature and level of its economic and technological development, particularly in the context of developing a knowledge society. Further, it needs to be realised that all levels of education are inter-dependent and, that an organic relationship exists among them. Indeed, the quality of primary and secondary education itself depends on the quality of higher education.

- Hike in fees would lead to elitism in higher education since high fees will force the poor not to opt for higher education or seek higher education of an indifferent quality such as that offered in poor quality colleges.
- High fees would accentuate inequities in the system as children from high income groups would spend more and be able to make more advantageous choices while children from low-income families would spend less and therefore would have to be content with the leftovers.
- Hike in fees is advocated on the basis of full cost recovery or no-profit-no-loss principles, which treatsS education just like any other commodity. This is contrary to the nature and philosophy of education. It also ignores the aspects of human capital investment.
- Except in case of tuition fee, other forms and kinds of fees are already high and are increasing substantially.

Though, there have been strong arguments for and against student funding, various committees and the government have clearly recommended a substantial increase in fees due to various considerations.

The Government of India constituted a number of committees to examine the issue of mobilisation of resources for central universities; technical education, etc. These committees have invariably recommended an increase in the level of fees. The important recommendations of these committees are recapitulated below.

Tuition Fees

Tuition fee may be revised upwards with immediate effect and may be periodically adjusted keeping in view inflation and rise in costs of providing higher education, among others, by increases in faculty remuneration. The revision of fees must be related in a meaningful manner to the recurring cost of the courses of study and employment opportunities offered by the course (suggesting a differential fee structure) (Justic D.K.

Punnayya Committee, UGC,1993, p.77). Full cost recovery is suggested in government and aided institutions suggesting, that the government funded/aided colleges may be allowed to start new specialised programmes for specific target groups on self-financing/net revenue earning basis (AICTE, 1994, p.19). Tuition fees should seek to recover the actual cost of imparting education. Tuition and all other fees, which are not to be charged on one time basis should be leviable for 12 months. Modified unit cost method i.e. 3 per cent of the unit cost worked out by Punnayya Committee should be the basis of fee structure, annual upward revisions may be made at 2 per cent of the suggested rate and after five years the University Grants Commission may consider the entire issue again for upward revision in the fee structure. It is recommended that certain mandatory provisions be made to ensure that the revised fee structure being suggested by the Committee is implemented (UGC 2000, p. 41-44 and p.16).

Other Fees

With regard to fees for admission and examination, it has been recommended that they should recover the recurring cost of operations. In the case of library, laboratory, sports and other similar facilities, it has been recommended that fees must be revised to recover a significant part of the recurring cost (UGC 1993, p.77). Further, that development fee be revised to meet actual recurring cost on no-profit-no-loss basis (UGC 1999, 2000).

Hostel and Mess Fees

Actual recurring cost and part of the capital cost over time be recovered (UGC 1993, 1999, and 2000).

Municipal, Civil and Other Services

Transport, telephone, postage and stationery, typing, computing, photocopying, etc. should be recovered to cover the expenditure incurred. (UGC 1993, 1999 and 2000).

Fees as a Source of Income

Various committees have recommended that institutions should raise fees in such a way that at least 15 to 25 per cent of the annual recurring cost per student is recovered from students in the form of fees and from other sources by the end of ten years. The government should, in course of time, shift funding of universities to a system of student funding (UGC 1993, 1999 and 2000). Tuition fee for the government funded and government aided institutions should be revised to cover at least 20 per cent of the recurring expenditure per student per year. Fees so fixed may be reviewed and refixed once every three years (AICTE 1994, pp.19).

The general perception is that fees are extremely low and have not been revised for decades. In reality most universities have not revised some components of fees, like tuition fee, which is only one of the components of total chargeable fees. For many

Figure 2.1: Share of various components of household expenditure on higher education

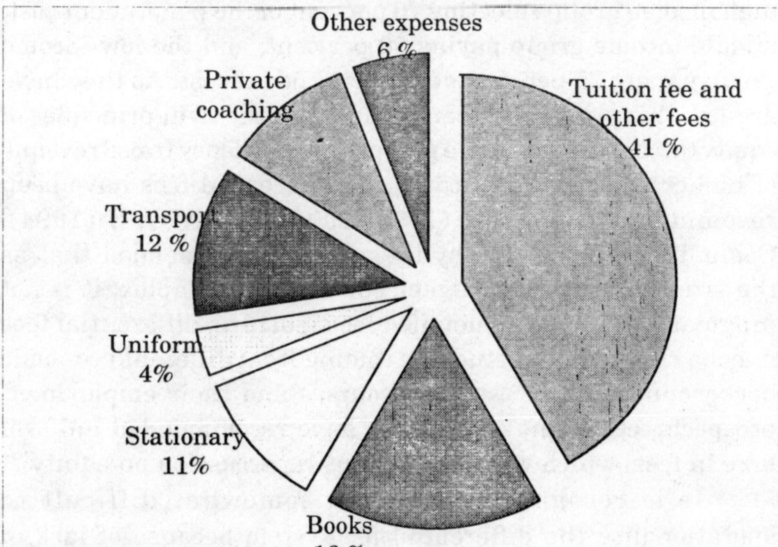

Source: Based on NSSO (1998), p. A117.

services, especially student welfare services, viz hostels, water, electricity, food charges, fees have been revised to a substantial extent. This can be evidenced from the components of household expenditure on education that showed that 41 per cent of higher education was in respect of tuition and other fees in the year 1995-96 (see Figure 2.1).

Confronted with fiscal crisis on account of reduced allocations and increasing expenditures on higher education, higher education institutions have to look for alternate sources of revenue and find ways and means of reducing costs. It becomes imperative for the system to explore alternatives for resource mobilisation. Following the recommendations of several committees, the policy directions and reduced resource allocations, many universities and other institutions of higher education have been required to reform their fee structures and introduce financial reforms. The first focused source of income is the fee income, which has serious ramifications on equity and access to higher education.

The differential fee structure proposed by Azad (1975) and Tilak and Varghese (1985) seems to be a viable alternative with high income groups meeting 75 per cent of the per student cost; middle income group paying 50 per cent; and the low-income group paying 25 per cent of the per student cost. As they have argued, this proposal attempts to ensure the twin principles of equity (access to low income groups) and efficiency (raise revenue of higher education institutions). Differential fees have been recommended by UGC (1993; 2000) and AICTE (1994). Committees constituted by them have recommended that as the size and variety of higher education is complex, it is not pragmatic to suggest a detailed fee structure; differential fees may be charged from students coming from different economic background and for subjects/courses and their employment prospects, etc. Some committees have recommended uniform hike in fees, which will have serious repercussion on equity[1].

It is recognised that it is somewhat difficult to operationalise the differential fee system because of lack of precise information about the economic capacity of all the beneficiaries. As noted by Azad (1975, 1984), "there are a number of difficulties involved in implementing this type of reform. The main arguments against this proposal are that it is not practicable to introduce such a scheme on a large scale and it is discriminatory.... However, the long term advantages of this proposal outweigh the disadvantages and the suggested reform in fee structure warrants serious consideration and implementation ...." (p.125-6).

Other Sources of Income

Income from other sources comprises income from endowments, university press, rent from university land, buildings, space, infrastructure, etc, income from consultancy services and research projects, etc. Income from sale of university publications, self-financing courses, and income from interest are some other sources of internal income of universities. The search for additional resources and the introduction of income-generating activities have been undertaken in many institutions. While such efforts need to continue, they should not be at the cost of primary goals of equity, academic excellence and relevance of higher education.

It is evident that the Government of India now encourages the augmentation of resources by each institution for covering a larger proportion of the cost of education. The recent policy direction in India suggests full cost recovery ('user pays' principle) from students even in public higher education institutions through hike in fees and introduction of self-financing courses and seats in tune with liberalisation policies[2]. Under the impact of globalisation and competitive market oriented economy, important economic rationale for government funding for higher education is often neglected. With economic reforms and other pressures, higher education is proposed to be shifted to the list of non-merit goods[3] from the list of merit goods. This tends to ignore expenditure on education as a social investment and the complementary nature of public and household expenditure on education. Funding of higher education requires both public and private resources even in a situation of economic austerity. However, the role of the state and public support to higher education remains essential to ensure its educational, social and institutional objectives.

Private investment in higher education alone would be socially *sub-optimal,* because households do not or are not able to invest on non-market oriented courses in higher education and research and development activities. This is also true of private enterprises. Increased role of market in determining nature and character of education is likely to jeopardise participation of meritorious students from economically disadvantaged groups, women and minorities. Very steep increase in fees might compel a large number of students from low and middle income families and women not to seek higher education, and some rich students to opt for studies abroad. Further, it is important to notice that self-financing courses are often of short duration; any heavy reliance on them will have repercussions on equity and quality of higher education system in the long run. This will also adversely affect the availability of qualified and competent teachers and researchers in pure and basic disciplines in the near future as is reported to be happening in the United Kingdom.

Student Loans

Student loans are currently in operation in more than 80 countries around the globe. Of late, educational loans have become popular among students because of their simple and appealing logic, despite their inherent weaknesses. It is argued that in order to safeguard poor students against rising costs of higher education (both tuition and maintenance), a number of countries in the developing and developed world have initiated student loan programmes. However, cost recovery cannot be implemented equitably without scholarship programmes that should guarantee necessary financial support to academically meritorious and economically backward students (Salmi, 1992; Tilak, 1997). Further, imperfections in capital markets related to lack of collateral security for education investments restricts the ability of poor students to take advantage of loans available for higher education.

There has been a paradigm shift in the attitude towards financing of higher education *per se* and student loans in particular. The features of second generation of loan programmes around the world seem to suffer from many problems which, among others, include: a loan is not guaranteed by government; sanction of the loan requires 100 per cent collateral security for amounts above a designated level and a guarantor/co-signatory of parent or family member; loan schemes are operated by commercial banks/private sector/private banks, since loan amounts are charged at market rates of interest; employment possibilities of a course has a higher probability of a loan being sanctioned. A major shift can be observed from the choice of administering agency from government/agency or institutions/ universities to commercial banks and private banks or private sector. There is gradual shift from a regime of interest-free loans to subsidised interest on student loans. With changes in economic reform polices around the world, there is a sudden shift to charge market rates of interest or more for student loans.

Second generation of loan programmes aim at full cost recovery and are not responsive to any equity considerations. It should be mentioned that such loan schemes involve a number of risks. Heavy reliance on such student loans will discourage students from low-income families, women and other weaker sections and minorities from participating in higher education programmes. More specifically for women a study loan is regarded as a negative dowry. Further, with globalisation and internationalisation of higher education under WTO and General Agreement on Trade in Services (GATS), there is a risk of greater student mobility from developing countries to developed countries.

Keeping in view the wave of changes around the world, the present Educational Loan Scheme was introduced in India following an announcement in the budget of 2000-01. The scheme administered by commercial banks covers a wide range of courses in higher studies from post-matric education to research studies, both in India and abroad. Eligibility criterion is that any student who secures admission in domestic/foreign educational institution is eligible for a loan, which covers both instructional cost and living expenses. The loan can be repaid in three to seven years and repayment would commence one year after completion of the course or six months after getting employment, whichever is earlier. Simple rate of interest is charged during the period of study and up to the commencement of repayment.

It has however to be noted that there is no income ceiling on students/parents for being eligible for loan. Academic achievement is also not considered as an eligibility criterion, that is, there is no minimum qualifying marks required. There are no special provisions of any kind for weaker sections in terms of security, government guarantee, lower rate of interest or repayment period, repayment in accordance with earnings, waivers, etc. The scheme does not adhere either to the efficiency or equity principles unlike in many other countries, where merit-cum-means determine the eligibility for student loan.

In this context, mention may be made of an important recommendation made by the AICTE Committee (1994) relating to the setting up of an Educational Development Bank. This Bank, whose equity capital will be provided equally by the central and state governments and NRIs, will provide soft loans to educational institutions in financial distress. It is also expected to administer student loans programmes, which are beneficiary friendly and not motivated by commercial considerations. The scheme is still at a conceptual stage.

Given the world experience on student loan schemes, the new scheme in India is insensitive to the needs of the poor and does not consider equity aspects; there are no special provisions of any kind for the weaker sections. The present loan scheme does not take into consideration various details, such as eligibility, interest rates, repayment terms and conditions as recommended by various committees. The scheme is a sheer commercial venture in tune with private commercial higher education and, in its present form, has the potentiality of doing more harm than good for the quantitative growth and qualitative development of higher education. Hence, an alternative scheme, which avoids the pitfalls of the present scheme and genuinely caters to the needs of the weaker sections of the society, should be worked out.

The world experience suggests that recovery rate from student loans is very low. In addition, administrative cost of student loan programme is generally quite high. Hence, total cost incurred on default and administration would be much higher and eventually the scheme may not be financially viable. Hence, the idea of self-sustaining student loan schemes in the long run seems to be elusive. Further, student loan schemes require a large initial investment. Apart from financial non-viability of a student loan, its psychological impact (burden) and societal attitude ("negative dowry" for women etc.) is adverse on students, family and society.

(c) Community Contributions

It has been mentioned that private donations, as a source of educational finance, are fast drying up. There are historical reasons for this phenomenon. The abolition of the Zamindari System, the extinction of Rajas and Maharajas and lack of incentives by way of relief in taxation could be cited as the main factors responsible for this problem. It is necessary that a concerted effort is made to mobilise community resources for meeting some part of educational expenditure. These should include, besides relief in taxation, the following measures:

1. Users of technical manpower should pay part of educational costs.
2. There should be collaboration between industrial establishments and universities which could take the form of sponsored research, creation of special chairs, consultancy, endowments for specialised discipline etc.
3. Educational institutions should approach the community for financial assistance. This would happen only if educational institutions shed their academic exclusiveness, become a part of the society around them and provide education, which is relevant to community needs. An educational institution should function as the centre for social life around it and not a place, which has nothing to do with its social and physical environment.

(d) Avoiding Wastage

While making a case for mobilizing additional resources, we have also to guard against mind boggling wastage of resources that occurs in the form of irrelevant courses and failures and drop-outs at various stages of education. The drop out rate at the primary and upper primary stage is 40 per cent and 57 per cent respectively. At secondary and higher education stages (in humanities and social science) about 50 per cent students fail to come out successfully in public examinations. According to a study conducted by the present author, only one out of 8 students, who enter universities, comes out with a reasonably good grade.

Another important aspect of this colossal wastage is the emigration of trained manpower to economically advanced countries. Thus we seem to finance education of these people without any tangible returns to the country although remittances from them have shown some increase. Further, an economically backward country like India seems to supply the cream of its professionally trained manpower to developed countries without any quid-pro-quo, giving rise to a form of foreign assistance in the reverse direction. While it is not intended to suggest that this outflow of the creamy layer of the professional manpower should be stopped, it would be desirable to tax these emigrants to the extent that they reimburse the full cost of their education in case they permanently settle down in foreign countries.

Concluding Remarks

Allocation of resources to higher education in GDP and intra-sectoral allocation to university and higher education and technical education have shown a declining trend, particularly at the beginning of the reform period, slight improvement in the middle of 1990s and again a decline in the late 1990s. The growth in enrolment has not been accompanied by commensurate growth in public expenditure. The rapid erosion of public resources has a negative impact on the quality of educational services. It is apparent that the recent policy of the Government of India and of state governments encourages augmentation of resources for covering a larger portion of cost of higher education through sources other than public funding.

Recent policy changes in India often favour diversion of resources from higher to primary level of education. While it is essential that the nation achieve universal elementary education, it cannot afford to neglect higher education in the context of globalisation. Further, it needs to be realised that different levels of education are inter-dependent; the principle should not be growth of one sector of education at the cost of another. It may also be mentioned that increased role of market jeopardises the participation of meritorious students from economically disadvantaged groups, women and minorities. Markets can also crowd out important educational opportunities. (UNESCO, 2000).

The policy directions in recent decade in India emphasise full cost recovery from students even in public higher education institutions through student funding including hike in fees. Important economic rationale for government funding for higher education is often neglected. Cost recovery measures, comprising increase in fees, student loans currently operated by commercial banks and privatisation will aggravate inequalities in the society. It needs to be noted that the maximum income that can be raised from fees will, on an average, be around 25 per cent of the total recurring expenditure in a span of ten years. Further, it is also important to realize that self-financing courses are short term in nature and heavy reliance on them will have repercussions on equity, content and quality of education system in the long run. This will also lead to lack of teachers and researchers in pure and basic disciplines in the near future as is happening in the United Kingdom.

Increasing reliance on student fees, student loans and privatisation without considering the interests of low-income groups may produce regressive effects in the society. An alternative student loan scheme specifically for the weaker sections needs to be formulated. Such a programme must be flexible enough to suit their requirements, which may involve government guaranteed loans, subsidised interest rates, liberal terms of repayment, waivers for those students with low future incomes, etc, in addition to a strong student support system. The proposal to set up an Educational Development Bank also merits serious consideration.

In the context of globalisation, economic rationale for government funding, especially for higher education tends to be neglected. This is a retrogressive development. Public support for higher education remains essential to ensure a balanced achievement of educational and social objectives, apart from ensuring national survival in the knowledge-based society. Sequencing of priorities, i.e., universal primary education first, secondary and higher education later (as and when resources are available or/leaving these sectors to private initiatives) will prove to be a very costly strategy in the era of globalisation.

It is equally important to bring about the required fundamental transformation at both the system level and institutional structure of higher education. Effective financial management at institutional level should be an essential pre-requisite. It is also necessary that funding sources be diversified; but cost-sharing with students has social and political limits, and excessive commercialization of higher education should be discouraged.

In the end, it may be stressed that challenge to public policy on higher education in India requires that private providers are encouraged to contribute to higher education in terms of finances, management and academic support. The government should, however, continue to discharge its responsibility of funding, regulating, guiding and monitoring the progress of institutions of higher education so that there is a balance between equity (assurance of access to low-income students) and efficiency (quality and academic coverage). It may also be ensured that increased access of private bodies to the financing and management of education and higher education in particular does not end up in commercialization of the system.

Appendix I
Public Expenditure on Education

	Expenditure (in billion of dollars)		Per Capita (Dollars)		Total Enrolment (000)		Per Student		% of Expenditure on Education		% of Enrolment	
	1980	*1994*	*1980*	*1994*	*1980*	*1994*	*1980*	*1994*	*1980*	*1994*	*1980*	*1994*
World	516.4	1329.9	126	252	857017	1078000	602.56	1233.67	100.00	100.00	100.00	100.00
Africa	22.9	29.1	48	41	78024	125746	293.50	231.42	4.43	2.19	9.10	11.66
America	188.6	481.7	307	623	147253	179066	1280.79	2690.07	36.52	36.22	17.18	16.61
Asia	93.8	302.1	37	93	494813	628247	189.57	480.86	18.16	22.72	57.74	58.28
Europe	200.6	492.6	418	982	132112	138196	1518.41	3564.50	38.85	37.04	15.42	12.82
Oceania	10.4	24.5	467	878	4815	6746	2159.92	3631.78	2.01	1.84	0.56	0.63
Developing Countries	101.6	206.6	31	48	626061	831989	162.28	248.32	19.67	15.54	73.05	77.18
Developed Countries	414.8	1123.3	487	1211	230956	246011	1796.01	4566.06	80.33	84.46	26.95	22.82

Source: UNESCO Statistical Year Book 1997 for Expenditure Pp. 2-29 and Enrolment 2-11 to 2-13.

Appendix II
Public Expenditure on Education in India

(Rs. in crore)

Year	*Govt. expenditure on education (Trg. & Rev) by education and other Deptt. (centre + state)*	*Total Govt. Expenditure on all sectors (Rev)*	*GDP at current prices (at factor cost) base year 1993-94*	*% of Expenditure on Education to Expenditure on all sectors*	*% of Education Expenditure to GDP*
1	*2*	*3*	*4*	*5*	*6*
1961-62	260.3	2225.4	17116	11.70	1.52
1962-63	278.76	2942.67	18302	9.47	1.52
1963-64	313.93	3488.97	20916	9.00	1.50
1964-65	369.29	3844.91	24436	9.60	1.51
1965-66	432.61	4404.82	25586	9.82	1.69
1966-67	487.83	5100.24	29123	9.56	1.63
1967-68	593.14	5619.77	34225	10.55	1.68
1968-69	649.13	6922.07	26092	9.38	1.80
1969-70	760.23	7908.09	39691	9.61	1.92
1970-71	892.36	8787.12	41111	10.16	2.11
1971-72	1011.07	10610.89	44923	9.53	2.25
1972-73	1150.43	11863.56	49415	9.70	2.33
1973-74	1300.72	12884.48	60560	10.10	2.15
1974-75	1570.67	14626.03	71283	10.74	2.20
1975-76	1849.47	17958.9	75709	10.30	2.44
1976-77	2039.09	20482.83	84381	9.96	2.51

(Contd.)

(Contd.Appendix II)

Year	Govt. expenditure on education (Trg. & Rev) by education and other Deptt. (centre + state)	Total Govt. Expenditure on all sectors (Rev)	GDP at current prices (at factor cost) base year 1993-94	% of Expenditure on Education to Expenditure on all sectors	% of Education Expenditure to GDP
1	*2*	*3*	*4*	*5*	*6*
1977-78	2630.6	22666.31	92881	11.61	2.83
1978-79	2994.69	26134.84	99823	11.46	3.00
1979-80	3347.57	30915.39	108927	10.83	3.07
1980-81	3884.2	36398.39	130178	10.67	2.98
1981-82	4298.29	41715.71	152056	10.30	2.83
1982-83	5509.17	43996.18	169525	12.52	3.25
1983-84	6229.53	61889.25	198630	10.52	3.25
1984-85	7455.88	63025.45	222705	10.80	3.35
1985-86	8713.05	67091.41	249547	12.99	3.49
1986-87	9479.13	80454.66	278258	11.78	3.41
1987-88	11798.35	92518.38	915993	12.75	3.73
1988-89	14069.82	107549.75	378491	13.08	3.72
1989-90	17192.5	126045.97	438020	13.64	3.93
1990-91	19615.85	146711.53	510954	13.37	3.84
1991-92	22393.69	170370.38	589086	13.14	3.80
1992-93	25030.3	190327.45	673221	13.15	3.72

(Contd.)

(Contd.Appendix II)

Year	*Govt. expenditure on education (Trg. & Rev) by education and other Deptt. (centre + state)*	*Total Govt. Expenditure on all sectors (Rev)*	*GDP at current prices (at factor cost) base year 1993-94*	*% of Expenditure on Education to Expenditure on all sectors*	*% of Education Expenditure to GDP*
1	*2*	*3*	*4*	*5*	*6*
1993-94	28279.69	218535.15	673221	13.15	3.72
1994-95	32606.22	251691.92	917058	12.95	3.56
1995-96	38178.09	286194.55	1073271	13.34	3.56
1996-97	43896.48	329389.92	917058	12.95	3.56
1997-98	48552.14	380728.45	1390148	12.75	3.49
1998-99	61578.91	439768.11	1598127	14.00	3.85
1999-2000	74816.09	512519.33	1761838	14.60	4.25
2000-2001	82486.88	572160.14	1902998	14.42	4.33
2001-2002*	79865.7	619713.15	2081474	12.89	3.84
2002-2003*	85507.34	678547.31	2254888	12.60	3.79
2003-2004*	89079.25	743668.96	2543396	11.98	3.50
2004-2005*	104566.00 (RE)	819231.90 (RE)	2843897 (Q)	12.76	3.68

P-Provisional estimates. Q-Quick estimates, RE – Revised estimates

Source:

1. National Accounts statistics published by C.S.O.
2. Expenditure on Education figure is taken from Ministry of Educations' Analysis of Budgeted Expenditure on Education' published Department of Secondary & Higher Education
3. Selected Educational Statistics, 2004-05, MHRD, New Delhi, 2007.

Appendix III
Percentage of GNP Spent on Education Selected Countries

		Educational Expenditure	
		As % of GNP	*As % of Government Expenditure*
Africa			
Egypt	1970	4.8	15.8
	1996	4.8	14.9
	2005	NA	NA
Kenya	1970	5.0	17.8
	1996	6.5	16.7
	2004	6.2	22.3
South Africa	1986	6.0	22.1 (1992)
	1996	8.0	23.9
	2005	5.3	NA
North America			
Canada	1970	8.6	17.8 (1975)
	1994	6.9	12.9
	2005	NA	NA
USA	1985	4.9	15.5
	1994	5.4	14.4
	2005	5.6	15.5
Asia			
Bangladesh	1975	0.8	13.6
	1996	2.2	8.7 (1992)
	2005	2.4	15.5
China	1970	1.3	4.3
	1996	2.3	12.2 (1993)
	2005	NA	NA
India	1970	2.6	10.7
	1996	3.2	11.6 (1995)
	2005	3.8	
Iran	1976	5.7	14.1
	1995	4.0	17.8
	2005	4.9	17.7

(Contd.)

(Contd.Appendix III)

		Educational Expenditure	
		As % of GNP	*As % of Government Expenditure*
Israel	1970	5.7	8.1
	1994	7.6	12.3 (1993)
	2005	NA	NA
Malaysia	1970	4.2	17.7
	1997	4.9	15.4 (1996)
	2005	8.1	20.3
Pakistan	1970	1.7	4.2
	1997	2.7	7.1
	2004	1.8	7.8
Sri Lanka	1970	4.0	13.6
	1996	3.4	8.9
	2005	NA	NA
Thailand	1970	3.2	17.3
	1996	4.8	20.1 (1995)
	2005	4.6	27.5
Europe			
Austria	1970	4.5	8.1 10.4
	1996	5.4	10.4
	2005	5.7	NA
Denmark	1970	6.7	16.9
	1996	8.1	13.1 (1995)
	2005	8.5	15.4
France	1970	4.8	24.9
	1996	6.0	10.9
	2005	5.4	NA
Italy	1970	3.7	11.9
	1996	4.9	9.1
	2005	4.7	10.3
Russia	1970	3.9	NA
	1995	3.0	NA
	2005	3.8	11.5

(Contd.)

(Contd.Appendix III)

		Educational Expenditure	
		As % of GNP	*As % of Government Expenditure*
Sweden	1970	7.6	13.4
	1996	8.3	12.2
	2005	7.3	12.8
UK	1970	5.3	14.1
Oceania	1995	5.3	11.6
	2005	NA	NA
Australia	1970	4.1	13.3
	1995	5.5	13.5 (1975)
	2005	4.9	N A
New Zealand	1970	4.7	17.1
	1996	7.3	NA
	2005	6.7	NA

(Figure in Parentheses indicate the years to which they belong)
Source: UNESCO, Statistical year Book 1999 and UNESCO Global Education Ddigest, 2005 , UNESCO Publishing Paris, France.

References

1. However, differential fee structure seems to be incompatible with the Supreme Court Judgement on the Writ Petition (Civil) 317 of 1993 in TMA Pai Foundation and Others and State of Karnataka and Others on October 31, 2002.
2. Some students in each department pay full cost fee, while the rest of the students pay normal (subsidised) fees. It is to be noted that the normal fee itself has been increasing.
3. Srivastava and Sen (1997).

3

University Finances: An Analytical Study

Higher education in India is financed largely by the government –Central as well as the states. Until late 1980s, state provided up to 90 per cent of the total funding for higher education. This proportion has steadily declined over the years. Almost all universities have been facing financial crises of various dimensions for quite some time with very little hope of the situation changing for the better. While the quantum of resources has been increasing at a rapid rate, the increase has not been commensurate with their requirements, which have been increasing at a much faster rate. Consequently, the gap between the two has widened. Several changes are taking place in the pattern of university finances. These include: introduction of self-financing courses, enhanced cost-recovery measures, emphasis on student loans instead of non-recoverable scholarships etc. There has also been a change in government policy, resulting in increased funding for elementary and secondary education and declining support for university education. Non-governmental resources for universities have declined. For instance, contribution of fees as a source of income of universities has declined. During the 1950s and 1960s, it was around 15 to 20 per cent, in mid 1980s, it declined to 15 per cent (Tilak, 2003), and during 1990s, it further declined to 2 to 3 per cent of the total income of universities.

This chapter attempts to review some critical aspects of university finances in respect of the universities from which information was received. Attempt has been made to examine the pattern of financing of twenty-nine universities, for which data were received through a structured questionnaire. The data are from three categories of universities: Central Universities, Deemed to be Universities and State Universities. State universities have been selected from five regions i.e. Central, Northern, North-Eastern, Western and Southern.

The interpretation of the data has been made keeping in view the facts as they emerge out of the information given by the universities. No attempt has been made to identify the causative factors responsible for the emerging situation. That would require a much more detailed investigation, which the present study does not warrant.

The sources of income and the pattern of expenditure of a university has been classified into:

Sources of Income

(A) Government Sources:

(i) **Grants**
- Central Government
- University Grants Commission
- All India Council for Technical Education
- Other Governmental Agencies
- State Governments
- Local Bodies

(B) Non-government Sources

(i) **Cost Recoveries**
- Tuition Fees
- Hostel Fees
- Examination Fees
- Other Charges

(ii) University Sources

- Computer
- Press
- Consultancy
- Project Grants

(iii) Other Sources

- Endowments, donations etc.

Pattern of Expenditure

(i) Recurring Expenditure

- Direct teaching expenditure
- Indirect teaching expenditure
- Student welfare activities

(ii) Non-Recurring Expenditure

- Buildings
- Furniture
- Library
- Laboratory
- Others

Sources of Income

For examining proportionate contribution of each component of the total income of universities, analysis has been classified into government and non-government sources. The relative share of income from both these sources has been calculated for 29 universities. Table 3.1 and Figure 3.1 indicate that the total income of the universities has shown a spectacular increase – about 106 per cent during the period 1996-97 and 2001-02. The increase in Deemed to be Universities, has been much larger (166.65 per cent) than in the case of State Universities (107.27 per cent) and Central University (93.20 per cent). Among the Deemed to be Universities, in Rashtriya Sanskrit Vidhyapeetham, Tirupathi, the increase in allocation

Table 3.1: Percentage increase/decrease in Universities income in 1996-97 and 2001-02

Name of the Universities	*Region*	*Year of Estt.*	*1996-97 (Rs. in Lakh)*	*2001-02 (Rs in Lakh)*	*Percentage Increase/ Decrease*
Central Unviersity					
AMU, Aligarh		1920	**8220.42**	**15882.01**	**93.20**
Deemed to be Universities					
Banasthali Vidhyapeeth, Rajasthan		1962	496.94	1398.82	181.49
Rashtriya Sanskrit Vidyapeethm,Tirupati		1961	107.94	331.49	207.11
Sri Sathya Sai Institute of H. Learning, AP		1981	214.46	454.42	111.89
Total Deemed to be Universities			**819.34**	**2184.73**	**166.65**
State Universities					
Devi Ahilya University, Indore	**Central**	1964	763.85	3365.22	340.56
Dr. Harisingh G.Vishdy. M.P.		1946	1521.56	2474.29	62.62
Barkatullah Univ. Bhopal		1970	1516.26	2282.95	50.56
Ranchi University, Bihar		1976	42.99	134.95	213.91
Magadh University, Bihar*		1960	4443.12	7307.38	64.47
Rani Durgawati University, Jabalpur		1935	805.11	746.25	-7.31
Deen Dayal Upad. University, Gorakhpur		1956	1005.45	2308.58	129.61

(Contd.)

(Contd. Table 3.1)

Name of the Universities	*Region*	*Year of Estt.*	*1996-97 (Rs. in Lakh)*	*2001-02 (Rs in Lakh)*	*Percentage Increase/ Decrease*
Punjab University, Chandigarh	**Northern**	1947	4824.59	8423.19	74.59
Kurukshetra University, Haryana		1957	2997.55	7311.71	143.92
M.D. Univ. Rohtak, Haryana		1956	1797.72	7688.33	327.67
Manipur University, Imphal	**North-Eastern**	1980	664.97	1143.44	71.95
Nagaland University, Kohima		1994	492.38	1394.52	183.22
Tirpura University, Tipura West		1987	286.80	811.11	182.81
Mizoram University		2001	0.00	1534.30	-
Bhavnagar University	**Western**	1979	418.26	1276.25	205.13
Swami Rmanand Univ., Nanded		1994	613.45	568.63	-7.31
Shivaji Univeristy, Kolhapur		1962	2217.15	3848.97	73.60
Nagpur University, Nagpur		1923	3166.58	5774.01	82.34

(Contd.)

(Contd. Table 3.1)

Name of the Universities	*Region*	*Year of Estt.*	*1996-97 (Rs. in Lakh)*	*2001-02 (Rs in Lakh)*	*Percentage Increase/ Decrease*
Karnatak Univ. Dharwad	**Southern**	1950	2746.25	4310.17	56.95
Banglore University		1961	3330.29	6670.62	100.30
Mangalore University, Mangalagangothri		1980	1061.93	1898.98	78.82
Cochin Univ. of Sc. & Tech., Kerala		1986	1484.23	2922.59	96.91
University of Kerala, Thiruvanauthapuram		1937	3186.81	5561.51	74.52
Sri Krishnadevaraya Univ., Anantapur		1981	823.69	1192.64	44.79
University of Madras, Chennai		1857	2827.40	8255.25	191.97
Total State Universities			**43038.39**	**89205.84**	**107.27**
All Universities Total			**52078.15**	**107272.58**	**105.98**

Note : * = Special assistance during IX plan.

Figure 3.1 : Total Income of the Universities in 1996-97 and 2001-02

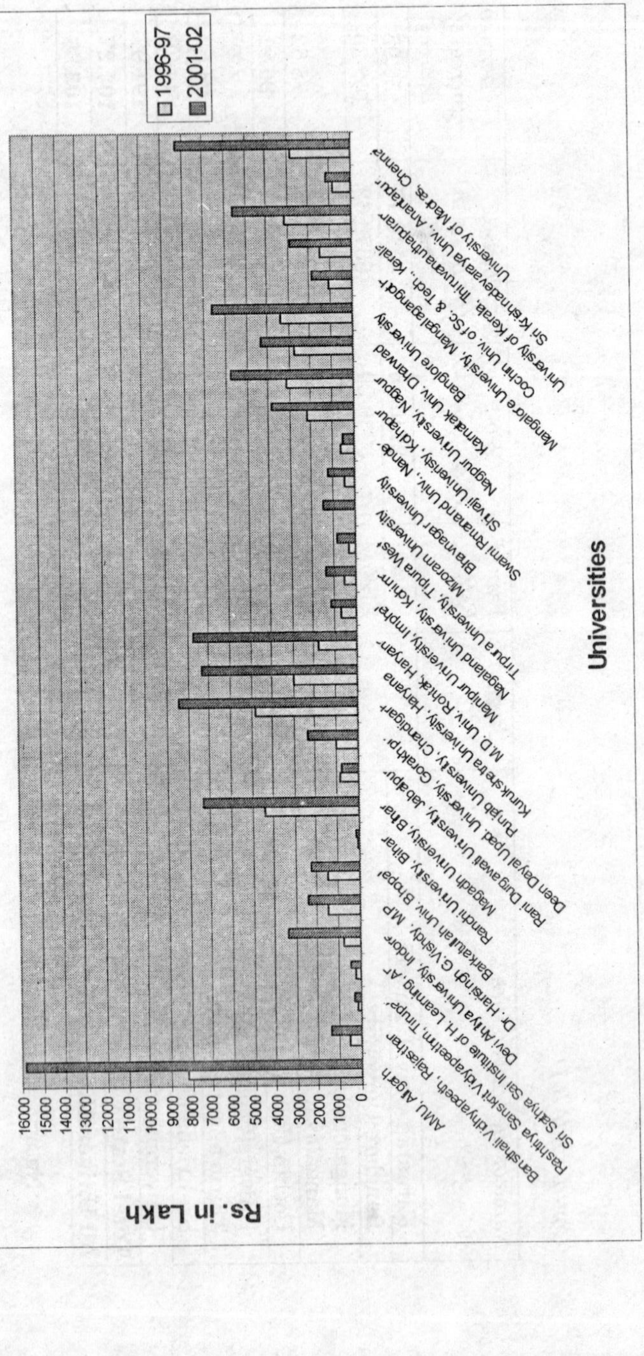

of resources is more than two hundred per cent followed by Banasthali Vidhypeeth i.e. 181.49 per cent. Among state Universities, (except for two i.e. Rani Durgawati University and Swami Ramanand University), there has been considerable enhancement, although according to their year of establishment and region, the two Universities are not comparable. Rani Durgawati of Central region is a very old University (1935), while Swami Ramanand University of Western region was established in 1994.

Among all the universities in the Central region, the minimum increase in the total income was in Barkatullah University (50.56 per cent) and maximum increase in Devi Ahilya University (340.56 per cent). In North-Eastern region also, there was an increase in percentage income of universities. In Southern region maximum increase in of income was in University of Madras (191.97 per cent) and minimum in Sri Krishnadevaraya University (44.79 per cent).

A. Government Sources

(i) Grants

The objective of government grants is to help universities to achieve optimum development. Government grants are important and a major source of income for universities. The sources of grants include: Central Government, University Grants Commission (UGC), All India Council for Technical Education (AICTE), Other Central Government Agencies, State Governments and Local Bodies. Out of these grants, state government grants and grants from the UGC are the major sources of income. State government grants are provided to state universities while grants from UGC are made available to Central and Deemed to be Universities for maintenance and development activities. The UGC also provides grants to state universities for their developmental activities.

Tables 3.2 and 3.3 indicate the income of universities from government and other sources. The present analysis of financing of universities is confined to one Central University, three

Table 3.2: Income from Different Sources in 1996-97 (In Percentage)

Name of the Universities	*Region*	*Year of Estt.*	*Central Govt.*	*UGC*	*AICTE*	*Other Govt. Agencies*	*State Govt.*
Central Universities							
AMU, Aligarh		**1920**	**0.000**	**91.307**	**0.000**	**0.000**	**0.026**
Deemed to be Universities							
Banasthali Vidyapeeth, Rajasthan		1935	0.000	0.000	0.000	0.000	37.085
Rashtriya Sanskrit Vidyapeethm,Tirupati		1961	1.881	91.366	0.000	0.000	0.389
Sri Sathya Sai Institute of H.Learning, AP		1981	0.000	5.143	11.116	0.000	0.000
Total Deemed to be Universities			**0.248**	**13.383**	**2.910**	**0.000**	**22.544**
State Universities							
Devi Ahilya University, Indore	Central	1964	0.000	2.199	0.000	0.000	63.986
Dr. Harisingh G.Vishdy. M.P.		1946	0.258	9.694	0.263	0.317	57.047
Barkatullah Univ. Bhopal		1970	0.000	4.518	0.204	0.000	17.515
Ranchi University, Bihar		1960	0.000	41.079	0.000	0.000	51.942
Magadh University, Bihar		1962	0.000	0.000	0.000	0.000	93.270
Rani Durgawati University, Jabalpur		1956	0.000	5.203	0.000	2.800	54.609
Deen Dayal Upad. University, Gorakhpur		1957	0.000	7.423	0.000	0.000	67.034
Punjab University, Chandigarh	Northern	1947	0.340	4.337	0.090	1.881	31.888
Kurukshetra University, Haryana		1956	0.048	5.430	0.000	0.000	41.967
M.D. Univ. Rohtak, Haryana		1976	0.000	1.646	0.000	0.000	49.501

(Contd.)

(Contd. Table 3.2)

Name of the Universities	*Region*	*Local Body*	*Total (Govt. Grant)*	*Total Fees*	*Univ. & Other Sources*	*Total Income*
Central Universities						
AMU, Aligarh		**0.000**	**91.333**	**3.237**	**5.430**	**100.000**
Deemed to be Universities						
Banasthali Vidyapeeth, Rajasthan		0.000	37.085	40.498	**22.417**	100.000
Rashtriya Sanskrit Vidyapeethni,Tirupati		1.853	95.488	3.215	**1.297**	100.000
Sri Sathya Sai Institute of H.Learning, AP		0.000	16.259	0.000	**83.741**	100.000
Total Deemed to be Universities		**0.244**	**39.328**	**24.986**	**35.686**	**100.000**
State Universities						
Devi Ahilya University, Indore	**Central**	0.000	66.186	25.786	**8.028**	100.000
Dr. Harisingh G.Vishdy. M.P.		0.000	67.579	30.688	**1.733**	100.000
Barkatullah Univ. Bhopal		22.284*	44.521	25.730	**29.749**	100.000
Ranchi University, Bihar		0.000	93.022	6.978	**0**	100.000
Magadh University, Bihar		0.000	93.270	6.497	**0.233**	100.000
Rani Durgawati University, Jabalpur		0.000	62.611	33.046	**4.343**	100.000
Deen Dayal Upad. University, Gorakhpur		0.000	74.456	17.446	**8.098**	100.000
Punjab University, Chandigarh	**Northern**	49.455	87.991	9.081	**2.928**	100.000
Kurukshetra University, Haryana		0.000	47.444	18.320	**34.236**	100.000
M.D. Univ. Rohtak, Haryana		0.000	51.147	9.884	**38.969**	100.000

(Contd.)

(Contd. Table 3.2)

Name of the Universities	Region	Year of Estt.	Central Govt.	UGC	AICTE	Other Govt. Agencies	State Govt.
Manipur University, Imphal	North-Eastern	1980	0.000	9.951	0.000	0.000	63.451
Nagaland University, Kohima		1994	0.000	75.531	0.000	0.000	0.000
Tirpura University, Tipura West		1987	0.000	18.026	0.000	0.000	69.282
Bhavnagar University	Western	1979	1.203	7.921	0.000	0.000	71.771
Swami Rmanand Univ., Nanded		1994	0.000	0.000	0.000	0.000	67.813
Shivaji Univeristy, Kolhapur		1962	0.614	1.795	0.000	5.058	39.188
Nagpur University, Nagpur		1923	0.350	0.767	0.363	0.722	27.143
Karnatak Univ. Dharwad	Southern	1950	0.000	4.038	0.000	0.000	58.407
Banglore University		1961	0.418	3.714	0.091	0.627	43.242
Mangalore University, Mangalagangothri		1980	0.000	9.057	0.000	0.000	49.011
Cochin Univ. of Sc. & Tech., Kerala		1986	0.000	2.043	0.000	1.120	67.665
University of Kerala, Thiruvanauthapuram		1937	2.064	5.067	0.000	1.120	59.671
Sri Krishnadevaraya Univ., Anantapur		1981	0.000	0.000	0.000	0.000	69.622
University of Madras, Chennai		1857	0.000	0.707	0.000	0.000	7.389
Total State Universities			0.305	4.398	0.060	0.758	48.586
All Universities Total			0.256	18.258	0.096	0.627	40.511

(Contd.)

(Contd.Table 3.2)

Name of the Universities	*Region*	*Local Body*	*Total (Govt. Grant)*	*Total Fees*	*Univ. & Other Sources*	*Total Income*
Manipur University, Imphal	**North-Eastern**	0.000	73.163	10.885	**15.952**	100.000
Nagaland University, Kohima		0.000	75.531	3.958	**20.511**	100.000
Tirpura University, Tipura West		0.656	87.964	3.835	**8.201**	100.000
Bhavnagar University	**Western**	0.423	81.318	10.615	**8.067**	100.000
Swami Rmanand Univ., Nanded		0.000	67.813	29.791	**2.396**	100.000
Shivaji Univeristy, Kolhapur		0.000	46.655	23.951	**29.394**	100.000
Nagpur University, Nagpur		0.000	29.344	24.329	**46.327**	100.000
Karnatak Univ. Dharwad	**Southern**	0.000	62.444	30.892	**6.664**	100.000
Banglore University		0.000	48.093	36.342	**15.565**	100.000
Mangalore University, Mangalagangothri		0.000	58.068	26.374	**15.558**	100.000
Cochin Univ. of Sc. & Tech., Kerala		0.065	70.894	10.737	**18.369**	100.000
University of Kerala, Thiruvanauthapuram		0.000	67.922	31.329	**0.749**	100.000
Sri Krishnadevaraya Univ., Anantapur		0.000	69.622	18.776	**11.602**	100.000
University of Madras, Chennai		0.000	8.096	61.657	**30.247**	100.000
Total State Universities		6.340	60.447	23.184	14.079	100.000
All Universities Total		5.243	64.990	20.064	24.862	100.000

Note : *= other loan.

Table 3.3: Income from Different Sources – 2001-02 (In Percentage)

Name of the Universities	*Region*	*Year of Estt.*	*Central Govt.*	*UGC*	*AICTE*	*Other Govt. Agencies*	*State Govt.*
Central University							
AMU, Aligarh		1920	0.000	93.734	0.000	0.000	0.000
Deemed to be Universities							
Banasthali Vidyapeeth, Rajasthan		1935	0.054	0.000	0.000	0.000	15.735
Rashtriya Sanskrit Vidyapeethm,Tirupati		1961	0.000	85.891	0.000	0.000	0.000
Sri Sathya Sai Institute of H.Learning, AP		1981	0.000	13.210	0.000	0.000	0.000
Total Deemed to be Universities			0.034	15.780	0.000	0.000	10.074
State Universities							
Devi Ahilya University, Indore	Central	1964	0.000	0.630	0.000	0.000	28.893
Dr. Harisingh G.Vishdy. M.P.		1946	0.658	8.566	0.249	1.079	54.480
Barkatullah Univ. Bhopal		1970	0.000	6.277	0.000	0.000	12.726
Ranchi University, Bihar		1960	0.000	58.444	0.000	0.000	38.888
Magadh University, Bihar		1962	0.000	0.000	0.000	0.000	90.754
Rani Durgawati University, Jabalpur		1956	0.000	8.173	0.000	2.637	10.129
Deen Dayal Upad. University, Gorakhpur		1957	0.000	4.453	0.000	0.000	47.215
Punjab University, Chandigarh	Northern	1947	0.520	3.534	0.071	3.497	20.250
Kurukshetra University, Haryana		1956	0.345	2.151	0.000	0.000	26.949
M.D. Univ. Rohtak, Haryana		1976	1.532	1.614	0.000	0.000	23.724

(Contd.)

(Contd. Table 3.3)

Name of the Universities	*Region*	*Year of Estt.*	*Local Body*	*Total (Govt. Grants)*	*Total Fees*	*Univ. & Other Sources*	*Total Income*
Central University							
AMU, Aligarh		1920	0.000	93.734	3.331	2.940	100.000
Deemed to be Universities							
Banasthali Vidyapeeth, Rajasthan		1935	0.036	15.824	67.091	17.090	100.000
Rashtriya Sanskrit Vidyapeethm, Tirupati		1961	0.000	85.891	2.205	11.900	100.000
Sri Sathya Sai Institute of H.Learning, AP		1981	0.000	13.210	0.000	86.790	100.000
Total Deemed to be Universities			0.023	25.912	43.291	30.800	100.000
State Universities							
Devi Ahilya University, Indore	**Central**	1964	0.125	29.648	62.529	7.820	100.000
Dr. Harisingh G.Vishdy. M.P.		1946	0.000	65.032	33.535	1.430	100.000
Barkatullah Univ. Bhopal		1970	0.000	19.003	61.739	19.260	100.000
Ranchi University, Bihar		1960	0.000	97.332	2.668	0.000	100.000
Magadh University, Bihar		1962	0.000	90.754	7.705	1.540	100.000
Rani Durgawati University, Jabalpur		1956	0.000	20.939	75.298	3.760	100.000
Deen Dayal Upad. University, Gorakhpur		1957	0.000	51.668	35.134	13.200	100.000
Punjab University, Chandigarh	**Northern**	1947	34.417	62.289	35.889	1.820	100.000
Kurukshetra University, Haryana		1956	0.000	29.445	21.487	49.070	100.000
M.D. Univ. Rohtak, Haryana		1976	0.000	26.870	19.135	54.000	100.000

(Contd.)

(Contd.Table 3.3)

Name of the Universities	*Region*	*Year of Estt.*	*Central Govt.*	*UGC*	*AICTE*	*Other Govt. Agencies*	*State Govt.*
Manipur University, Imphal	**North-Eastern**	1980	0.000	4.574	0.000	0.118	68.215
Nagaland University, Kohima		1994	0.000	80.165	0.000	0.000	0.000
Tirpura University, Tipura West		1987	0.000	3.637	0.000	0.635	91.663
Mizoram Univeristy, Aizawl-Mizoram		2001	0.000	34.361	61.643	0.000	0.674
Bhavnagar University	**Western**	1979	0.000	35.685	0.000	0.000	52.881
Swami Rmanand Univ., Nanded		1994	0.000	23.741	0.000	0.000	58.771
Shivaji Univeristy, Kolhapur		1962	0.604	0.930	0.000	11.815	44.216
Nagpur University, Nagpur		1923	0.173	1.217	0.526	0.000	35.350
Karnatak Univ. Dharwad	**Southern**	1950	0.000	3.450	0.000	0.000	66.121
Banglore University		1961	1.305	2.795	0.300	0.893	39.571
Mangalore University, Mangalagangothri		1980	0.000	5.284	0.000	0.000	50.058
Cochin Univ. of Sc. & Tech., Kerala		1986	0.000	5.204	0.692	0.930	53.035
University of Kerala, Thiruvanauthapuram		1937	3.347	3.872	0.000	0.271	66.650
Sri Krishnadeva--raya Univ., Anantapur		1981	0.000	0.000	0.000	0.000	75.517
University of Madras, Chennai		1857	0.000	0.428	0.000	0.000	8.845
Total State Universities			0.571	4.999	1.153	1.013	39.879
All Universities Total			0.476	18.356	0.959	0.843	33.368

(Contd.)

(Contd.Table 3.3)

Name of the Universities	*Region*	*Year of Estt.*	*Local Body*	*Total (Govt. Grants)*	*Total Fees*	*Univ. & Other Sources*	*Total Income*
Manipur University, Imphal	**North-Eastern**	1980	0.000	72.907	11.787	15.310	100.000
Nagaland University, Kohima		1994	0.000	80.165	6.249	13.590	100.000
Tirpura University, Tipura West		1987	0.000	95.935	2.980	1.080	100.000
Mizoram Univeristy, Aizawl-Mizoram		2001	0.000	96.678	2.852	0.470	100.000
Bhavnagar University	**Western**	1979	0.000	88.566	7.835	3.600	100.000
Swami Rmanand Univ., Nanded		1994	0.000	82.512	13.933	3.560	100.000
Shivaji Univeristy, Kolhapur		1962	0.000	57.564	29.741	12.700	100.000
Nagpur University, Nagpur		1923	0.000	37.267	16.475	46.260	100.000
Karnatak Univ. Dharwad	**Southern**	1950	0.000	69.572	21.452	8.980	100.000
Banglore University		1961	0.000	44.863	43.181	11.960	100.000
Mangalore University, Mangalagangothri		1980	0.000	55.342	26.318	8.340	100.000
Cochin Univ. of Sc. & Tech., Kerala		1986	0.039	59.900	18.109	21.990	100.000
University of Kerala, Thiruvanauthapuram		1937	0.000	74.139	25.779	0.080	100.000
Sri Krishnadeva--raya Univ., Anantapur		1981	0.823	76.340	16.394	7.270	100.000
University of Madras, Chennai		1857	0.000	9.272	62.385	28.340	100.000
Total State Universities			3.267	50.883	29.737	19.380	100.000
All Universities Total			2.717	56.719	26.103	17.180	100.000

Deemed to be Universities and a number of state universities for 1996-97 and 2001-02. They indicate that:

1. The total government grants in selected universities have declined. The decline is from 64.99 per cent to 56.71 per cent.
2. In AMU, which is a Central University, total government grants in 2001-02 increased to 93.73 per cent from 91.33 in 1996-97
3. In state universities, total government grants declined from 60.44 per cent to 50.88 per cent respectively.
4. In Deemed to be Universities, a declining trend has been observed. The total government grants received by these universities declined from 39.32 per cent to 25.91 per cent of the total income. In Bansathali Vidyapeeth, however, the decline was more than 50 per cent.
5. Large disparities in funding from state governments (have been observed) in all types of universities. Some universities receive grants on a more liberal scale than others. The grant ranged from 7.38 per cent (University of Madras) to 71.77 per cent (Bhavnagar University) in 1996-97 and 8.84 per cent (University of Madras) to 75.51 per cent (Sri Krishnadevaraya University) in 2001-02. Within universities also, disparities in grants received were observed in all state universities except in North-Eastern region.
6. Other grants given to universities, by Central government, All India Council for Technical Education (AICTE), other government agencies and local bodies, are meagre, except in the case of Punjab University which received 49.45 per cent from local body in 1996-97. That too has declined over the period of five years i.e. to 34.41 per cent.
7. Total funding from local bodies in all universities decreased sharply during the period under review i.e. 5.24 per cent to 2.71 per cent. There is a marginal decline in Deemed to be Universities also. However, for state universities, the decline was again quite high i.e. 6.34 per cent to 3.26 per cent.

8. In Cochin University of Science and Technology, which provides professional education courses, grants from the government decreased from 70.89 per cent to 59.90 per cent from 1996-97 to 2001-02.
9. Contribution from fees, which includes tuition, hostel and examination fees, increased from 20.06 per cent to 26.10 per cent. In Central University, there was a marginal increase. However, in Deemed to be Universities income from fees was quite substantial, ranging between 24.98 per cent to 43.29 per cent.
10. Income from 'other sources' that include endowments and donations from trusts, contribution from alumni, general public, industries, corporate houses, sale of publications, project grants, fellowship and others was 24.86 per cent during 1996-97 which declined to 17.18 per cent during 2001-02.

Table 3.4 and Figure 3.2 show that there is no relationship between the income of universities and the year of their establishment. The percentage allocation of resources decreased from 1996-97 to 2001-02 in two universities i.e. Rani Durgawati which is very old (established in 1935) and Swami Ramanand University which is a new University (established in 1994). Only two universities, which were established in 1950s and 1960s, show more than 300 per cent increase in income from different sources viz. Devi Ahilya University (1964) and MD University (1956). Universities, which were established before 1950, have generally less income than those established later. However, there are a few exceptions.

B. Non-government Sources

In view of the sharp decline in government sources of income, universities have to mobilize resources from non-government sources. These sources consist generally of fees from students, (tuition fees, examination fees, hostel fees etc), university resources, endowments, donations, etc. It is generally accepted that government contribution for education is very important and non-government sources can be utilized for

Table 3.4: Distribution of Universities by share in Income (increase or decrease and year of establishment from 1996-97 to 2001-02) (In Percentage)

Decreased	*Increased* *Less than 100*	*100 to 200*	*201 to 300*	*Above 300*
·Rani Durgawati	· AMU (1920)	· Deen Dayal Upadhayay	· Rashtriya Sanskrit Vidyapeetha	· M.D. University (1956)
	University, (1956)			
· Swami Ramanand	· Nagpur (1923)	· Madras (1957)	· Ranchi (1976)	· Devhi Ahilya (1964)
	· Kerala (1937)	· Kurukshetra (1957)	· Ranchi (1976)	
	· Dr. Hari Singh Gaur (1946)	· Bangalore	· Bhavnagar (1979)	
	· Punjab (1947)	· Banasthali (1962)		
	· Karnataka (1950)	· Sri Sathya Sai		
	Instt. (1981)			
	· Shivaji (1962)	· Tripura (1987)		
	· Barkatullahj (1970)	· Nagaland (1994)		
	· Manipur (1980)			
	· Mangalore (1980)			
	· Sri Krishnadevaraya (1981)			
	· Cochin (Sc. & Tech.) (1986)			

Note: Figures in parenthesis denote the year of establishment of the Universities.

Figure : 3.2 Distribution of Universities by % Share of Increase and Decrease in Income and Year of Establishment

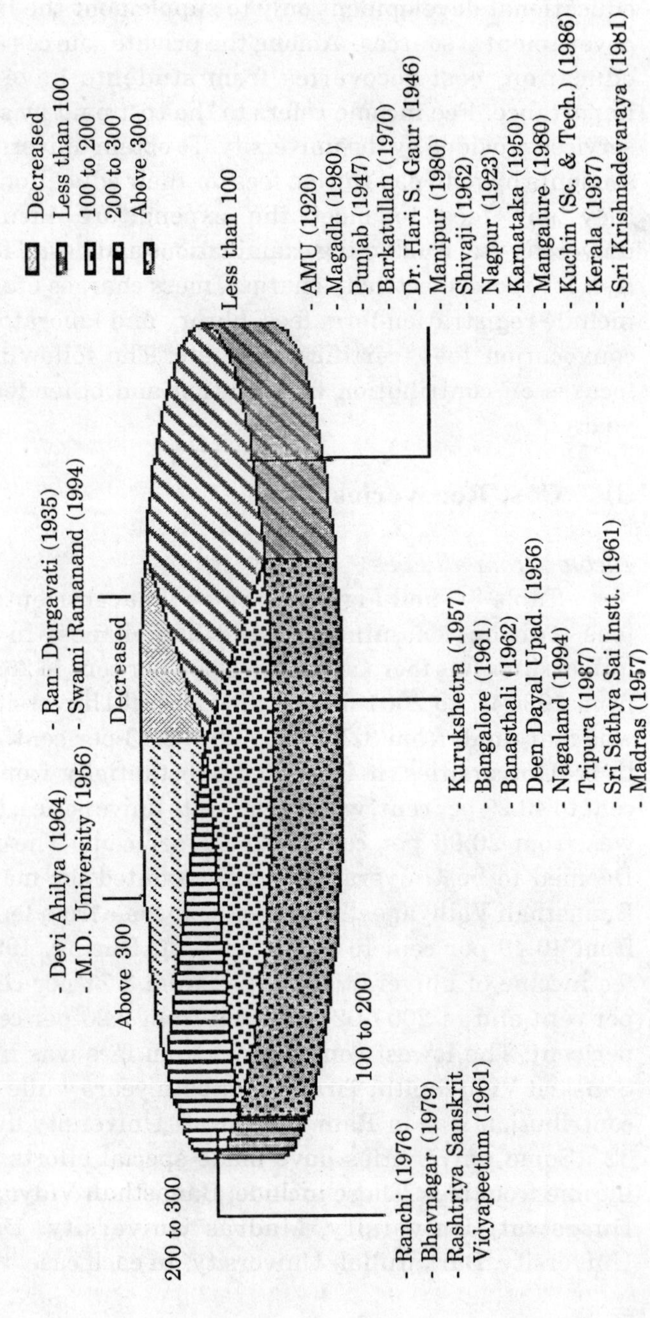

educational development only to supplement the income from governmental sources. Among the private sources of financing education, cost recoveries from students have their own importance. Fee income refers to the cost paid by students for services provided by the university. To obtain university degrees, students have to pay tuition fees for their education. Similarly, they pay fees to meet the expenditure incurred by a university in conducting examinations and hostel fees towards rent for room, electricity charges, mess charges etc. Other fees include registration form fees, library and laboratory charges, convocation fees, certificate fee etc. The following analysis focuses on contribution from tuition and other fees over the years.

(i) Cost Recoveries

Income from all Fees

Table 3.5 and Figure 3.3 show that contribution from all fees (tuition, examination and hostel fees) in all the 29 universities has increased from 20.06 per cent to 26.10 per cent from 1996-97 to 2001-02. In the Central University, increase was marginal, from 3.23 per cent to 3.33 per cent. In Deemed to be Universities, it increased substantially from 24.98 per cent to 43.29 per cent, while in all state universities, the increase was from 20.06 per cent to 26.10 per cent. The increase in Deemed to be Universities was accounted for mainly by the Banasthali Vidhyapeeth, where the income from fees increased from 40.49 per cent to 67.09 per cent. During, 1996-97, total fee income of universities ranged from 3.21 per cent to 61.65 per cent and in 2001-02 it ranged from 2.20 per cent to 75.29 per cent. The lowest contribution from fees was in Rasthriya Sanskrit Vidhyapith, Tirupati for both years while the highest contribution was in Rani Durgawati University during 2001-02. Some universities have made special efforts to increase income from fees. These include: Banasthali Vidyapeeth, Rani Durgawati University, Madras University, Devi Ahilya University, Barkatullah University. In each case, the increase

Table 3.5: Percentage distribution of share of total fees to the total income in 1996-97 and 2001-02

Name of the Universities	*Region*	*Year of Estt.*	*1996-97*		
			Total Income (Rs. in lakh)	*All Fees (Rs. in lakh)*	*% of All Fees*
Central Unviersity					
AMU, Aligarh		1920	**8220.42**	**266.12**	**3.237**
Deemed to be Universities					
Banasthali Vidhyapeeth, Rajasthan		1962	496.94	201.25	40.498
Rashtriya Sanskrit Vidyapeethm,Tirupati		1961	107.94	3.47	3.215
Sri Sathya Sai Institute of H.Learning, AP		1981	214.46	0.00	0.000
Total Deemed to be Universities			**819.34**	**204.72**	**24.986**
State Universities					
Devi Ahilya University, Indore		1964	763.85	196.97	25.786
Dr. Harisingh G.Vishdy. M.P.		1946	1521.56	466.93	30.688
Barkatullah Univ. Bhopal		1970	1516.26	390.13	25.730
Ranchi University, Bihar	**Central**	1976	42.99	3.00	6.978
Magadh University, Bihar		1960	4443.12	288.68	6.497
Rani Durgawati University, Jabalpur		1935	805.11	266.06	33.046
Deen Dayal Upad. University, Gorakhpur		1956	1005.45	175.41	17.446

(Contd.)

(Contd. Table 3.5)

Name of the Universities	*Region*	*Year of Estt.*	*2001-02*		
			Total Income (Rs. in lakh)	*All Fees (Rs. in lakh)*	*% of All Fees*
Central Unviersity					
AMU, Aligarh		1920	**15882.01**	**528.99**	**3.331**
Deemed to be Universities					
Banasthali Vidhyapeeth, Rajasthan		1962	1398.82	938.48	67.091
Rashtriya Sanskrit Vidyapeethm,Tirupati		1961	331.49	7.31	2.205
Sri Sathya Sai Institute of H.Learning, AP		1981	454.42	0	0.000
Total Deemed to be Universities			**2184.73**	**945.79**	**43.291**
State Universities					
Devi Ahilya University, Indore	**Central**	1964	3365.22	2104.25	62.529
Dr. Harisingh G.Vishdy. M.P.		1946	2474.29	829.75	33.535
Barkatullah Univ. Bhopal		1970	2282.95	1409.46	61.739
Ranchi University, Bihar		1976	134.95	3.6	2.668
Magadh University, Bihar		1960	7307.38	563.05	7.705
Rani Durgawati University, Jabalpur		1935	746.25	561.91	75.298
Deen Dayal Upad. University, Gorakhpur		1956	2308.58	811.1	35.134

(Contd.)

(Contd.Table 3.5)

Name of the Universities	*Region*	*Year of Estt.*	*1996-97*		
			Total Income (Rs. in lakh)	*All Fees (Rs. in lakh)*	*% of All Fees*
Punjab University, Chandigarh	**Northern**	1947	4824.59	438.12	9.081
Kurukshetra University, Haryana		1957	2997.55	549.16	18.320
M.D. Univ. Rohtak, Haryana		1956	1797.72	177.68	9.884
Manipur University, Imphal	**North-Eastern**	1980	664.97	72.38	10.885
Nagaland University, Kohima		1994	492.38	19.49	3.958
Tirpura University, Tipura West		1987	286.80	11.00	3.835
Mizoram University		2001	0.00	0.00	0.00
Bhavnagar University	**Western**	1979	418.26	44.40	10.615
Swami Rmanand Univ., Nanded		1994	613.45	182.75	29.791
Shivaji Univeristy, Kolhapur		1962	2217.15	531.03	23.951
Nagpur University, Nagpur		1923	3166.58	770.41	24.329

(Contd.)

(Contd. Table 3.5)

Name of the Universities	*Region*	*Year of Estt.*	*2001-02*		
			Total Income (Rs. in lakh)	*All Fees (Rs. in lakh)*	*% of All Fees*
Manipur University, Imphal	**North-Eastern**	1980	1143.44	134.78	11.787
Nagaland University, Kohima		1994	1394.52	87.15	6.249
Tirpura University, Tipura West		1987	811.11	24.17	2.980
Mizoram University		2001	1534.30	43.76	2.852
Bhavnagar University	**Western**	1979	1276.25	99.99	7.835
Swami Rmanand Univ., Nanded		1994	568.63	79.23	13.933
Shivaji Univeristy, Kolhapur		1962	3848.97	1144.72	29.741
Nagpur University, Nagpur		1923	5774.01	951.29	16.475

(Contd.)

(Contd.Table 3.5)

Name of the Universities	*Region*	*Year of Estt.*	*1996-97*		
			Total Income (Rs. in lakh)	*All Fees (Rs. in lakh)*	*% of All Fees*
Karnatak Univ. Dharwad	**Southern**	1950	2746.25	848.36	30.892
Banglore University		1961	3330.29	1210.29	36.342
Mangalore University, Mangalagangothri		1980	1061.93	280.07	26.374
Cochin Univ. of Sc. & Tech., Kerala		1986	1484.23	159.36	10.737
University of Kerala, Thiruvanauthapuram		1937	3186.81	998.40	31.329
Sri Krishnadevaraya Univ., Anantapur		1981	823.69	154.66	18.776
University of Madras, Chennai		1857	2827.40	1743.29	61.657
Total State Universities			**43038.39**	**9978.03**	**23.184**
All Universities Total			**52078.15**	**10448.87**	**20.064**

(Contd.)

(Contd.Table 3.5)

Name of the Universities	*Region*	*Year of Estt.*	*2001-02*		
			Total Income (Rs. in lakh)	*All Fees (Rs. in lakh)*	*% of All Fees*
Karnatak Univ. Dharwad	**Southern**	1950	4310.17	924.6	21.452
Banglore University		1961	6670.62	2880.46	43.181
Mangalore University, Mangalagangothri		1980	1898.98	499.78	26.318
Cochin Univ. of Sc. & Tech., Kerala		1986	2922.59	529.25	18.109
University of Kerala, Thiruvanauthapuram		1937	5561.51	1433.71	25.779
Sri Krishnadevaraya Univ., Anantapur		1981	1192.64	195.52	16.394
University of Madras, Chennai		1857	8255.25	5150.01	62.385
Total State Universities			**89205.84**	**26526.8**	**29.737**
All Universities Total			**107272.58**	**28001.53**	**26.103**

(Contd.)

Figure 3.3 : Pattern of Fee Income

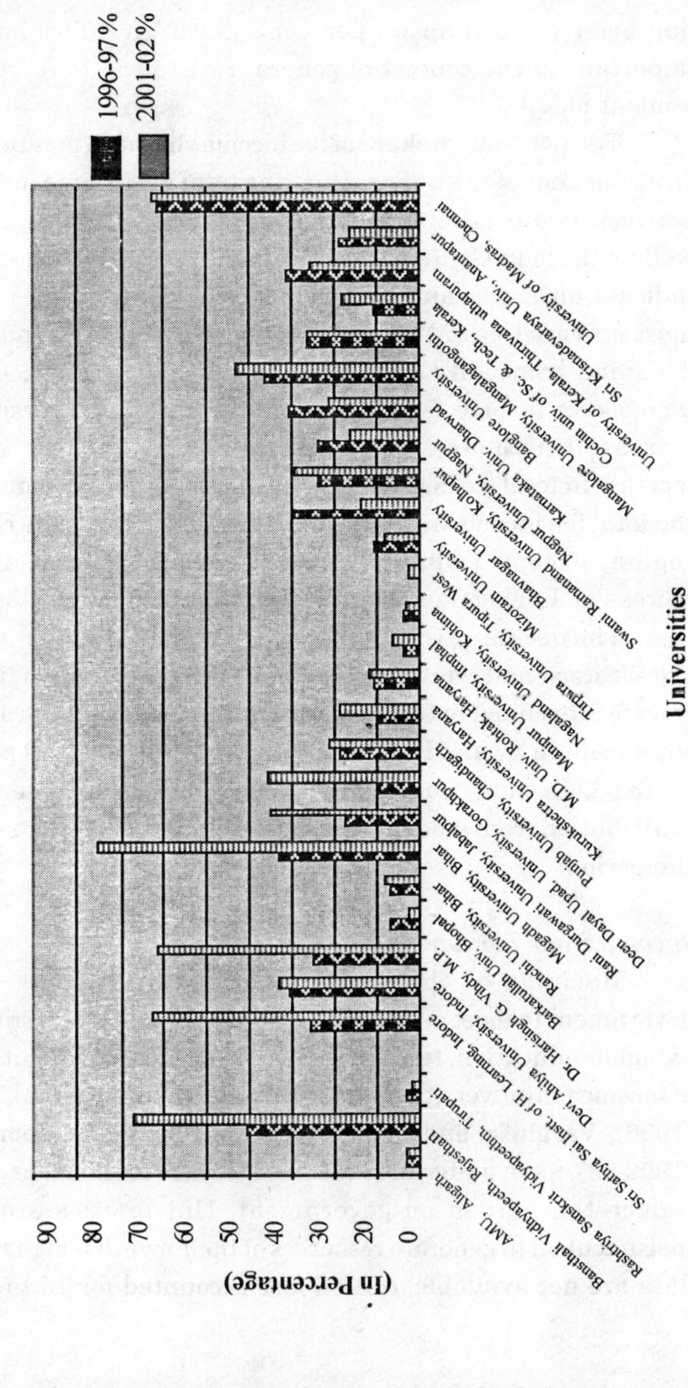

has been more than 60 per cent. Such an effort becomes important in the context of general resistance to increase in student fees.

The percentage share of fee income shows an erratic trend. In 35 per cent of the universities, the total fee income increased between two periods under consideration. All universities as well as those in Central, Northern and North-Eastern regions indicate an increasing trend for income from all fees. While most universities in Western and Southern regions, indicate a declining trend, in Central region, there was a spectacular increase in income from fees. In Devi Ahilya University, the increase was more than seven times. In Northern region, increase in total fee income was quite high. In Punjab University, the total fee income increased almost 4 times. In North-Eastern region, except Tripura University, income from all fees increased. In Nagaland University, it doubled itself.

The declining trend was observed in most universities of the Western and Southern regions. In Western region, income from fees declined in three universities. The decrease was quite significant in Swami Ramanand University from 29.79 per cent to 13.93. In sum, no uniform pattern has been observed in contribution from student fees in university institutions during the period.

Income from Tuition Fees

Because of the inability or unwillingness of the government to meet all the financial requirements of institutions of higher education, tuition fee has become an important source of income for universities. Azad (1975, 1984), World Bank Report (1986), Varghese and Tilak (1991) and Punnayya Committee (1992-93), have underlined the need to raise tuition fees so as to reduce the burden on government. Universities are being insisted upon to generate resources of their own. Though reliable data are not available, tuition fees accounted for 15 to 20 per cent of the total recurring expenditure during 1950s. For more than five decades now, though cost of education has gone up substantially, tuition fees accounted for only 2-3 per cent of the total income of universities (see Table 3.6).

Table 3.6 and figure 3.4 indicates that the share of tuition fees to total income in all universities was 1.89 per cent in 1996-97; it increased to 4.19 per cent in 2001-02. In state universities, income from tuition fees increased in the two years from 1.83 per cent and to 4.12 per cent. In Deemed to be Universities, it increased 11 times viz. from 2.40 per cent to 26.19 per cent. But in Central University, it decreased from 2.2 per cent to 1.56 per cent. University-wise data show that except in Devi Ahilya, Banasthali, Punjab, Karnataka and Bangalore Universities, tuition fees accounted for 2 to 3 per cent of the total income in 2001-02. The marginal increase in the income from tuition fees – from 2 per cent to 4 per cent – indicates that despite rising costs of education, universities have not made any substantial effort to transfer part of the burden of financing higher education to students who are its direct beneficiaries.

The table also indicates that in most universities, whether Central or State, income from tuition fees has been on the decline, except for two universities viz. Devi Ahilya (State University) and Banasthali Vidypeeth (Deemd to be University). In 1996-97, Devi Ahilya, which was recovering only 0.73 per cent of the total income from tuition fees, increased the share of fees to 40.79 per cent in 2001-02. Banasthali Vidyapeeth's income from tuition fees also rose from 3.97 per cent to 40.91 per cent. The reason for increase in tuition fees in these universities was mainly the introduction of professional or job-oriented courses. In other universities in the same region, the proportion of income from tuition fees has been on the decline. Even in Cochin University of Science and Technology, which is a university offering professional courses, the decline in its income from tuition fees was from 6.89 per cent to 4.77 per cent. This would seem to indicate that professional courses and those related to jobs, need not necessarily result in their financing by their direct beneficiaries.

Table 3.6: Share of Tuition Fees to Total Income in 1996-97 and 2001-02

Name of the Universities	*Region*	*Year of Estt.*	*1996-97*		
			Total Income (Rs. in lakh)	*Tuition Fees (Rs. in lakh)*	*Tuition Fees (in %)*
Central Unviersity					
AMU, Aligarh		1920	**8220.42**	**179.25**	**2.181**
Deemed to be Universities					
Banasthali Vidhyapeeth, Rajasthan		1962	496.94	19.73	3.970
Rashtriya Sanskrit Vidyapeethm,Tirupati		1961	107.94	0.00	0.000
Sri Sathya Sai Institute of H.Learning, AP		1981	214.46	0.00	0.000
Total Deemed to be Universities			**819.34**	**19.73**	**2.408**
State Universities					
Devi Ahilya University, Indore	**Central**	1964	763.85	5.61	0.734
Dr. Harisingh G.Vishdy. M.P.		1946	1521.56	15.41	1.013
Barkatullah Univ. Bhopal		1970	1516.26	7.18	0.474
Ranchi University, Bihar		1976	42.99	2.2	5.117
Magadh University, Bihar*		1960	4443.12	134.48	3.027
Rani Durgawati University, Jabalpur		1935	805.11	6.93	0.861
Deen Dayal Upad. University, Gorakhpur		1956	1005.45	32.99	3.281

(Contd.)

(Contd. Table 3.6)

Name of the Universities	*Region*	*Year of Estt.*	*2001-02*		
			Total Income (Rs. in lakh)	*Tuition Fees (Rs. in lakh)*	*Tuition Fees (in %)*
Central Unviersity					
AMU, Aligarh		1920	**15882.01**	**248.29**	**1.563**
Deemed to be Universities					
Banasthali Vidhyapeeth, Rajasthan		1962	1398.82	572.29	40.912*
Rashtriya Sanskrit Vidyapeethm, Tirupati		1961	331.49	0.00	0.000
Sri Sathya Sai Institute of H.Learning, AP		1981	454.42	0.00	0.000
Total Deemed to be Universities			**2184.73**	**572.29**	**26.195**
State Universities					
Devi Ahilya University, Indore	**Central**	1964	3365.22	1372.85	40.795*
Dr. Harisingh G.Vishdy. M.P.		1946	2474.29	35.13	1.420
Barkatullah Univ. Bhopal		1970	2282.95	2.47	0.108
Ranchi University, Bihar		1976	134.95	2.20	1.630
Magadh University, Bihar*		1960	7307.38	135.70	1.857
Rani Durgawati University, Jabalpur		1935	746.25	12.73	1.706
Deen Dayal Upad. University, Gorakhpur		1956	2308.58	78.42	3.397

(Contd.)

(Contd.Table 3.6)

Name of the Universities	*Region*	*Year of Estt.*	*1996-97*		
			Total Income (Rs. in lakh)	*Tuition Fees (Rs. in lakh)*	*Tuition Fees (in %)*
Punjab University, Chandigarh	**Northern**	1947	4824.59	56.68	1.175
Kurukshetra University, Haryana		1957	2997.55	46.96	1.567
M.D. Univ. Rohtak, Haryana		1956	1797.72	17.73	0.986
Manipur University, Imphal	**North-Eastern**	1980	664.97	21.03	3.163
Nagaland University, Kohima		1994	492.38	2.58	0.524
Tirpura University, Tipura West		1987	286.80	8.96	3.124
Mizoram University		2001	0.00	0.00	0.00
Bhavnagar University	**Western**	1979	418.26	3.59	0.858
Swami Rmanand Univ., Nanded		1994	613.45	0.11	0.018
Shivaji Univeristy, Kolhapur		1962	2217.15	65.74	2.965
Nagpur University, Nagpur		1923	3166.58	74.35	2.348

(Contd.)

(Contd.Table 3.6)

Name of the Universities	*Region*	*Year of Estt.*	*2001-02*		
			Total Income (Rs. in lakh)	*Tuition Fees (Rs. in lakh)*	*Tuition Fees (in %)*
Punjab University, Chandigarh	**Northern**	1947	8423.19	721.44	8.565
Kurukshetra University, Haryana		1957	7311.71	53.26	0.728
M.D. Univ. Rohtak, Haryana		1956	7688.33	22.22	0.289
Manipur University, Imphal	**North-Eastern**	1980	1143.44	37.57	3.286
Nagaland University, Kohima		1994	1394.52	4.71	0.338
Tirpura University, Tipura West		1987	811.11	6.37	0.785
Mizoram University		2001	1534.30	5.47	0.357
Bhavnagar University	**Western**	1979	1276.25	14.44	1.131
Swami Rmanand Univ., Nanded		1994	568.63	11.44	2.012
Shivaji Univeristy, Kolhapur		1962	3848.97	111.71	2.902
Nagpur University, Nagpur		1923	5774.01	129.81	2.248

(Contd.)

(Contd. Table 3.6)

Name of the Universities	*Region*	*Year of Estt.*	*1996-97*		
			Total Income (Rs. in lakh)	*Tuition Fees (Rs. in lakh)*	*Tuition Fees (in %)*
Karnatak Univ. Dharwad	**Southern**	1950	2746.25	51.73	1.884
Banglore University		1961	3330.29	46.26	1.389
Mangalore University, Mangalagangothri		1980	1061.93	9.47	0.892
Cochin Univ. of Sc. & Tech., Kerala		1986	1484.23	102.31	6.893
University of Kerala, Thiruvanauthapuram		1937	3186.81	24.74	0.776
Sri Krishnadevaraya Univ., Anantapur		1981	823.69	11.72	1.423
University of Madras, Chennai		1857	2827.40	41.44	1.466
Total State Universities			**43038.39**	**790.2**	**1.836**
All Universities Total			**52078.15**	**989.18**	**1.899**

(Contd.)

(Contd.Table 3.6)

Name of the Universities	*Region*	*Year of Estt.*	*2001-02*		
			Total Income (Rs. in lakh)	*Tuition Fees (Rs. in lakh)*	*Tuition Fees (in %)*
Karnatak Univ. Dharwad	**Southern**	1950	4310.17	244.56	5.674
Banglore University		1961	6670.62	348.08	5.218
Mangalore University, Mangalagangothri		1980	1898.98	16.52	0.870
Cochin Univ. of Sc. & Tech., Kerala		1986	2922.59	139.51	4.774
University of Kerala, Thiruvanauthapuram		1937	5561.51	55.01	0.989
Sri Krishnadevaraya Univ., Anantapur		1981	1192.64	9.81	0.823
University of Madras, Chennai		1857	8255.25	110.88	1.343
Total State Universities			**89205.84**	**3682.31**	**4.128**
All Universities Total			**107272.58**	**4502.89**	**4.198**

Note : * = started self financing courses to accrue income from tuition fees.

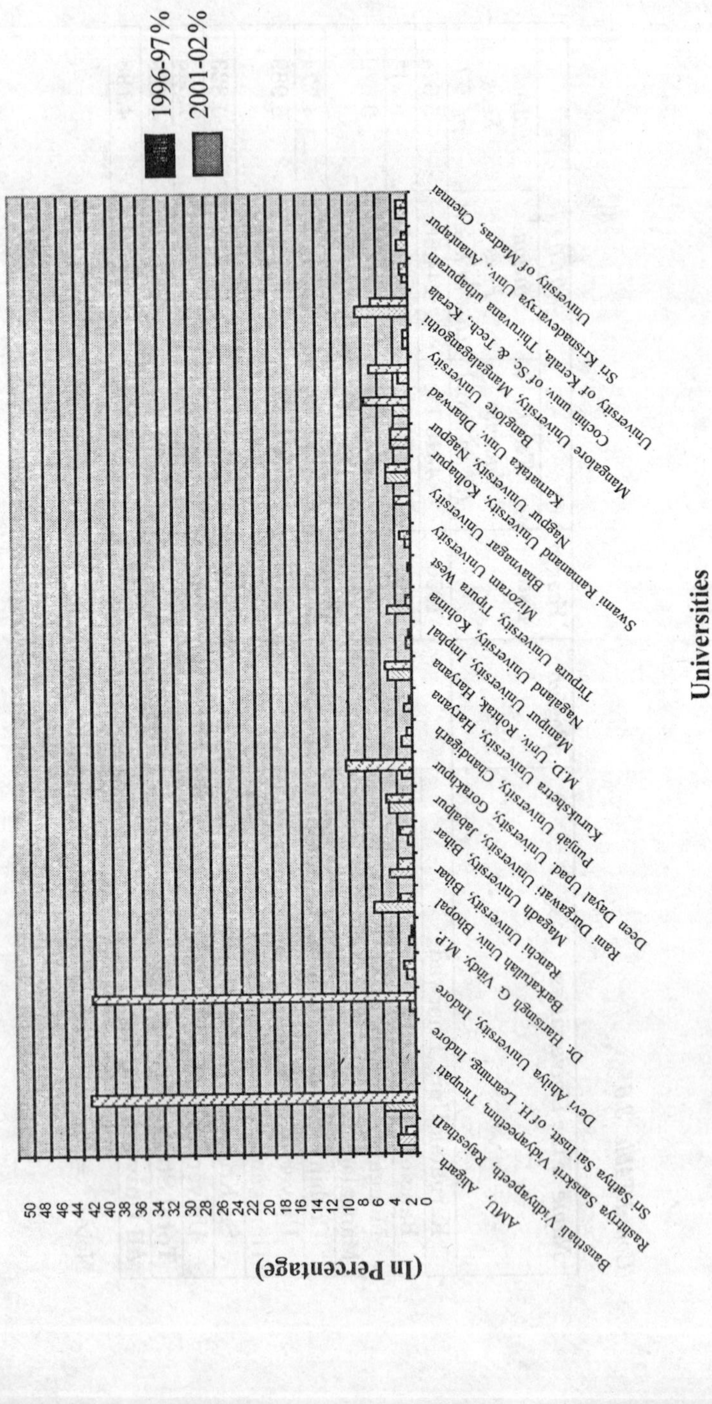

Figure 3.4 : Percentage of Tuition Fees

Income from Examination Fees

Examination fees from students are charged for conduct and management of examinations. The expenditure incurred includes: payment of honorarium to examiners, invigilators, paper setters, moderators, and evaluators, printing of question papers, answer books and meetings, computation costs, etc.

Table 3.7 and Figure 3.5 show that there has been a substantial increase in percentage of income from examination fees, the share of all the 29 universities increased in aggregate from 11.52 per cent to 14.18 per cent from 1996-97 to 2001-02. However, the increasing trend was observed in state universities only. In Central University and Deemed to be Universities, there was a decline in percentage of income from examination fees. In more than 50 per cent of universities, the percentage of income from examination fees increased during the period. In Central, Northern and North-Eastern regions, income from examination fees increased in all universities except in Devi Ahilya University (from 16.24 to 15.15) of Central region. Aligarh Mulsim University, a Central University had the lowest percentage as far as income from examination fees was concerned (0.32 & 0.14) for two years i.e. 1996-97 and 2001-02 respectively. On the other hand, Rani Durgawati University and Barkatullah University had shown more than two times increase from 1996-97 to 2001-02 viz. 29.73 per cent to 63.23 and 25.22 per cent to 61.27 per cent respectively mainly because of the introduction of self-financing courses. In Southern region, increase was observed in two universities only i.e. Mangalore University and Cochin University of Science and Technology. In remaining universities, income from examination fees shows a decreasing trend.

In Cochin University of Science and Technology, increase in examination fees was 3 times between 1996-97 to 2001-02; the main reason might be that the University runs technology courses, which are in great demand and costly to provide, and therefore along with other charges, the University finds it easier to charge higher fees for the conduct of examinations for these courses.

Table 3.7: Percentage distribution of share of examination fees to total income in 1996-97 and 2001-02

Name of the Universities	*Region*	*Year of Estt.*	*1996-97*		
			Total Income (Rs. in lakh)	*Exam. Fees (Rs. in lakh)*	*Exam. Fees (in %)*
Central Unviersity					
AMU, Aligarh		1920	**8220.42**	**26.98**	**0.328**
Deemed to be Universities					
Banasthali Vidhyapeeth, Rajasthan		1962	496.94	3.51	0.706
Rashtriya Sanskrit Vidyapeethm,Tirupati		1961	107.94	3.47	3.215
Sri Sathya Sai Institute of H.Learning, AP		1981	214.46	0.00	0.000
Total Deemed to be Universities			**819.34**	**6.98**	**0.852**
State Universities					
Devi Ahilya University, Indore	**Central**	1964	763.85	124.11	16.248
Dr. Harisingh G.Vishdy. M.P.		1946	1521.56	265.00	17.416
Barkatullah Univ. Bhopal		1970	1516.26	382.42	25.221
Ranchi University, Bihar		1976	42.99	0.80	1.861
Magadh University, Bihar*		1960	4443.12	154.20	3.471
Rani Durgawati University, Jabalpur		1935	805.11	239.39	29.734
Deen Dayal Upad. University, Gorakhpur		1956	1005.45	125.48	12.480

(Contd.)

(Contd.Table 3.7)

Name of the Universities	Region	Year of Estt.	2001-02		
			Total Income (Rs. in lakh)	Exam. Fees (Rs. in lakh)	Exam. Fees (in %)
Central Unviersity					
AMU, Aligarh		1920	**15882.01**	**23.27**	**0.147**
Deemed to be Universities					
Banasthali Vidhyapeeth, Rajasthan		1962	1398.82	9.10	0.651
Rashtriya Sanskrit Vidyapeethm, Tirupati		1961	331.49	7.31	2.205
Sri Sathya Sai Institute of H.Learning, AP		1981	454.42	0.00	0.000
Total Deemed to be Universities			**2184.73**	**16.41**	**0.751**
State Universities					
Devi Ahilya University, Indore	**Central**	1964	3365.22	510.00	15.155
Dr. Harisingh G.Vishdy. M.P.		1946	2474.29	473.00	19.117
Barkatullah Univ. Bhopal		1970	2282.95	1398.95	61.278
Ranchi University, Bihar		1976	134.95	1.40	1.037
Magadh University, Bihar*		1960	7307.38	320.51	4.386
Rani Durgawati University, Jabalpur		1935	746.25	471.86	63.231
Deen Dayal Upad. University, Gorakhpur		1956	2308.58	689.45	29.865

(Contd.)

(Contd. Table 3.7)

Name of the Universities	*Region*	*Year of Estt.*	*1996-97*		
			Total Income (Rs. in lakh)	*Exam. Fees (Rs. in lakh)*	*Exam. Fees (in %)*
Punjab University, Chandigarh	**Northern**	1947	4824.59	205.53	4.260
Kurukshetra University, Haryana		1957	2997.55	220.21	7.346
M.D. Univ. Rohtak, Haryana		1956	1797.72	117.67	6.546
Manipur University, Imphal	**North-Eastern**	1980	664.97	44.46	6.686
Nagaland University, Kohima		1994	492.38	13.05	2.650
Tirpura University, Tipura West		1987	286.80	0.02	0.007
Mizoram University		2001	0.00	0.00	0
Bhavnagar University	**Western**	1979	418.26	36.28	8.674
Swami Rmanand Univ., Nanded		1994	613.45	107.50	17.524
Shivaji Univeristy, Kolhapur		1962	2217.15	311.60	14.054
Nagpur University, Nagpur		1923	3166.58	630.71	19.918

(Contd.)

(Contd. Table 3.7)

Name of the Universities	Region	Year of Estt.	2001-02		
			Total Income (Rs. in lakh)	Exam. Fees (Rs. in lakh)	Exam. Fees (in %)
Punjab University, Chandigarh	Northern	1947	8423.19	1618.78	19.218
Kurukshetra University, Haryana		1957	7311.71	823.85	11.268
M.D. Univ. Rohtak, Haryana		1956	7688.33	1007.10	13.099
Manipur University, Imphal	North-Eastern	1980	1143.44	91.67	8.017
Nagaland University, Kohima		1994	1394.52	57.14	4.097
Tirpura University, Tipura West		1987	811.11	14.98	1.847
Mizoram University		2001	1534.30	24.31	1.584
Bhavnagar University	Western	1979	1276.25	70.74	5.543
Swami Rmanand Univ., Nanded		1994	568.63	26.75	4.704
Shivaji Univeristy, Kolhapur		1962	3848.97	810.79	21.065
Nagpur University, Nagpur		1923	5774.01	712.98	12.348

(Contd.)

(Contd. Table 3.7)

Name of the Universities	*Region*	*Year of Estt.*	*1996-97*		
			Total Income (Rs. in lakh)	*Exam. Fees (Rs. in lakh)*	*Exam. Fees (in %)*
Karnatak Univ. Dharwad	Southern	1950	2746.25	641.37	23.354
Banglore University		1961	3330.29	501.11	15.047
Mangalore University, Mangalagangothri		1980	1061.93	127.36	11.993
Cochin Univ. of Sc. & Tech., Kerala		1986	1484.23	18.46	1.244
University of Kerala, Thiruvanauthapuram		1937	3186.81	293.75	9.218
Sri Krishnadevaraya Univ., Anantapur		1981	823.69	139.24	16.904
University of Madras, Chennai		1857	2827.40	1266.57	44.796
Total State Universities			**43038.39**	**5966.29**	**13.863**
All Universities Total			**52078.15**	**6000.25**	**11.522**

(Contd.)

(Contd. Table 3.7)

Name of the Universities	Region	Year of Estt.	2001-02		
			Total Income (Rs. in lakh)	Exam. Fees (Rs. in lakh)	Exam. Fees (in %)
Karnatak Univ. Dharwad	Southern	1950	4310.17	500.78	11.619
Banglore University		1961	6670.62	1156.60	17.339
Mangalore University, Mangalagangothri		1980	1898.98	117.97	6.212
Cochin Univ. of Sc. & Tech., Kerala		1986	2922.59	135.86	4.649
University of Kerala, Thiruvanauthapuram		1937	5561.51	324.01	5.826
Sri Krishnadevaraya Univ., Anantapur		1981	1192.64	182.32	15.287
University of Madras, Chennai		1857	8255.25	3632.17	43.998
Total State Universities			**89205.84**	**15173.97**	**17.010**
All Universities Total			**107272.58**	**15213.65**	**14.182**

Figure 3.5 : Percentage of Income from Examination Fees to Total Income

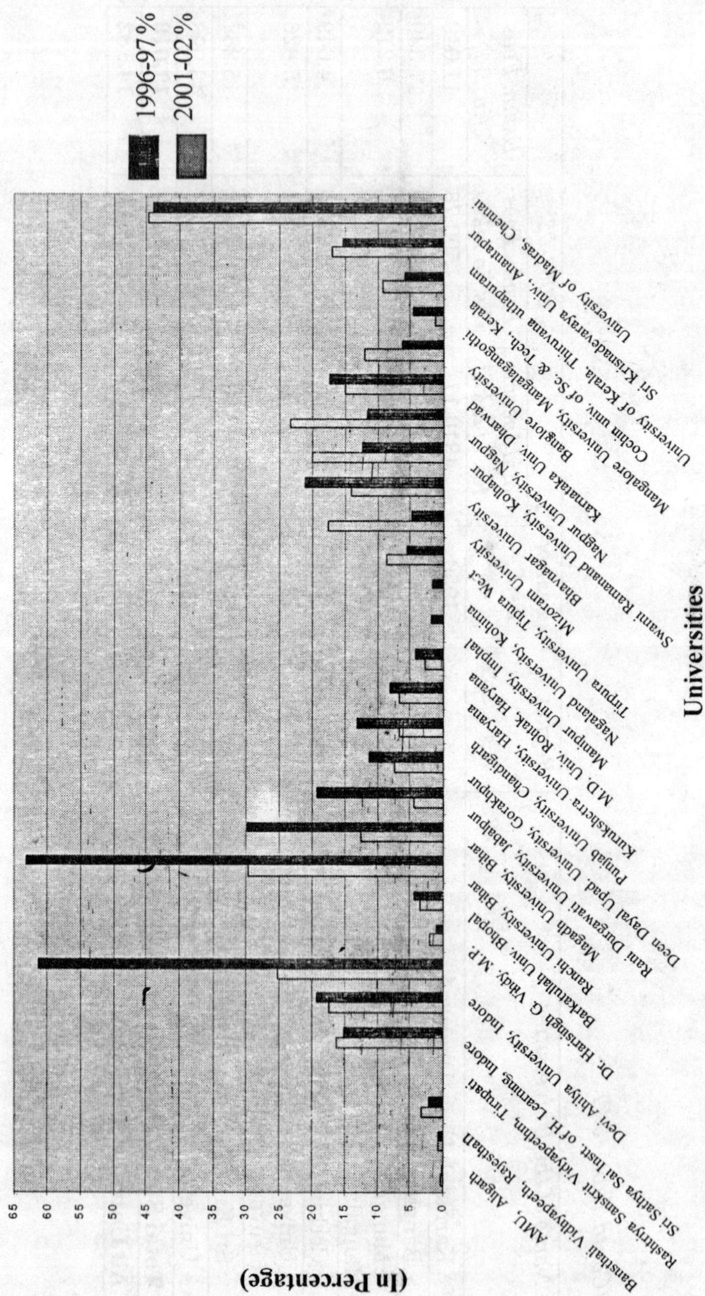

Universities where the percentage from examination fees shows a declining trend would need to find out the reasons and to adopt suitable measures so that they can, along with examination fees, mobilize additional resources through non-governmental sources. As a matter of policy examination fees should meet the entire expenditure under this head.

Income from Hostel Rent

In all the 29 universities, a marginal declining trend was observed in the share of hostel rent to total income of universities, which has slightly decreased from 0.53 per cent to 0.51 per cent during 1996-97 and 2001-02. In Central University the share declined from 0.30 per cent to 0.25 per cent, while in Deemed to be Universities, the decline was quite substantial, from 21.66 per cent to 14.62. In State universities, however, a marginal increase was observed; form 0.17 per cent to 0.21 per cent. Table 3.8 and Figure 3.6 show a declining trend in the income from hostel fees in more than 34 per cent of the universities. The largest decline was in Bansathali Vidyapeeth, from 35.72 per cent to 22.84 per cent during the period under review.

Income from Projects

Besides the usual on-going activities, specific time-bound projects are undertaken by universities from time-to-time. Apart from their significance to the fulfilment of university's objectives, they help in mobilizing additional resources and provide various departments and their faculty, opportunities for undertaking research and other activities, which have implications for enhancing research and relevance of education. These project grants come mainly from the UGC and to some extent from other agencies such as CSIR, ICAR, DAE, DST, ICSSR etc. The projects are generally in the nature of introduction of new courses, development of a particular specialization, qualitative improvement of specific activities/ facilities, establishment of a new school or centre of study, time bound research, extension or consultancy, construction of new

Table 3.8: Share of hostel rent to the total income in 1996-97 and 2001-02

Name of the Universities	*Region*	*Year of Estt.*	*1996-97*		
			Total Income (Rs. in lakh)	*Hostel Rent (Rs. in lakh)*	*Hostel Rent (in %)*
Central Unviersity					
AMU, Aligarh		1920	**8220.42**	**24.63**	**0.300**
Deemed to be Universities					
Banasthali Vidhyapeeth, Rajasthan		1962	496.94	177.52	35.723
Rashtriya Sanskrit Vidyapeethm,Tirupati		1961	107.94	0.00	0.000
Sri Sathya Sai Institute of H.Learning, AP		1981	214.46	0.00	0.000
Total Deemed to be Universities			**819.34**	**177.52**	**21.666**
State Universities					
Devi Ahilya University, Indore	**Central**	1964	763.85	3.00	0.393
Dr. Harisingh G.Vishdy. M.P.		1946	1521.56	2.52	0.166
Barkatullah Univ. Bhopal		1970	1516.26	0.43	0.028
Ranchi University, Bihar		1976	42.99	0.00	0.000
Magadh University, Bihar*		1960	4443.12	0.00	0.000
Rani Durgawati University, Jabalpur		1935	805.11	0.72	0.089
Deen Dayal Upad. University, Gorakhpur		1956	1005.45	1.29	0.128

(Contd.)

(Contd.Table 3.8)

Name of the Universities	*Region*	*Year of Estt.*	*2001-02*		
			Total Income (Rs. in lakh)	*Hostel Rent (Rs. in lakh)*	*Hostel Rent (in %)*
Central Unviersity					
AMU, Aligarh		1920	**15882.01**	**40.98**	**0.258**
Deemed to be Universities					
Banasthali Vidhyapeeth, Rajasthan		1962	1398.82	319.49	22.840
Rashtriya Sanskrit Vidyapeethm,Tirupati		1961	331.49	0.00	0.000
Sri Sathya Sai Institute of H.Learning, AP		1981	454.42	0.00	0.000
Total Deemed to be Universities			**2184.73**	**319.49**	**14.624**
State Universities					
Devi Ahilya University, Indore	**Central**	1964	3365.22	7.00	0.208
Dr. Harisingh G.Vishdy. M.P.		1946	2474.29	4.62	0.187
Barkatullah Univ. Bhopal		1970	2282.95	5.25	0.230
Ranchi University, Bihar		1976	134.95	0.00	0.000
Magadh University, Bihar*		1960	7307.38	0.00	0.000
Rani Durgawati University, Jabalpur		1935	746.25	2.16	0.289
Deen Dayal Upad. University, Gorakhpur		1956	2308.58	7.48	0.324

(Contd.)

(Contd.Table 3.8)

Name of the Universities	Region	Year of Estt.	1996-97		
			Total Income (Rs. in lakh)	Hostel Rent (Rs. in lakh)	Hostel Rent (in %)
Punjab University, Chandigarh	Northern	1947	4824.59	0.87	0.018
Kurukshetra University, Haryana		1957	2997.55	12.84	0.428
M.D. Univ. Rohtak, Haryana		1956	1797.72	6.12	0.340
Manipur University, Imphal	North-Eastern	1980	664.97	1.30	0.195
Nagaland University, Kohima		1994	492.38	0.60	0.122
Tirpura University, Tipura West		1987	286.80	2.02	0.704
Mizoram University		2001	0.00	0.00	0.00
Bhavnagar University	Western	1979	418.26	0.34	0.081
Swami Rmanand Univ., Nanded		1994	613.45	0.00	0.000
Shivaji Univeristy, Kolhapur		1962	2217.15	6.78	0.306
Nagpur University, Nagpur		1923	3166.58	10.07	0.318

(Contd.)

(Contd.Table 3.8)

Name of the Universities	Region	Year of Estt.	2001-02		
			Total Income (Rs. in lakh)	Hostel Rent (Rs. in lakh)	Hostel Rent (in %)
Punjab University, Chandigarh	**Northern**	1947	8423.19	6.99	0.083
Kurukshetra University, Haryana		1957	7311.71	28.38	0.388
M.D. Univ. Rohtak, Haryana		1956	7688.33	25.65	0.334
Manipur University, Imphal	**North-Eastern**	1980	1143.44	1.03	0.090
Nagaland University, Kohima		1994	1394.52	1.82	0.131
Tirpura University, Tipura West		1987	811.11	0.03	0.004
Mizoram University		2001	1534.30	0.19	0.012
Bhavnagar University	**Western**	1979	1276.25	2.35	0.184
Swami Rmanand Univ., Nanded		1994	568.63	1.94	0.341
Shivaji Univeristy, Kolhapur		1962	3848.97	8.38	0.218
Nagpur University, Nagpur		1923	5774.01	20.11	0.348

(Contd.)

(Contd.Table 3.8)

Name of the Universities	Region	Year of Estt.	2001-02		
			Total Income (Rs. in lakh)	Hostel Rent (Rs. in lakh)	Hostel Rent (in %)
Karnatak Univ. Dharwad	Southern	1950	4310.17	24.71	0.573
Banglore University		1961	6670.62	0.00	0.000
Mangalore University, Mangalagangothri		1980	1898.98	14.64	0.771
Cochin Univ. of Sc. & Tech., Kerala		1986	2922.59	6.28	0.215
University of Kerala, Thiruvanauthapuram		1937	5561.51	8.53	0.153
Sri Krishnadevaraya Univ., Anantapur		1981	1192.64	3.39	0.284
University of Madras, Chennai		1857	8255.25	9.33	0.113
Total State Universities			**89205.84**	**190.26**	**0.213**
All Universities Total			**107272.58**	**550.73**	**0.513**

(Contd.)

(Contd. Table 3.8)

Name of the Universities	*Region*	*Year of Estt.*	*2001-02*		
			Total Income (Rs. in lakh)	*Hostel Rent (Rs. in lakh)*	*Hostel Rent (in %)*
Karnatak Univ. Dharwad	**Southern**	1950	4310.17	24.71	0.573
Banglore University		1961	6670.62	0.00	0.000
Mangalore University, Mangalagangothri		1980	1898.98	14.64	0.771
Cochin Univ. of Sc. & Tech., Kerala		1986	2922.59	6.28	0.215
University of Kerala, Thiruvanauthapuram		1937	5561.51	8.53	0.153
Sri Krishnadevaraya Univ., Anantapur		1981	1192.64	3.39	0.284
University of Madras, Chennai		1857	8255.25	9.33	0.113
Total State Universities			**89205.84**	**190.26**	**0.213**
All Universities Total			**107272.58**	**550.73**	**0.513**

(Contd.)

Figure 3.6 : Hostel Charges to Total Income

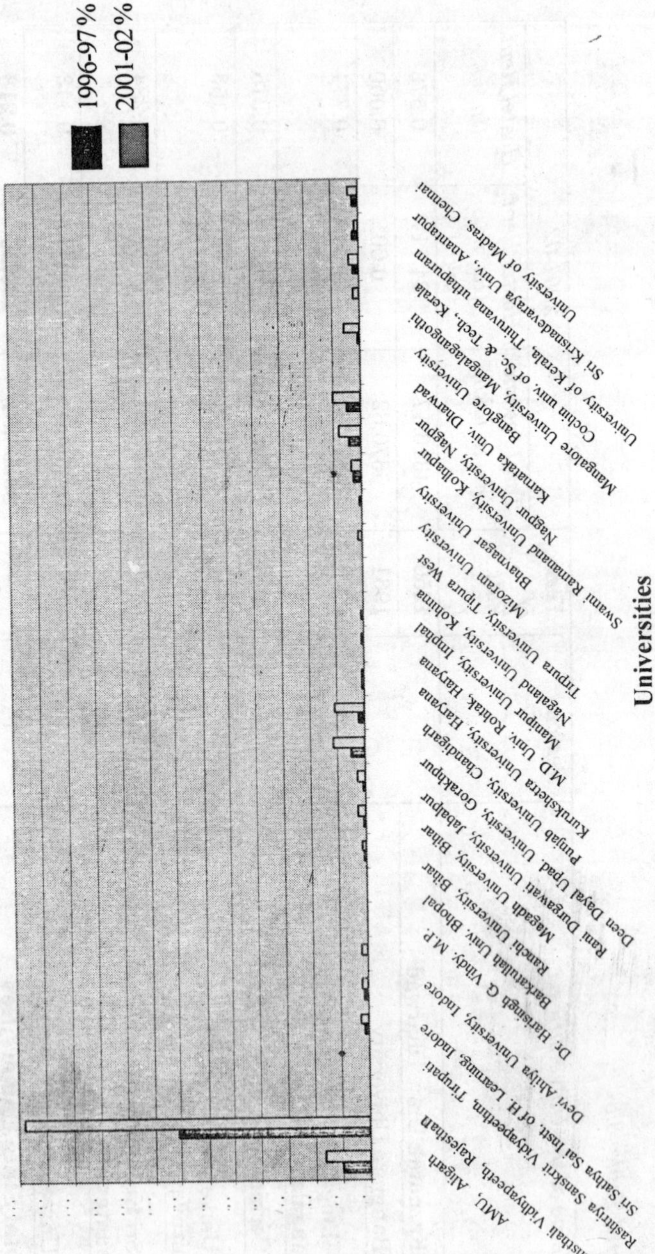

buildings (or adding to the existing ones). Each of these projects has to be closely monitored, both in terms of progress of expenditure and benefits derived.

Table 3.9 shows that there is a wide variation in the amount received by universities for research projects sponsored either by the government or by non-governmental organizations. The share of income from project grants by government sources in all 29 Universities has shown a declining trend. It declined from 1.91 per cent to 1.52 per cent during 1996-97 and 2001-02. On the other hand the share of grants from non-government sources increased from 0.61 per cent to 1.75 per cent. In Central University, no income seems to have occurred from this source, which is unlikely. On the other hand, in Deemed to be Universities, percentage of project grants from government sources increased from 0.15 per cent to 2.21 per cent. In state universities, income from project grants by government sources declined from 2.31 per cent to 1.77 per cent and increased to 0.74 per cent to 2.10 per cent from non-government sources. University wise data show that the percentage of project grants by government organizations to total income ranged between 0.12 per cent (Rashtriya Sanskrit Vidhypeetham, Tirupati) and 13.66 per cent (Manipur University) during 1996-97; during 2001-02 there was marginal change in the share of income from project grants. It ranged from 0.13 per cent in Bhavnagar University to 12.54 in Manipur University.

The percentage of project grants to total income by non-government organizations was negligible in universities except in Bhavnagar University, Cochin University of Science and Technology, University of Madras and Manipur University. In Madras University, the NGO's project grant increased from 10.27 per cent to 19.07 per cent of the income for the selected years.

The total income from project grants has declined in more than 50 per cent of the universities. The reasons for this downslide need to be explored. In Madras University, project grants in absolute terms increased, from government and NGO

Table 3.9: Percentage distribution of project grants to the total income in 1996-97 and 2001-02

Name of the Universities	*Region*	*Years of Estt.*	*1996-97*				
			Total income (Rs. in lakh)	*Project Grants (Rs. in lakh)*		*Project Grants (in %)*	
				Govt.	*NGOs*	*Govt.*	*NGOs*
Central Unviersity							
AMU, Aligarh		1920	**8220.42**	**0.00**	**0.00**	**0.000**	**0.000**
Deemed to be Universities							
Banasthali Vidhyapeeth, Rajasthan		1962	496.94	0.00	0.00	0.000	0.000
Rashtriya Sanskrit Vidyapeethm,Tirupati		1961	107.94	1.00	0.00	0.926	0.000
Sri Sathya Sai Institute of H.Learning, AP		1981	214.46	0.27	0	0.126	0.000
Total Deemed to be Universities			**819.34**	**1.27**	**0.00**	**0.155**	**0.000**
State Universities							

(Contd.)

(Contd.Table 3.9)

Name of the Universities	*Region*	*Years of Estt.*	*2001-02*				
			Total income (Rs. in lakh)	*Project Grants (Rs. in lakh)*		*Project Grants (in %)*	
				Govt.	*NGOs*	*Govt.*	*NGOs*
Central Unviersity							
AMU, Aligarh		1920	**15882.01**	**0.00**	**0.00**	**0.000**	**0.000**
Deemed to be Universities							
Banasthali Vidhyapeeth, Rajasthan		1962	1398.82	0.00	0.00	0.000	0.000
Rashtriya Sanskrit Vidyapeethm,Tirupati		1961	331.49	38.02	0.00	11.469	0.000
Sri Sathya Sai Institute of H.Learning, AP		1981	454.42	10.31	0.00	2.269	0.000
Total Deemed to be Universities			**2184.73**	**48.33**	**0.00**	**2.212**	**0.000**
State Universities							

(Contd.)

(Contd.Table 3.9)

Name of the Universities	*Region*	*Years of Estt.*	*1996-97*				
			Total income (Rs. in lakh)	*Project Grants (Rs. in lakh)*		*Project Grants (in %)*	
				Govt.	*NGOs*	*Govt.*	*NGOs*
Devi Ahilya University, Indore	**Central**	1964	763.85	55.30	0.00	7.240	0.000
Dr. Harisingh G.Vishdy. M.P.		1946	1521.56	17.77	0.00	1.168	0.000
Barkatullah Univ. Bhopal		1970	1516.26	30.55	0.00	2.015	0.000
Ranchi University, Bihar		1976	42.99	0.00	0.00	0.000	0.000
Magadh University, Bihar		1960	4443.12	0.00	0.00	0.000	0.000
Rani Durgawati University, Jabalpur		1935	805.11	17.12	0	2.126	0.000
Deen Dayal Upad. University, Gorakhpur		1956	1005.45	0.00	0.00	0.000	0.000
Punjab University, Chandigarh	**Northern**	1947	4824.59	74.90	0.00	1.552	0.000
Kurukshetra University, Haryana		1957	2997.55	20.63	0.00	0.688	0.000
M.D. Univ. Rohtak, Haryana		1956	1797.72	16.25	0.00	0.904	0.000
Manipur University, Imphal	**North-Eastern**	1980	664.97	90.89	0.80	13.668	0.120
Nagaland University, Kohima		1994	492.38	2.35	0.00	0.477	0.000
Tirpura University, Tipura West		1987	286.80	20.21	0.00	7.047	0.000
Mizoram University		2001	0.00	0.00	0.00	0.00	0.00

(Contd.)

(Contd. Table 3.9)

Name of the Universities	Region	Years of Estt.	2001-02				
			Total income (Rs. in lakh)	Project Grants (Rs. in lakh)		Project Grants (in %)	
				Govt.	NGOs	Govt.	NGOs
Devi Ahilya University, Indore	Central	1964	3365.22	168.15	0.00	4.997	0.000
Dr. Harisingh G.Vishdy. M.P.		1946	2474.29	27.63	0.00	1.117	0.000
Barkatullah Univ. Bhopal		1970	2282.95	23.36	0.00	1.023	0.000
Ranchi University, Bihar		1976	134.95	0.00	0.00	0.000	0.000
Magadh University, Bihar		1960	7307.38	0.00	0.00	0.000	0.000
Rani Durgawati University, Jabalpur		1935	746.25	14.00	0.00	1.876	0.000
Deen Dayal Upad. University, Gorakhpur		1956	2308.58	0.00	0.00	0.000	0.000
Punjab University, Chandigarh	Northern	1947	8423.19	57.45	0.00	0.682	0.000
Kurukshetra University, Haryana		1957	7311.71	18.89	0.00	0.258	0.000
M.D. Univ. Rohtak, Haryana		1956	7688.33	25.71	0.00	0.334	0.000
Manipur University, Imphal	North-Eastern	1980	1143.44	143.46	0.96	12.546	0.084
Nagaland University, Kohima		1994	1394.52	51.78	61.64	3.713	4.420
Tirpura University, Tipura West		1987	811.11	8.34	0.00	1.028	0.000
Mizoram University		2001	1534.30	0.00	3.74	0.000	0.244

(Contd.)

(Contd. Table 3.9)

Name of the Universities	*Region*	*Years of Estt.*	*1996-97*				
			Total income (Rs. in lakh)	*Project Grants (Rs. in lakh)*		*Project Grants (in %)*	
				Govt.	*NGOs*	*Govt.*	*NGOs*
Bhavnagar University	**Western**	1979	418.26	4.05	24.01	0.968	5.740
Swami Rmanand Univ., Nanded		1994	613.45	0.00	0.00	0.000	0.000
Shivaji Univeristy, Kolhapur		1962	2217.15	28.24	0.00	1.274	0.000
Nagpur University, Nagpur		1923	3166.58	41.73	0	1.318	0.000
Karnatak Univ. Dharwad	**Southern**	1950	2746.25	23.42	0.41	0.853	0.015
Banglore University		1961	3330.29	76.21	0.00	2.288	0.000
Mangalore University, Mangalagangothri		1980	1061.93	98.03	0	9.231	0.000
Cochin Univ. of Sc. & Tech., Kerala		1986	1484.23	112.11	2.67	7.553	0.180
Univ. of Kerala, Thiruvanauthapuram		1937	3186.81	0.00	0.00	0.000	0.000
Sri Krishnadevaraya Univ., Anantapur		1981	823.69	86.28	0.00	10.475	0.000
University of Madras, Chennai		1857	2827.40	179.35	290.47	6.343	10.273
Total State Universities			**43038.39**	**995.39**	**318.36**	**2.313**	**0.740**
All Universities Total			**52078.15**	**996.66**	**318.36**	**1.914**	**0.611**

(Contd.)

(Contd. Table 3.9)

Name of the Universities	Region	Years of Estt.	2001-02				
			Total income (Rs. in lakh)	Project Grants (Rs. in lakh)		Project Grants (in %)	
				Govt.	NGOs	Govt.	NGOs
Bhavnagar University	Western	1979	1276.25	1.67	43.49	0.131	3.408
Swami Rmanand Univ., Nanded		1994	568.63	0.00	0.00	0.000	0.000
Shivaji Univeristy, Kolhapur		1962	3848.97	52.76	0.00	1.371	0.000
Nagpur University, Nagpur		1923	5774.01	56.70	0.00	0.982	0.000
Karnatak Univ. Dharwad	Southern	1950	4310.17	90.60	0.00	2.102	0.000
Banglore University		1961	6670.62	14.13	0.00	0.212	0.000
Mangalore University, Mangalagangothri		1980	1898.98	203.60	0.00	10.722	0.000
Cochin Univ. of Sc. & Tech., Kerala		1986	2922.59	300.76	196.33	10.291	6.718
Univ. of Kerala, Thiruvanauthapuram		1937	5561.51	0.00	0.00	0.000	0.000
Sri Krishnadevaraya Univ., Anantapur		1981	1192.64	80.42	0.00	6.743	0.000
University of Madras, Chennai		1857	8255.25	239.61	1574.77	2.903	19.076
Total State Universities			**89205.84**	**1579.02**	**1880.93**	**1.770**	**2.109**
All Universities Total			**107272.58**	**1627.35**	**1880.93**	**1.517**	**1.753**

(Contd.)

sources, from Rs. 179.35 lakh and Rs. 290.47 lakh to Rs. 239.61 and Rs. 1574.77 lakh respectively during the period 1996-97 to 2001-02.

Pattern of Expenditure

This section discusses the behaviour of expenditure of selected universities for 1996-97 and 2001-02; the main purpose being to analyse expenditure incurred on various activities. The analysis is expected to reveal the type of activities that are considered important in the working of universities in terms of financial allocations. In order to examine the pattern and its changing behavior over the years, expenditure was broken down into its recurring and non-recurring components. The recurring expenditure covers direct teaching and non-teaching expenditure, indirect teaching expenditure and student welfare services. Non-recurring expenditure includes universities' expenditure on buildings' and their maintenance and equipment etc.

Table 3.10 and Figure 3.7 show that during the five years of 1996-97 to 2001-02, there was significant increase in expenditure in all the selected universities; the total expenditure of all universities increasing from Rs. 50,850.99 lakh to Rs. 107134.86 lakh, or an increase of 116 per cent. The expenditure of Central University more than doubled, from Rs. 7855.52 to 16850.25 lakh; of Deemed to be Universities, it increased from Rs. 1028.68 lakh to Rs. 2216.46 lakh and in all state universities, the expenditure increased from Rs. 41966.79 lakh to Rs. 88868.15 lakh. Although expenditure increased by 112 per cent in their case, in some state universities, increase in expenditure was substantially less. The increase in percentage terms ranged from 26.49 in Dr. Hari Singh Gaur University to 657.26 in Swami Ramanand University. The total expenditure has registered a continuous upward trend in all regions.

The distribution of universities by increase or decrease of total expenditure on the basis of their year of establishment (Table 3.11 and Figure 3.8) indicates that the maximum number of universities (12) fall under the category of 50 to 100 per cent

Table 3.10: Distribution of total expenditure in selected Universities

Name of the Universities	*Region*	*Year of Estt.*	*1996-97 (Rs. in Lakh)*	*2001-02 (Rs in Lakh)*	*Percentage Increase/ Decrease*
			Expenditure	*Expenditure*	
Central Unviersity					
AMU, Aligarh		1920	**7855.52**	**16050.25**	**104.32**
Deemed to be Universities					
Banasthali Vidhyapeeth, Rajasthan		1962	596.63	1409.62	136.26
Rashtriya Sanskrit Vidyapeethm,Tirupati		1961	198.26	366.39	84.80
Sri Sathya Sai Institute of H.Learning, AP		1981	233.79	440.45	88.40
Total Deemed to be Universities			**1028.68**	**2216.46**	**115.47**
State Universities					

(Contd.)

(Contd.Table 3.10)

Name of the Universities	*Region*	*Year of Estt.*	*1996-97 (Rs. in Lakh)*	*2001-02 (Rs in Lakh)*	*Percentage Increase/ Decrease*
			Expenditure	*Expenditure*	
Devi Ahilya University, Indore	**Central**	1964	979.57	3544.42	261.83
Dr. Harisingh G.Vishdy. M.P.		1946	1289.84	1631.51	26.49
Barkatullah Univ. Bhopal		1970	1474.71	3371.94	128.65
Ranchi University, Bihar		1976	70.40	166.17	136.04
Magadh University, Bihar*		1960	4345.92	6757.77	55.50
Rani Durgawati University, Jabalpur		1935	883.59	1436.51	62.58
Deen Dayal Upad. University, Gorakhpur		1956	979.97	1792.19	82.88
Punjab University, Chandigarh	**Northern**	1947	4615.33	8021.55	73.80
Kurukshetra University, Haryana		1957	3348.67	7295.27	117.86
M.D. Univ. Rohtak, Haryana		1956	2739.22	5773.26	110.76
Manipur University, Imphal	**North-Eastern**	1980	577.39	1199.11	107.68
Nagaland University, Kohima		1994	465.86	1274.49	173.58
Tirpura University, Tipura West		1987	223.82	827.09	269.53
Mizoram University		2001	0.00	5253.75	-

(Contd.)

(Contd.Table 3.10)

Name of the Universities	*Region*	*Year of Estt.*	*1996-97 (Rs. in Lakh)*	*2001-02 (Rs in Lakh)*	*Percentage Increase/ Decrease*
			Expenditure	*Expenditure*	
Bhavnagar University	**Western**	1979	324.23	644.94	98.91
Swami Rmanand Univ., Nanded		1994	127.34	964.30	657.26
Shivaji Univeristy, Kolhapur		1962	2040.62	4043.19	98.14
Nagpur University, Nagpur		1923	2118.35	6258.58	195.45
Karnatak Univ. Dharwad	**Southern**	1950	1983.49	3911.12	97.18
Banglore University		1961	3336.90	5729.64	71.71
Mangalore University, Mangalagangothri		1980	974.78	1779.05	82.51
Cochin Univ. of Sc. & Tech., Kerala		1986	1433.35	2899.92	102.32
Univ. of Kerala, Thiruvanauthapuram		1937	3298.46	5690.24	72.51
Sri Krishnadevaraya Univ., Anantapur		1981	1123.66	1605.50	42.88
University of Madras, Chennai		1857	3211.32	6996.64	117.87
Total State Universities			**41966.79**	**88868.15**	**111.76**
All Universities Total			**50850.99**	**107134.86**	**110.68**

Note : * = Special assistance during IX plan.

Figure 3.7 : Distribution of Selected Universities in terms of Total Expenditure

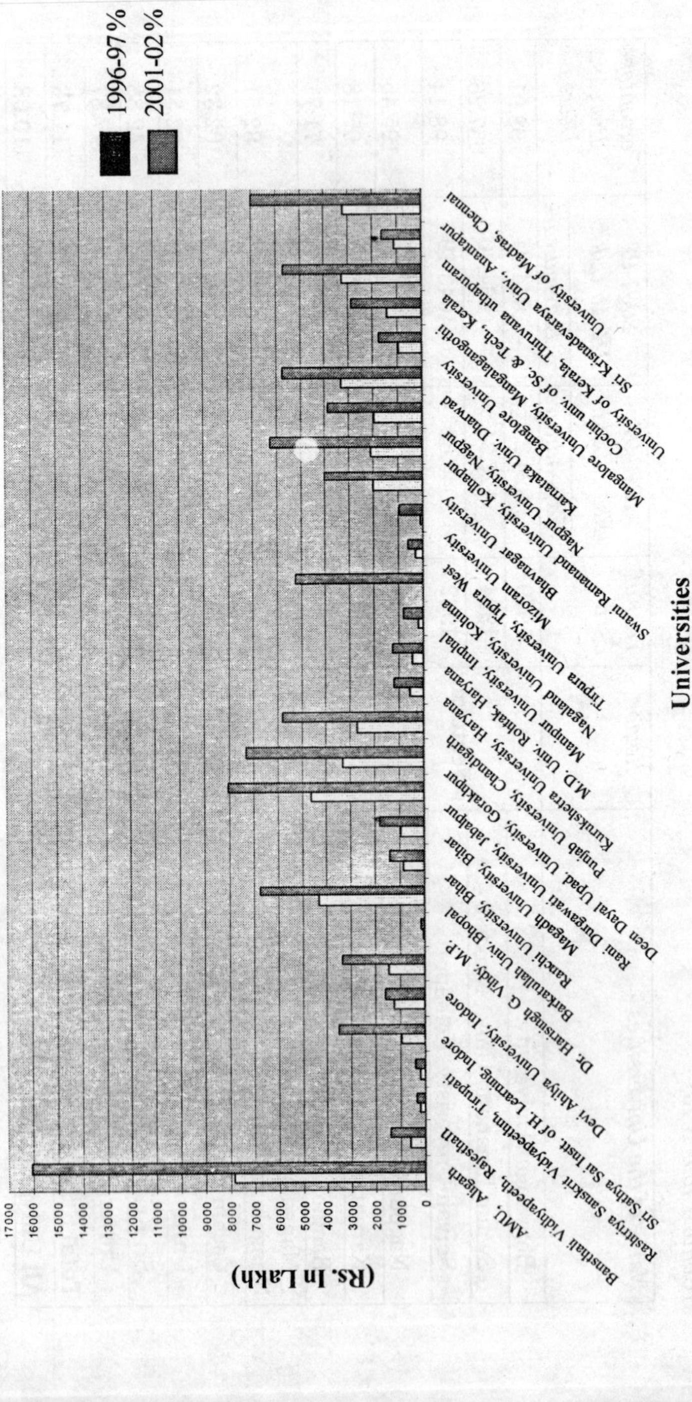

Table 3.11: Distribution of Universities by increase of total expenditure with year of establishment

(in percentage)

Less than 50	*50 – 100*	*100 – 150*	*150 – 200*	*Above 200*
Dr. Hari Singh Gaur (1946) Sri Krishna Dev Raya (1981)	Rani Durgawati (1935) Kerala (1937) Punjab (1947) Karnataka (1950) Gorakhpur (1956) Magadh (1960) Bangalore (1961) Rashtriya Sanskrit (1961) Shivaji (1962) Bhavnagar (1979) Mangalore (1980) Sri Satya Sai Institute (1981)	AMU (1920) M.D. Univ. (1956) Madras (1857) Kurukshetra (1957) Banasthali (1962) Barkatullah (1970) Ranchi (1976) Manipur (1980) Cochin Univ. of Sc. & Tech. (1986)	Nagpur (1923) Nagaland (1994)	Devi Ahilya (1964) Tripura (1987) Swami Ramanand (1994)

Note: Figures in the parenthesis are year of establishment of University.

increase from the years 1996-97 to 2001-02. The years of establishment of these universities range from 1935 to 1981. Only two universities fall under the category of less than 50 per cent increase (Dr. Hari Singh Gaur and Sri Krishnadevraya). Out of these, one university was established in 1946 and the other in 1981. The maximum increase in expenditure i.e. above 200 per cent, was observed in three universities. The year of establishment of these universities ranges from 1964 (Devi Ahilya University) to 1994 (Swami Ramanand University). This shows that the quantum of expenditure is not determined by the age of the university. It also indicates that most universities fall within the range of 50 to 150 per cent increase in their expenditure during the years under study.

Per Student Cost

Table 3.12 shows university-wise per student cost. Although the quality of programmes of universities can to some extent be evaluated by comparing per unit cost, the position is much more complex. Considering that salaries of teaching and non-teaching staff account for bulk of the university expenditure, the cost per student is likely to be higher in universities with higher pay scales. The other determining factors are student enrolment and the nature of courses. Per unit cost is calculated by dividing the total recurring expenditure by the total number of students enrolled during 1995-96 and 2001-02. All universities supplied information on enrolment. Since some discrepancies were found, enrolment data have been collected from University Handbook of the Association of Indian Universities (AIU) for the year 1996 and 2002. It has been found that in Central University and Deemed to be Universities, cost per student was higher than State Universities. In Deemed to be Universities cost per student ranges from Rs. 18,720 to Rs. 56,970 for the year 1996-97 and for 2001-02, it ranged from Rs. 35,106 to Rs. 59,582. In state universities, it ranged from Rs. 946 to Rs. 11,236 and Rs. 7,450 to Rs. 1,422 for the years 1996-97 and 2001-02

Figure 3.8 : Distribution of Universities by Increase/Decrease of Total Expenditure with Year of Establishment

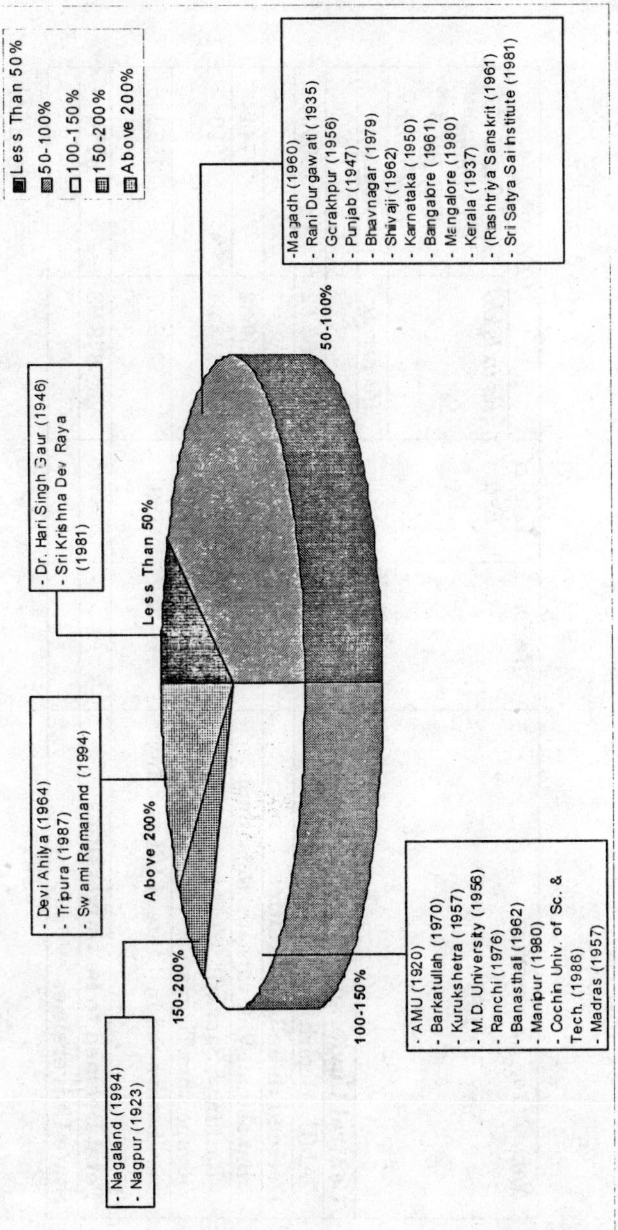

Table 3.12: University-wise per student cost during 1996-97 and 2001-02

Name of the Universities	*Region*	*Year of Estt.*	*1996-97*	
			(Rs in lakh)	*Total Enrolment** (UG, PG & Research)*
			Recurring	*Regular*
Central Unviersity				
AMU, Aligarh		1920	**7855.52**	**15000**
Deemed to be Universities				
Banasthali Vidhyapeeth, Rajasthan		1962	556.82	2744
Rashtriya Sanskrit Vidyapeethm,Tirupati		1961	113.94	320
Sri Sathya Sai Institute of H.Learning, AP		1981	208.17	1112
Total Deemed to be Universities			**878.93**	**4176**
State Universities				

(Contd.)

(Contd. Table 3.12)

Name of the Universities	*Region*	*Year of Estt.*	*2001-02*		*Cost per student*	
			(Rs in lakh)	*Total Enrolment** (UG, PG & Research)*	*1996-97*	*2001-02*
			Recurring	*Regular*		
Central Unviersity						
AMU, Aligarh		1920	15847.21	**18562**	**52370**	**86468**
Deemed to be Universities						
Banasthali Vidhyapeeth, Rajasthan		1962	1241.19	2763	**20292**	44922
Rashtriya Sanskrit Vidyapeethm,Tirupati		1961	292.55	491	56970	59582
Sri Sathya Sai Institute of H.Learning, AP		1981	392.49	1118	18720	35106
Total Deemed to be Universities			1926.23	**4372**	**21047**	**44058**
State Universities						

(Contd.)

(Contd.Table 3. 12)

Name of the Universities	*Region*	*Year of Estt.*	*1996-97*	
			(Rs in lakh)	*Total Enrolment** (UG, PG & Research)*
			Recurring	*Regular*
Devi Ahilya University, Indore	**Central**	1964	883.32	56089
Dr. Harisingh G.Vishdy. M.P.		1946	1284.81	11434
Barkatullah Univ. Bhopal		1970	1447.23	-
Ranchi University, Bihar		1976	52.74	-
Magadh University, Bihar*		1960	4166.42	100000
Rani Durgawati University, Jabalpur		1935	755.19	50083
Deen Dayal Upad. University, Gorakhpur		1956	932.00	98504
Punjab University, Chandigarh	**Northern**	1947	4512.18	99792
Kurukshetra University, Haryana		1957	2791.80	75549
M.D. Univ. Rohtak, Haryana		1956	2012.03	54538
Manipur University, Imphal	**North-Eastern**	1980	503.38	33159
Nagaland University, Kohima		1994	455.42	-
Tirpura University, Tipura West		1987	180.90	6446
Mizoram University		2001	0.00	-

(Contd.)

(Contd.Table 3.12)

Name of the Universities	Region	Year of Estt.	2001-02 (Rs in lakh) Recurring	2001-02 Total Enrolment** (UG, PG & Research) Regular	Cost per student 1996-97	Cost per student 2001-02
Devi Ahilya University, Indore	Central	1964	3345.13	63053	1742	5305
Dr. Harisingh G.Vishdy. M.P.	Central	1946	1612.93	40454	11236	3987
Barkatullah Univ. Bhopal	Central	1970	3367.47	-	-	-
Ranchi University, Bihar	Central	1976	87.30	-	-	-
Magadh University, Bihar*	Central	1960	6757.77	114199	4166	5917
Rani Durgawati University, Jabalpur	Central	1935	1231.17	86563	1508	1422
Deen Dayal Upad. University, Gorakhpur	Central	1956	1779.03	77809	946	2286
Punjab University, Chandigarh	Northern	1947	7958.79	106822	4522	7450
Kurukshetra University, Haryana	Northern	1957	6189.74	114941	3695	5385
M.D. Univ. Rohtak, Haryana	Northern	1956	5410.44	151753	3689	3565
Manipur University, Imphal	North-Eastern	1980	1007.70	-	-	-
Nagaland University, Kohima	North-Eastern	1994	1228.72	873	-	-
Tirpura University, Tipura West	North-Eastern	1987	402.87	18425	2806	2186
Mizoram University	North-Eastern	2001	5042.17	6840	-	-

(Contd.)

(Contd.Table 3.12)

Name of the Universities	*Region*	*Year of Estt.*	*1996-97*	
			(Rs in lakh)	*Total Enrolment** (UG, PG & Research)*
			Recurring	*Regular*
Bhavnagar University	Western	1979	298.23	4929
Swami Rmanand Univ., Nanded		1994	127.34	-
Shivaji Univeristy, Kolhapur		1962	1791.86	135843
Nagpur University, Nagpur		1923	1673.91	118165
Karnatak Univ. Dharwad	Southern	1950	1862.81	-
Banglore University		1961	2740.67	121850
Mangalore University, Mangalagangothri		1980	842.67	-
Cochin Univ. of Sc. & Tech., Kerala		1986	1186.24	53602
University of Kerala, Thiruvanauthapuram		1937	2829.21	-
Sri Krishnadevaraya Univ., Anantapur		1981	1123.66	-
University of Madras, Chennai		1857	3187.25	160022
Total State Universities			37641.27	
All Universities Total			46375.72	

(Contd.)

(Contd.Table 3. 12)

Name of the Universities	*Region*	*Year of Estt.*	*2001-02*		*Cost per student*	
			(Rs in lakh)	*Total Enrolment** (UG, PG & Research)*	*1996-97*	*2001-02*
			Recurring	*Regular*		
Bhavnagar University	**Western**	1979	563.48	15872	6050	3550
Swami Rmanand Univ., Nanded		1994	646.51	515	-	-
Shivaji Univeristy, Kolhapur		1962	3666.79	166386	1319	2203
Nagpur University, Nagpur		1923	5057.39	152364	1416	3319
Karnatak Univ. Dharwad	**Southern**	1950	3568.57	-	-	-
Banglore University		1961	4911.33	152774	2249	3215
Mangalore University, Mangalagangothri		1980	1623.98	-	-	-
Cochin Univ. of Sc. & Tech., Kerala		1986	2705.17	77809	2213	3477
University of Kerala, Thiruvanauthapuram		1937	5152.20	-	-	-
Sri Krishnadevaraya Univ., Anantapur		1981	1605 50	-	-	-
University of Madras, Chennai		1857	6878.31	205514	1992	3347
Total State Universities			81800.96			
All Universities Total			99574.40			

Note : * = Special assistance during IX plan. **= University Handbook, AIU, 2002 and 1998.

respectively. In State Universities, the cost per student has escalated in all universities, except Dr. Hari Singh Gaur University, Rani Durgawati, M.D. University (Rohtak), Tripura University and Bhavnagar University. In these universities sharp increase in enrolment seems to have resulted in a decline in per student cost from 1996-97 to 2001-02. Among all the universities, the highest cost per student for 1996-97 was in Rashtirya Sanskrit Vidypeetham and the lowest in Rani Durgawati University. For 2001-02, the highest per student cost was in Aligarh Muslim University and the lowest in Barkatullah University. The wide variations in per student cost need to be investigated not only in terms of the reasons for variations but more so in relation to the components of the cost and their implications for relevance and quality of higher education.

Comparative Picture of Recurring and Non-recurring Expenditure

Table 3.13 indicates breakup of recurring and non-recurring expenditure of the universities. It shows that bulk of the expenditure in universities is on recurring items. The percentage of recurring expenditure to total expenditure of all universities as well as Deemed to be Universities and state universities shows an increasing trend. The percentage increased from 91.20 to 92.94 in all universities, 85.44 to 86.91 in Deemed to be Universities and 89.69 to 92.05 in state universities. The percentage of non-recurring expenditure has on the other hand decreased, from 8.80 to 7.06 for all universities; for Deemed to be Universities from 14.56 to 13.09 and for state universities from 10.31 to 7.15. In most universities, recurring expenditure accounted for more than 80 per cent of the total expenditure both in 1996-97 and 2001-02. However, in Ranchi and Tripura Universities recurring expenditure decreased substantially, from 74.91 per cent to 52.54 per cent and 80.82 per cent to 48.71 per cent respectively.

In most universities, non-recurring expenditure accounts for very low percentage of total expenditure. In 1996-97, it ranged from less than 0.39 per cent to 20 per cent except in Rashtriya Sanskrit Vidyapeetham Tirupati, Barakatullha University and M.D. University Rohtak. In 2001-02, the range was from 0.13 per cent to 20 per cent except in Barkatullah University, Tripura University and Swami Rama Nand University. The table also indicates a decreasing trend in more than 45 per cent of the universities, except in Dr. Hari Singh Gaur, Bansthali Vidhyapeeth, Barkatullah, Manipur, Nagaland, Tripura, Bhavnagar, Karnataka and Madras Universities.

The decreasing percentage of non-recurring expenditure would seem to indicate inadequate attention on the part of universities to development and up- gradation of infrastructure. In non-recurring expenditure, buildings have received a major share (see Table 3.18).

Recurring Expenditure

Direct Teaching Expenditure

Expenditure on Salaries of Teaching Faculty

Direct expenditure on teaching consists of salaries of teaching and non-teaching staff. Table 3.14 and Figure 3.9 and 3.9(a) provide information about the expenditure on teachers' salaries as percentage of total recurring expenditure. Information about salaries of teaching and non-teaching staff is available separately for 23 universities for 1996-97 and 24 universities for 2001-02. During 1996-97, a majority of the universities were in the category of 'less than 25 per cent' and '25 to 50 per cent' and only one University was in the category of above 50 per cent expenditure on salaries. The situation changed in 2001-02. No university spent more than 50 per cent on teachers' salaries. Generally, out of the total recurring expenditure, share of teachers' salary ranged between less than 25 per cent to 50 per cent.

Table 3.13: Percentage distribution of recurring and non-recurring expenditure to total expenditure of the Universities

(Figures in percentage)

Name of the Universities	*Region*	*Year of Estt.*	*Recurring Expenditure*	
			1996-97	*2001-02*
Central Unviersity				
AMU, Aligarh		1920	**100.00**	**98.73**
Deemed to be Universities				
Banasthali Vidhyapeeth, Rajasthan		1962	93.33	88.05
Rashtriya Sanskrit Vidyapeethm,Tirupati		1961	57.47	79.85
Sri Sathya Sai Institute of H.Learning, AP		1981	89.04	89.11
Total Deemed to be Universities			**85.44**	**86.91**
State Universities				
Devi Ahilya University, Indore	**Central**	1964	90.17	94.38
Dr. Harisingh G.Vishdy. M.P.		1946	99.61	98.86
Barkatullah Univ. Bhopal		1970	98.14	99.87
Ranchi University, Bihar		1976	74.91	52.54
Magadh University, Bihar*		1960	95.87	100.00
Rani Durgawati University, Jabalpur		1935	85.47	85.71
Deen Dayal Upad. University, Gorakhpur		1956	95.10	99.27

(Contd.)

(Contd. Table 3. 13)

Name of the Universities	*Region*	*Year of Estt.*	*Non-Recurring Expenditure*		*Total Expenditure*	
			1996-97	*2001-02*	*1996-97*	*2001-02*
Central Unviersity						
AMU, Aligarh		1920	**0.00**	**1.27**	**7855.52**	**16050.25**
Deemed to be Universities						
Banasthali Vidhyapeeth, Rajasthan		1962	6.67	11.95	596.63	1409.62
Rashtriya Sanskrit Vidyapeethm,Tirupati		1961	42.53	20.15	198.26	366.39
Sri Sathya Sai Institute of H.Learning, AP		1981	10.96	10.89	233.79	440.45
Total Deemed to be Universities			**14.56**	**13.09**	**1028.68**	**2216.46**
State Universities						
Devi Ahilya University, Indore	**Central**	1964	9.83	5.62	979.57	3544.42
Dr. Harisingh G.Vishdy. M.P.		1946	0.39	1.14	1289.84	1631.51
Barkatullah Univ. Bhopal		1970	1.86	0.13	1474.71	3371.94
Ranchi University, Bihar		1976	25.09	47.46	70.40	166.17
Magadh University, Bihar*		1960	4.13	0.00	4345.92	6757.77
Rani Durgawati University, Jabalpur		1935	14.53	14.29	883.59	1436.51
Deen Dayal Upad. University, Gorakhpur		1956	4.90	0.73	979.97	1792.19

(Contd.)

(Contd.Table 3.13)

Name of the Universities	*Region*	*Year of Estt.*	*Recurring Expenditure*	
			1996-97	*2001-02*
Punjab University, Chandigarh	**Northern**	1947	97.77	99.22
Kurukshetra University, Haryana		1957	83.37	84.85
M.D. Univ. Rohtak, Haryana		1956	73.45	93.72
Manipur University, Imphal	**North-Eastern**	1980	87.18	84.04
Nagaland University, Kohima		1994	97.76	96.41
Tirpura University, Tipura West		1987	80.82	48.71
Mizoram University		2001	0	95.97
Bhavnagar University	**Western**	1979	91.98	87.37
Swami Rmanand Univ., Nanded		1994	100.00	67.04
Shivaji Univeristy, Kolhapur		1962	87.81	90.69
Nagpur University, Nagpur		1923	79.02	80.82

(Contd.)

(Contd.Table 3.13)

Name of the Universities	*Region*	*Year of Estt.*	*Non-Recurring Expenditure*		*Total Expenditure*	
			1996-97	*2001-02*	*1996-97*	*2001-02*
Punjab University, Chandigarh	**Northern**	1947	2.23	0.78	4615.33	8021.55
Kurukshetra University, Haryana		1957	16.63	15.15	3348.67	7295.27
M.D. Univ. Rohtak, Haryana		1956	26.55	6.28	2739.22	5773.26
Manipur University, Imphal	**North-Eastern**	1980	12.82	15.96	577.39	1199.11
Nagaland University, Kohima		1994	2.24	3.59	465.86	1274.49
Tirpura University, Tipura West		1987	19.18	51.29	223.82	827.09
Mizoram University		2001	0.000	4.03	0.00	5253.75
Bhavnagar University	**Western**	1979	8.02	12.63	324.23	644.94
Swami Rmanand Univ., Nanded		1994	0.00	32.96	127.34	964.30
Shivaji Univeristy, Kolhapur		1962	12.19	9.31	2040.62	4043.19
Nagpur University, Nagpur		1923	20.98	19.18	2118.35	6258.58

(Contd.)

(Contd.Table 3.13)

Name of the Universities	*Region*	*Year of Estt.*	*Recurring Expenditure*	
			1996-97	*2001-02*
Karnatak Univ. Dharwad	**Southern**	1950	93.92	91.24
Banglore University		1961	82.13	85.72
Mangalore University, Mangalagangothri		1980	86.45	91.28
Cochin Univ. of Sc. & Tech., Kerala		1986	82.76	93.28
University of Kerala, Thiruvanauthapuram		1937	85.77	90.54
Sri Krishnadevaraya Univ., Anantapur		1981	100.00	100.00
University of Madras, Chennai		1857	99.25	98.31
Total State Universities			**89.69**	**92.05**
All Universities Total			**91.20**	**92.94**

(Contd.)

(Contd. Table 3.13)

Name of the Universities	*Region*	*Year of Estt.*	*Non-Recurring Expenditure*		*Total Expenditure*	
			1996-97	*2001-02*	*1996-97*	*2001-02*
Karnatak Univ. Dharwad	**Southern**	1950	6.08	8.76	1983.49	3911.12
Banglore University		1961	17.87	14.28	3336.90	5729.64
Mangalore University, Mangalagangothri		1980	13.55	8.72	974.78	1779.05
Cochin Univ. of Sc. & Tech., Kerala		1986	17.24	6.72	1433.35	2899.92
University of Kerala, Thiruvanauthapuram		1937	14.23	9.46	3298.46	5690.24
Sri Krishnadevaraya Univ., Anantapur		1981	0.00	0.00	1123.66	1605.50
University of Madras, Chennai		1857	0.75	1.69	3211.32	6996.64
Total State Universities			**10.31**	**7.95**	**41966.79**	**88868.15**
All Universities Total			**8.80**	**7.06**	**50850.99**	**107134.86**

Table 3.14: Distribution of Universities by share of salary of teaching staff to total recurring expenditure (in percentages)

1996-97			*2001-02*		
Less than 25	*25 – 50*	*Above 50*	*Less than 25*	*25 – 50*	*Above 50*
Barkatullah (7.26)	Tripura (25.12)	Sri Krishna Devaraya (51.82)	Barkatullah (3.60)	AMU (27.34)	Nil
Shivaji (13.11)	Bangalore (26.61)		Mizoram (3.81)	Bangalore (26.38)	
Nagpur (13.93)	Rani Durgawati (27.80)		Madras (13.94)	Rashitriya Sanskrit (28.08)	
Madras (14.82)	M.D. Univ. (31.69)		Nagpur (15.44)	Mangalore (29.44)	
Swami Ramanand (15.16)	Bansathali (31.94)		Devi Ahilya (18.77)	Rani Durgawati (29.45)	
Nagalanad (16.09)	Rashtriya Sanskrit Vidya. (32.07)		Nagaland (21.66)	Bansthali (29.64)	
Cochin Univ. of Sc. & Tech. (19.24)	Devi Ahilya (34.19)		Cochin Univ. of Sc. & Tech. (22.14)	M.D. Univ. (30.71)	
Mangalore (21.38)	Manipur (39.94)		Shivaji (22.37)	Kurukshetra (35.13)	
Bhavnagar (23.36)	Deen Dayal Upadhyay Univ. (37.18)		Swami Ramanand (23.85)	Tripura (36.70)	
AMU (23.48)	Punjab (42.03)			Bhavnagar (37.18)	
Rani Durgawati (23.76)	Sri Sathya Sai Institute of Hr. Lrng. (43.94)			Deen Dayal Upadhyay (40.26)	
				Manipur (41.32)	
				Sri Krisha-Devaraya Univ. (38.98)	
				Sri Sathya Sai Instt. (45.82)	
				Punjab (47.58)	

Note: 1. The above table include only those Universities where bifurcation of teaching salaries of teaching staff is available.
2. Figures in the parenthesis denote percentage of teaching salaries.

Comparative Picture of Teaching and Non-Teaching Staff Salaries

Expenditure on salaries of teaching and non-teaching staff as a proportion of the total expenditure gives insight into the behaviour of university finances. It is evident from Table 3.15 that during a span of five years, expenditure on both teaching and non-teaching staff had shown a declining trend in all the 29 universities. In all of them, expenditure on salaries of teaching staff as a proportion of direct teaching costs decreased from 40.23 per cent to 35.54 per cent and non-teaching staff salary expenditure decreased from 23.64 per cent to 22.61 per cent. Bhavnagar University had the highest percentage (48.90) of non-teaching staff salary for the year 1996-97, followed by Aligarh Muslim University (46.49). However, in Aligarh Mulsim University, being a Central University, the percentage share of expenditure on non-teaching staff salaries declined relatively to 42.71 per cent from 1996-97 to 2001-02. The University, however, continues to spend more on non-teaching staff salaries than that on teaching faculty. On the other hand in Punjab, Manipur, Bangalore, Sri Krishna Devaraya and Mangalore Universities situation is opposite. These universities spend more on teaching faculty than on non-teaching staff. It also seems that Devi Ahilya and M.D. Universities have almost equal percentage of expenditure on teaching and non-teaching staff for both the years.

An important point to note is that some of the North-Eastern and Southern Universities and Bansathali Vidyapeeth show a faster increase in salary expenditure on non-teaching staff. Considering that the primary function of universities is teaching and research, increase in non-teaching staff salaries would seem to indicate the existence of a large number of non-teaching positions whose contribution to the realization of the academic objectives of the institutions might not be significant. An analytical study of expenditure on salaries of non-teaching staff seems worthwhile.

Figure 3.9 : Distribution of Universities by Share of Teaching Staff Salary to Total Recurring Expenditure (1996-97)

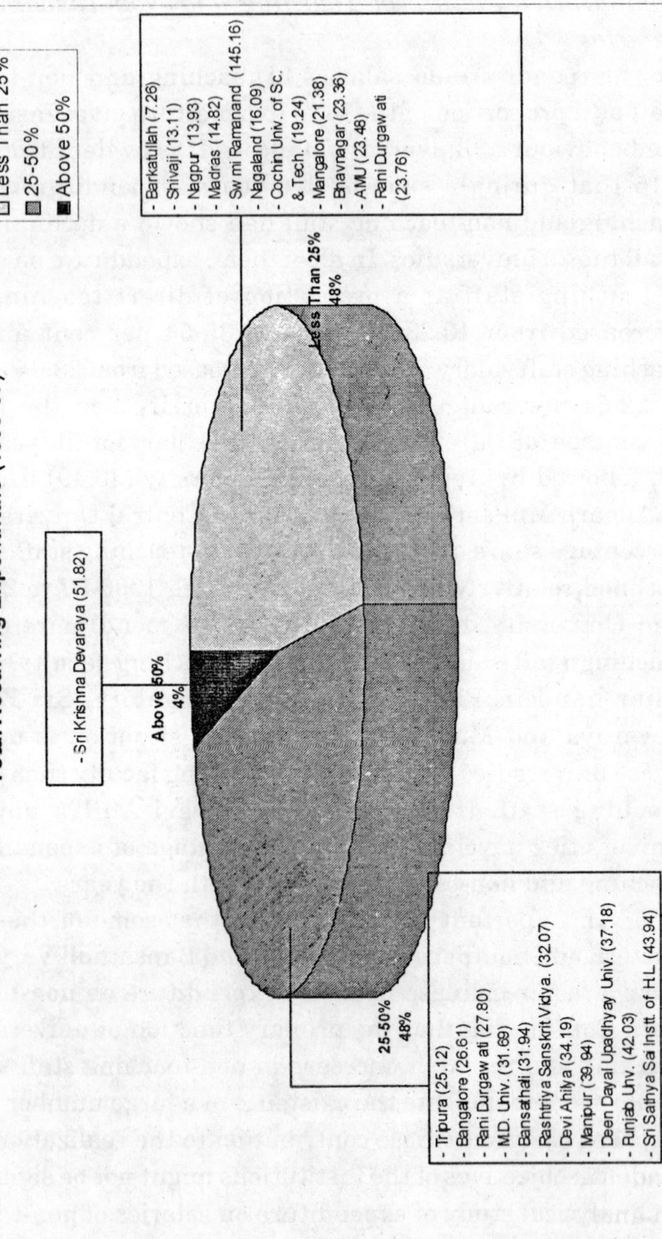

Figure 3.9a : Distribution of Universities by Share of Salary of Teaching Staff to Total Recurring Expenditure (2001-02)

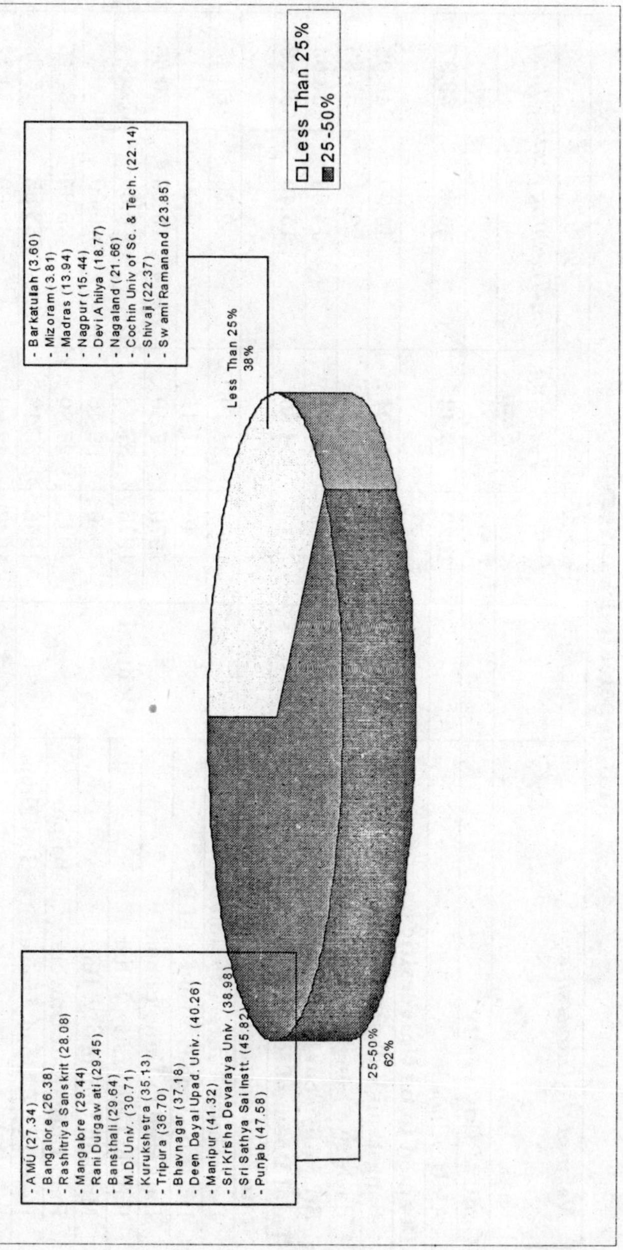

Table 3.15: Percentage distribution of salary expenditure of teaching and non-teaching staff in selected Universities

Name of the Universities	*Region*	*Year of Estt.*	*1996-97*		
			Teaching Staff	*Non-Teaching Staff*	*Total*
Central Unviersity					
AMU, Aligarh		1920	**23.48**	**46.49**	**69.97**
Deemed to be Universities					
Banasthali Vidhyapeeth, Rajasthan		1962	31.94	14.09	46.02
Rashtriya Sanskrit Vidyapeethm,Tirupati		1961	32.07	23.81	55.88
Sri Sathya Sai Institute of H.Learning, AP		1981	43.94	14.68	58.63
Total Deemed to be Universities			**34.80**	**15.49**	**50.29**
State Universities					
Devi Ahilya University, Indore	**Central**	1964	34.19	32.26	66.45
Dr. Harisingh G.Vishdy. M.P.*		1946	61.41	0.00	61.41**
Barkatullah Univ. Bhopal		1970	7.40	13.26	20.66
Ranchi University, Bihar		1976	87.28	0.00	87.28**
Magadh University, Bihar*		1960	99.46	0.00	99.46**
Rani Durgawati University, Jabalpur		1935	27.80	36.35	64.15
Deen Dayal Upad. University, Gorakhpur		1956	37.18	38.85	76.03
Punjab University, Chandigarh	**Northern**	1947	42.03	32.69	74.72
Kurukshetra University, Haryana*		1957	57.09	0.00	57.09*
M.D. Univ. Rohtak, Haryana		1956	31.69	29.85	61.54

(Contd.)

(Contd. Table 3.15)

Name of the Universities	Region	Year of Estt.	2001-02		
			Teaching Staff	Non-Teaching Staff	Total
Central Unviersity					
AMU, Aligarh		1920	**27.34**	**42.71**	**70.04**
Deemed to be Universities					
Banasthali Vidhyapeeth, Rajasthan		1962	29.64	18.81	48.45
Rashtriya Sanskrit Vidyapeethm, Tirupati		1961	28.08	17.05	45.13
Sri Sathya Sai Institute of H.Learning, AP		1981	45.82	13.05	58.87
Total Deemed to be Universities			**32.70**	**17.37**	**50.07**
State Universities					
Devi Ahilya University, Indore	**Central**	1964	18.77	17.46	36.23
Dr. Harisingh G.Vishdy. M.P.*		1946	83.64	0.00	83.64**
Barkatullah Univ. Bhopal		1970	3.60	13.16	16.76
Ranchi University, Bihar		1976	89.92	0.00	89.92**
Magadh University, Bihar*		1960	98.14	0.00	98.14**
Rani Durgawati University, Jabalpur		1935	29.45	36.12	65.57
Deen Dayal Upad. University, Gorakhpur		1956	40.26	32.23	72.49
Punjab University, Chandigarh	**Northern**	1947	47.58	31.14	78.72
Kurukshetra University, Haryana*		1957	35.13	22.08	57.21
M.D. Univ. Rohtak, Haryana		1956	30.71	27.28	57.99

(Contd.)

(Contd.Table 3.15)

Name of the Universities	*Region*	*Year of Estt.*	*1996-97*		
			Teaching Staff	*Non-Teaching Staff*	*Total*
Manipur University, Imphal	**North-Eastern**	1980	39.94	31.71	71.65
Nagaland University, Kohima		1994	16.09	35.81	51.90
Tirpura University, Tipura West		1987	31.08	31.08	62.16
Mizoram University		2001	0	0	0*
Bhavnagar University	**Western**	1979	25.40	48.90	74.29
Swami Rmanand Univ., Nanded		1994	15.67	44.97	60.65
Shivaji Univeristy, Kolhapur		1962	14.93	30.73	45.66
Nagpur University, Nagpur		1923	17.63	45.90	63.53
Karnatak Univ. Dharwad*	**Southern**	1950	70.59	0.00	70.59**
Banglore University		1961	32.40	13.43	45.83
Mangalore University, Mangalagangothri		1980	24.73	19.80	44.53
Cochin Univ. of Sc. & Tech., Kerala		1986	19.24	34.68	53.91
University of Kerala, Thiruvanauthapuram*		1937	61.80	0.00	61.80**
Sri Krishnadevaraya Univ., Anantapur*		1981	51.82	29.02	80.83
University of Madras, Chennai		1857	14.93	25.53	40.45
Total State Universities			**43.86**	**19.06**	**62.92**
All Universities Total			**40.23**	**23.64**	**63.87**

(Contd.)

(Contd.)

Name of the Universities	*Region*	*Year of Estt.*	*2001-02*		
			Teaching Staff	*Non-Teaching Staff*	*Total*
Manipur University, Imphal	**North-Eastern**	1980	41.32	34.01	75.33
Nagaland University, Kohima		1994	21.66	33.12	54.78
Tirpura University, Tipura West		1987	36.70	36.70	73.40
Mizoram University		2001	3.81	2.82	6.63
Bhavnagar University	**Western**	1979	37.18	41.25	78.43
Swami Rmanand Univ., Nanded		1994	23.85	26.05	49.90
Shivaji Univeristy, Kolhapur		1962	22.37	22.15	44.53
Nagpur University, Nagpur		1923	15.44	22.85	38.29
Karnatak Univ. Dharwad*	**Southern**	1950	78.18	0.00	78.18**
Banglore University		1961	26.38	19.95	46.34
Mangalore University, Mangalagangothri		1980	29.44	16.86	46.30
Cochin Univ. of Sc. & Tech., Kerala		1986	22.14	28.06	50.20
University of Kerala, Thiruvanauthapuram*		1937	61.68	0.00	61.68**
Sri Krishnadevaraya Univ., Anantapur*		1981	38.98	40.19	79.17
University of Madras, Chennai		1857	13.94	28.73	42.67
Total State Universities			**37.19**	**18.84**	**56.03**
All Universities Total			**35.54**	**22.61**	**58.14**

Note: *= no expenditure on teaching and non-teaching staff, as it established in 2001, **= bifurcation for expenditure on teaching and non-teaching staff not available.

Indirect Teaching Expenditure

Expenditure on Staff Development, Libraries, Laboratories and Computers

Indirect teaching expenditure is an important factor contributing to teaching-learning process. It consists of expenditure on staff development, libraries, laboratories and computers etc. Table 3.16 shows that the percentage share of expenditure on indirect-teaching activities is either negligible or has been declining from 1996-97 to 2001-02, except for staff development activity, which helps faculty and non-teaching, personnel to upgrade their competencies. The total expenditure on staff development activities increased from 0.18 per cent to 2.54 per cent. In Deen Dayal Upadhyay University, expenditure on this item increased from 0.017 per cent to 1.137 per cent. The expenditure on libraries has decreased during the five-year period in most universities except in Manipur University where it increased from 4.50 per cent to 5.39 per cent. Although in any academic institution libraries occupy a pivotal place, their declining share in the expenditure shows that they are not receiving importance in the allocation of resources. The decline in expenditure on libraries might be due to decrease in the number of journals subscribed, mainly on account of the substantial increase in subscription charges. Further, with their rising prices, university libraries seem to be finding it difficult to purchase books. The low expenditure on laboratories and computers indicates the inadequate priority given to them although they are significant for universities' teaching and research functions. Although most universities incurred expenditure on computers and software, amounts spent were insignificant and in percentage terms, they showed a declining trend.

Expenditure on Student Welfare Services

Expenditure on student welfare services consists of expenditure on hostels, scholarships/stipends and other student support services, like games and sports, NCC, NSS, cultural activities etc. Table 3.17 gives a comparative picture of the

Table 3.16: Percentage distribution of expenditure of selected Universities on indirect teaching services

Name of the Universities	*Region*	*Year of Estd.*	*Staff Dev.*		*Library (Books & Journals)*	
			96-97	*01-02*	*96-97*	*01-02*
Central Unviersity						
AMU, Aligarh		1920	**0.000**	**0.000**	**0.979**	**0.820**
Deemed to be Universities						
Banasthali Vidhyapeeth, Rajasthan		1962	0.000	0.000	2.238	2.073
Rashtriya Sanskrit Vidyapeethm,Tirupati		1961	0.000	0.000	0.412	0.543
Sri Sathya Sai Institute of H.Learning, AP		1981	0.000	0.000	4.400	4.647
Total Deemed to be Universities			**0.000**	**0.000**	**2.513**	**2.365**
State Universities						
Devi Ahilya University, Indore	**Central**	1964	0.000	0.000	2.265	1.329
Dr. Harisingh G.Vishdy. M.P.		1946	0.114	0.147	0.367	0.033
Barkatullah Univ. Bhopal		1970	0.000	0.000	1.121	0.492
Ranchi University, Bihar		1976	0.000	0.000	0.190	0.115
Magadh University, Bihar		1960	0.000	0.000	0.000	0.000
Rani Durgawati University, Jabalpur		1935	0.000	0.000	0.086	0.054
Deen Dayal Upad. University, Gorakhpur		1956	0.017	1.137	0.830	0.561

(Contd.)

(Contd.Table 3.16)

Name of the Universities	*Region*	*Year of Estd.*	*Laboratory And Workshop*		*Computer (Software & Maintenance)*		*Total*	
			96-97	*01-02*	*96-97*	*01-02*	*96-97*	*01-02*
Central Unviersity								
AMU, Aligarh		1920	**0.697**	**0.810**	**0.165**	**0.175**	**1.841**	**1.805**
Deemed to be Universities								
Banasthali Vidhyapeeth, Rajasthan		1962	1.259	2.888	0.000	0.000	3.497	4.961
Rashtriya Sanskrit Vidyapeethm,Tirupati		1961	0.000	0.000	0.000	0.000	0.412	0.543
Sri Sathya Sai Institute of H.Learning, AP		1981	1.379	0.747	0.259	0.250	6.038	5.643
Total Deemed to be Universities			**1.124**	**2.013**	**0.061**	**0.051**	**3.699**	**4.429**
State Universities								
Devi Ahilya University, Indore	**Central**	1964	1.019	0.598	0.566	0.658	3.850	2.585
Dr. Harisingh G.Vishdy. M.P.		1946	24.906	0.437	0.000	0.062	25.273	0.533
Barkatullah Univ. Bhopal		1970	0.000	0.000	0.000	0.000	1.121	0.492
Ranchi University, Bihar		1976	5.726	4.582	0.000	0.115	5.916	4.811
Magadh University, Bihar		1960	0.000	0.000	0.000	0.000	0.000	0.000
Rani Durgawati University, Jabalpur		1935	0.539	0.432	0.099	0.033	0.724	0.519
Deen Dayal Upad. University, Gorakhpur		1956	1.361	0.861	0.044	0.144	2.235	1.566

(Contd.)

(Contd.Table 3.16)

Name of the Universities	*Region*	*Year of Estd.*	*Staff Dev.*		*Library (Books & Journals)*	
			96-97	*01-02*	*96-97*	*01-02*
Punjab University, Chandigarh	**Northern**	1947	0.023	0.021	2.009	1.750
Kurukshetra University, Haryana		1957	0.000	0.000	1.049	1.026
M.D. Univ. Rohtak, Haryana		1956	0.000	0.000	0.110	0.044
Manipur University, Imphal	**North-Eastern**	1980	0.000	0.000	4.502	5.391
Nagaland University, Kohima		1994	0.101	0.026	1.506	1.034
Tirpura University, Tipura West		1987	0.000	0.000	5.920	3.133
Mizoram University		2001	0	45.025	0	0.113
Bhavnagar University	**Western**	1979	0.000	0.018	2.334	1.658
Swami Rmanand Univ., Nanded		1994	0.000	0.000	1.154	1.641
Shivaji Univeristy, Kolhapur		1962	0.038	2.291	1.759	1.031
Nagpur University, Nagpur		1923	1.648	0.790	0.352	0.445

(Contd.)

(Contd.Table 3.16)

Name of the Universities	Region	Year of Estd.	Laboratory And Workshop		Computer (Software & Maintenance)		Total	
			96-97	01-02	96-97	01-02	96-97	01-02
Punjab University, Chandigarh	Northern	1947	0.529	0.217	0.182	0.115	2.720	2.081
Kurukshetra University, Haryana		1957	0.346	0.332	0.074	0.069	1.469	1.427
M.D. Univ. Rohtak, Haryana		1956	0.196	0.237	0.148	0.047	0.453	0.328
Manipur University, Imphal	North-Eastern	1980	0.805	0.592	0.000	0.000	5.306	5.984
Nagaland University, Kohima		1994	0.228	1.252	0.000	0.224	1.735	2.509
Tirpura University, Tipura West		1987	0.763	0.154	0.431	0.000	7.114	3.286
Mizoram University		2001	0	0.079	0	0.202	0	0.394
Bhavnagar University	Western	1979	3.370	3.090	0.000	0.161	5.704	4.909
Swami Rmanand Univ., Nanded		1994	0.000	0.000	0.000	0.000	1.154	1.641
Shivaji Univeristy, Kolhapur		1962	0.845	0.531	0.269	0.187	2.873	1.748
Nagpur University, Nagpur		1923	0.287	0.050	0.836	0.223	1.475	0.719

(Contd.)

(Contd. Table 3.16)

Name of the Universities	*Region*	*Year of Estd.*	*Staff Dev.*		*Library (Books & Journals)*	
			96-97	*01-02*	*96-97*	*01-02*
Karnatak Univ. Dharwad	**Southern**	1950	0.000	0.000	2.339	1.728
Banglore University		1961	0.000	0.134	1.490	1.290
Mangalore University, Mangalagangothri		1980	0.000	0.039	2.706	2.785
Cochin Univ. of Sc. & Tech., Kerala		1986	2.097	1.307	6.365	3.054
University of Kerala, Thiruvanauthapuram		1937	0.863	1.194	0.965	1.208
Sri Krishnadevaraya Univ., Anantapur		1981	0.000	0.000	0.485	0.421
University of Madras, Chennai		1857	0.167	0.185	1.939	1.567
Total State Universities			**0.229**	**3.100**	**1.421**	**1.067**
All Universities Total			**0.186**	**2.547**	**1.367**	**1.053**

(Contd.)

(Contd.Table 3.16)

Name of the Universities	*Region*	*Year of Estd.*	*Laboratory And Workshop*		*Computer (Software & Maintenance)*		*Total*	
			96-97	*01-02*	*96-97*	*01-02*	*96-97*	*01-02*
Karnatak Univ. Dharwad		1950	0.000	0.000	0.070	0.282	2.409	2.011
Banglore University		1961	0.712	0.946	0.204	0.187	2.406	2.424
Mangalore University, Mangalagangothri		1980	1.558	2.962	1.982	0.000	6.246	5.746
Cochin Univ. of Sc. & Tech., Kerala	**Southern**	1986	0.835	0.334	1.898	0.194	9.097	3.582
University of Kerala, Thiruvanauthapuram		1937	0.784	0.934	0.012	0.107	1.761	2.249
Sri Krishnadevaraya Univ., Anantapur		1981	0.890	0.685	0.000	0.128	1.375	1.235
University of Madras, Chennai		1857	1.925	6.284	0.335	0.243	4.199	8.094
Total State Universities			**1.484**	**0.932**	**0.255**	**0.150**	**3.161**	**2.149**
All Universities Total			**1.344**	**0.934**	**0.236**	**0.152**	**2.948**	**2.139**

(Contd.)

percentage share of expenditure on these services in selected universities for 1996-97 and 2001-02. The table shows that in spite of their importance, universities spend a very small proportion of their budget on student welfare services. Further, a declining trend is visible for all the three services, regardless of the fact whether the university is a Central, Deemed to be or state.

The comparative picture of expenditure on hostel services for 1996-97 and 2001-02 shows that Banasthali Vidyapeeth of Rajasthan spent quite a substantial amount on hostels for students, although over the five year period, the share of expenditure on them declined from 34.46 per cent to 26.32 per cent. Bangalore university spent almost one half of the amount on hostel services during 2001-02 as compared to 1996-97; the expenditure declined from 7.09 to 3.29 per cent.

On scholarships, stipends, games and sports, etc. the share of expenditure has declined in a majority of the universities.

Non-Recurring Expenditure

Table 3.18 indicates that non-recurring expenditure forms a very low proportion of the total budget of universities. Further, it has declined over the years. During 1996-97, all the universities incurred 8.80 per cent of the total expenditure on non-recurring items; the percentage declined to 7.06 by 2001-02. The table indicates that universities seem to be spending more on construction of buildings, with very little amounts being spent on library, laboratory equipment, furniture, computers etc. The notable exceptions are Rashtriya Sanskrit Vidyapeetham and Deen Dayal Upadhyay, Punjab, Tripura and Mangalore Universities.

The Table also indicates that during 1996-97, non-recurring expenditure ranged from 0.39 per cent of the total expenditure in Dr. Hari Singh Gaur Vishvavidyalaya to 42.53 per cent in Rashtriya Sanskrit Vidyapeetham, Tirupati. In 2001-02, it ranged between 0.13 per cent in Barkatullah University to 51.29 per cent in Tripura University. There was substantial increase in non-recurring expenditure of Tripura University during 2001-

Table 3.17: Distribution of expenditure on student welfare services (in percentage)

Name of the Universities	*Region*	*Year of Estt.*	*Hostel*		*Stipends*	
			96-97	*01-02*	*96-97*	*01-02*
Central Unviersity						
AMU, Aligarh		1920	**0.558**	**0.519**	**0.310**	**0.216**
Deemed to be Universities						
Banasthali Vidhyapeeth, Rajasthan		1962	34.464	26.322	0.334	0.666
Rashtriya Sanskrit Vidyapeethm,Tirupati		1961	0.000	0.000	2.062	2.454
Sri Sathya Sai Institute of H.Learning, AP		1981	0.000	0.000	0.730	0.132
Total Deemed to be Universities			**21.833**	**16.961**	**0.652**	**0.829**
State Universities						
Devi Ahilya University, Indore	**Central**	1964	1.426	0.509	0.068	0.018
Dr. Harisingh G.Vishdy. M.P.		1946	0.000	0.000	0.000	0.033
Barkatullah Univ. Bhopal		1970	0.012	0.156	1.106	0.216
Ranchi University, Bihar		1976	0.000	0.000	0.000	0.000
Magadh University, Bihar		1960	0.000	0.007	0.000	0.000
Rani Durgawati University, Jabalpur		1935	0.007	0.010	0.000	0.000
Deen Dayal Upad. University, Gorakhpur		1956	0.025	0.008	0.000	0.000
Punjab University, Chandigarh	**Northern**	1947	1.586	1.599	0.153	0.108
Kurukshetra University, Haryana		1957	1.828	1.337	0.918	0.901
M.D. Univ. Rohtak, Haryana		1956	0.391	0.358	0.205	0.141

(Contd.)

(Contd.Table 3.17)

Name of the Universities	*Region*	*Year of Estt.*	*Student Support Services*		*Total*	
			96-97	*01-02*	*96-97*	*01-02*
Central Unviersity						
AMU, Aligarh		1920	**0.137**	**0.159**	**1.006**	**0.893**
Deemed to be Universities						
Banasthali Vidhyapeeth, Rajasthan		1962	1.043	1.423	35.841	28.411
Rashtriya Sanskrit Vidyapeethm,Tirupati		1961	0.000	0.000	2.062	2.454
Sri Sathya Sai Institute of H.Learning, AP		1981	0.408	0.627	1.138	0.759
Total Deemed to be Universities			**0.758**	**1.045**	**23.243**	**18.835**
State Universities						
Devi Ahilya University, Indore	**Central**	1964	5.356	0.557	6.850	1.084
Dr. Harisingh G.Vishdy. M.P.		1946	0.000	0.002	0.000	0.036
Barkatullah Univ. Bhopal		1970	0.182	0.013	1.300	0.385
Ranchi University, Bihar		1976	0.000	0.000	0.000	0.000
Magadh University, Bihar		1960	0.000	0.000	0.000	0.007
Rani Durgawati University, Jabalpur		1935	0.000	0.000	0.007	0.010
Deen Dayal Upad. University, Gorakhpur		1956	0.456	0.182	0.481	0.189
Punjab University, Chandigarh	**Northern**	1947	0.005	0.126	1.745	1.833
Kurukshetra University, Haryana		1957	0.109	0.017	2.855	2.255
M.D. Univ. Rohtak, Haryana		1956	0.912	0.579	1.507	1.078

(Contd.)

(Contd.Table 3.17)

Name of the Universities	*Region*	*Year of Estt.*	*Hostel*		*Stipends*	
			96-97	*01-02*	*96-97*	*01-02*
Manipur University, Imphal	**North-Eastern**	1980	1.136	1.086	0.095	0.032
Nagaland University, Kohima		1994	0.165	0.525	2.349	2.804
Tirpura University, Tipura West		1987	0.000	0.005	6.031	5.384
Mizoram University		2001	0	0.000	0	0.281
Bhavnagar University	**Western**	1979	0.040	0.032	0.000	0.000
Swami Rmanand Univ., Nanded		1994	0.000	0.000	0.000	0.000
Shivaji Univeristy, Kolhapur		1962	0.359	0.272	0.259	0.923
Nagpur University, Nagpur		1923	1.195	0.722	3.637	2.166
Karnatak Univ. Dharwad	**Southern**	1950	1.301	1.213	1.184	1.801
Banglore University		1961	7.089	3.292	0.946	0.384
Mangalore University, Mangalagangothri		1980	0.000	0.000	0.227	0.060
Cochin Univ. of Sc. & Tech., Kerala		1986	0.384	0.274	4.543	2.226
University of Kerala, Thiruvanauthapuram		1937	0.625	0.494	0.821	1.462
Sri Krishnadevaraya Univ., Anantapur		1981	3.934	5.324	0.593	0.435
University of Madras, Chennai		1857	0.023	0.024	0.357	0.585
Total State Universities			**1.228**	**0.784**	**0.760**	**0.686**
All Universities Total			**1.505**	**1.055**	**0.682**	**0.614**

(Contd.)

(Contd.Table 3.17)

Name of the Universities	*Region*	*Year of Estt.*	*Student Support Services*		*Total*	
			96-97	*01-02*	*96-97*	*01-02*
Manipur University, Imphal	**North-Eastern**	1980	0.234	0.011	1.466	1.128
Nagaland University, Kohima		1994	0.000	0.020	2.514	3.348
Tirpura University, Tipura West		1987	0.580	1.251	6.611	6.640
Mizoram University		2001	0	0.084	0	0.365
Bhavnagar University	**Western**	1979	1.187	0.855	1.227	0.887
Swami Rmanand Univ., Nanded		1994	0.000	0.565	0.000	0.565
Shivaji Univeristy, Kolhapur		1962	0.588	0.684	1.206	1.878
Nagpur University, Nagpur		1923	1.013	0.459	5.845	3.347
Karnatak Univ. Dharwad	**Southern**	1950	0.505	0.846	2.990	3.859
Banglore University		1961	0.231	0.066	8.266	3.742
Mangalore University, Mangalagangothri		1980	0.441	0.114	0.668	0.174
Cochin Univ. of Sc. & Tech., Kerala		1986	0.130	0.062	5.057	2.562
University of Kerala, Thiruvanauthapuram		1937	1.247	0.772	2.692	2.729
Sri Krishnadevaraya Univ., Anantapur		1981	0.000	0.000	4.526	5.758
University of Madras, Chennai		1857	0.314	0.312	0.995	0.921
Total State Universities			**0.491**	**0.280**	**2.479**	**1.751**
All Universities Total			**0.436**	**0.276**	**2.623**	**1.945**

(Contd.)

Table 3.18: Distribution of non-recurring expenditure (in percentage)

Name of the Universities	*Region*	*Year of Estt.*	*Buildings*		*Furniture*		*Library*	
			1996-97	*2001-02*	*1996-97*	*2001-02*	*1996-97*	*2001-02*
Central University								
AMU, Aligarh		1920	**0.000**	**0.227**	**0.000**	**0.000**	**0.000**	**0.078**
Deemed to be Universities								
Banasthali University, Rajasthan		1962	5.415	3.544	1.257	1.530	0.000	0.000
Rashtriya Sanskrit Vidyapeethm, Tirupati		1961	11.389	16.523	0.000	0.000	2.315	0.328
Sri Sathya Sai Institute of H.Learning, AP		1981	0.000	0.334	1.052	1.567	0.000	0.000
Total Deemed to be Universities			**5.336**	**5.051**	**0.968**	**1.284**	**0.446**	**0.054**
State Universities								
Devi Ahilya University, Indore		1964	6.533	3.112	1.123	0.339	0.408	0.141
Dr. Harisingh G.Vishdy. M.P.		1946	0.390	1.139	0.000	0.000	0.000	0.000
Barkatullah Univ. Bhopal		1970	0.000	0.000	1.322	0.066	0.000	0.000
Ranchi University, Bihar	**Central**	1976	1.397	7.949	0.000	0.000	1.659	0.564
Magadh University, Bihar		1960	0.000	0.000	0.244	0.483	0.000	0.000
Rani Durgawati University, Jabalpur		1935	1.781	0.025	0.062	0.060	0.005	0.436
Deen Dayal Upad. University, Gorakhpur		1956	13.460	12.268	0.280	0.266	0.358	0.499
Punjab University, Chandigarh		1947	23.668	4.785	0.104	0.043	2.397	1.105
Kurukshetra University, Haryana	**Northern**	1957	0.000	0.000	0.000	0.000	0.000	0.000
M.D. Univ. Rohtak, Haryana		1956	1.496	0.000	0.150	0.000	1.151	0.000

(Contd.)

(Contd.Table 3. 18)

Name of the Universities	Region	Year of Estt.	Laboratory		Other		Total Non-Recurring	
			1996-97	2001-02	1996-97	2001-02	1996-97	2001-02
Central University								
AMU, Aligarh		1920	**0.000**	**0.959**	**0.000**	**0.000**	**0.000**	**1.27**
Deemed to be Universities								
Banasthali University, Rajasthan		1962	0.000	6.875	0.000	0.000	6.67	11.95
Rashtriya Sanskrit Vidyapeethm,Tirupati		1961	0.000	0.000	28.826	3.302	42.53	20.15
Sri Sathya Sai Institute of H.Learning, AP		1981	9.906	8.989	0.000	0.000	10.96	10.89
Total Deemed to be Universities			**2.251**	**6.158**	**5.556**	**0.546**	**14.56**	**13.09**
State Universities								
Devi Ahilya University, Indore		1964	1.455	0.564	0.306	1.467	9.83	5.62
Dr. Harisingh G.Vishdy. M.P.		1946	0.000	0.000	0.000	0.000	0.39	1.14
Barkatullah Univ. Bhopal		1970	0.542	0.066	0.000	0.000	1.86	0.13
Ranchi University, Bihar	**Central**	1976	1.927	1.637	9.549	4.145	14.53	14.29
Magadh University, Bihar		1960	0.000	0.000	4.651	0.251	4.90	0.73
Rani Durgawati University, Jabalpur		1935	0.213	0.210	0.174	0.051	2.23	0.78
Deen Dayal Upad. University, Gorakhpur		1956	0.839	0.353	1.693	1.768	16.63	15.15
Punjab University, Chandigarh		1947	0.379	0.352	0.000	0.000	26.55	6.28
Kurukshetra University, Haryana	**Northern**	1957	0.000	0.000	25.085	47.463	25.09	47.46
M.D. Univ. Rohtak, Haryana		1956	1.335	0.000	0.000	0.000	4.13	0.00

(Contd.)

(Contd. Table 3.18)

Name of the Universities	*Region*	*Year of Estt.*	*Buildings*		*Furniture*		*Library*	
			1996-97	*2001-02*	*1996-97*	*2001-02*	*1996-97*	*2001-02*
Manipur University, Imphal	**North-Eastern**	1980	6.843	5.440	0.294	0.128	1.635	4.548
Nagaland University, Kohima		1994	0.000	0.159	2.205	1.468	0.036	0.964
Tirpura University, Tipura West		1987	6.684	45.306	0.259	0.669	0.121	0.175
Mizoram Univeristy, Aizawl-Mizoram		2001	0	1.736	0	1.189	0	0.120
Bhavnagar University	**Western**	1979	1.249	7.184	0.000	0.000	1.558	0.335
Swami Rmanand Univ., Nanded		1994	0.000	0.000	0.000	18.148	0.000	0.061
Shivaji Univeristy, Kolhapur		1962	9.638	3.122	0.063	0.000	0.149	0.466
Nagpur University, Nagpur		1923	3.559	2.091	3.817	0.334	2.462	1.130
Karnatak Univ. Dharwad	**Southern**	1950	5.295	8.044	0.359	0.363	0.000	0.000
Banglore University		1961	2.336	4.367	0.010	0.154	0.349	0.096
Mangalore University, Mangalagangothri		1980	12.211	7.765	1.071	0.780	0.271	0.172
Cochin Univ. of Sc. & Tech., Kerala		1986	10.914	6.241	0.775	0.141	0.040	0.007
Univ. of Kerala, Thiruvanauthapuram		1937	1.947	0.360	0.424	0.100	1.072	0.748
Sri Krishnadevaraya Univ., Anantapur		1981	0.000	0.000	0.000	0.000	0.000	0.000
University of Madras, Chennai		1857	0.201	0.756	0.365	0.327	0.002	0.000
Total State Universities			**5.212**	**3.612**	**0.486**	**0.454**	**0.636**	**0.412**
All Universities Total			**4.409**	**3.135**	**0.421**	**0.403**	**0.534**	**0.355**

(Contd.)

(Contd. Table 3.18)

Name of the Universities	Region	Year of Estt.	Laboratory		Other		Total Non-Recurring	
			1996-97	2001-02	1996-97	2001-02	1996-97	2001-02
Manipur University, Imphal	North-Eastern	1980	1.557	4.143	2.489	1.705	12.82	15.96
Nagaland University, Kohima		1994	0.000	0.326	0.000	0.675	2.24	3.59
Tirpura University, Tipura West		1987	11.040	4.199	1.072	0.942	19.18	51.29
Mizoram Univeristy, Aizawl-Mizoram		2001	0	0.054	0	0.928	0	4.03
Bhavnagar University	Western	1979	3.115	5.112	2.097	0.000	8.02	12.63
Swami Rmanand Univ., Nanded		1994	0.000	0.234	0.000	14.512	0.00	32.96
Shivaji Univeristy, Kolhapur		1962	2.056	5.018	0.284	0.704	12.19	9.31
Nagpur University, Nagpur		1923	1.197	2.216	9.945	13.413	20.98	19.18
Karnatak Univ. Dharwad	Southern	1950	0.430	0.352	0.000	0.000	6.08	8.76
Banglore University		1961	0.755	0.108	14.417	9.557	17.87	14.28
Mangalore University, Mangalagangothri		1980	0.000	0.000	0.000	0.000	13.55	8.72
Cochin Univ. of Sc. & Tech., Kerala		1986	5.511	0.327	0.000	0.000	17.24	6.72
Univ. of Kerala, Thiruvanauthapuram		1937	2.962	2.388	7.821	5.859	14.23	9.46
Sri Krishnadevaraya Univ., Anantapur		1981	0.000	0.000	0.000	0.000	0.00	0.00
University of Madras, Chennai		1857	0.135	0.608	0.046	0.000	0.75	1.69
Total State Universities			**1.123**	**0.883**	**2.850**	**2.591**	**10.31**	**7.95**
All Universities Total			**0.973**	**1.004**	**2.464**	**2.160**	**8.80**	**7.06**

Note : *= bifurcation is not given.

02; it increased more than two times. On the other hand, Dr. Hari Singh Gaur Vishvavidhyalaya spent the largest amount on non-recurring items during 1996-97, but after five years i.e. 2001-02, the percentage declined from 42.53 per cent to 20.15 per cent. The amount spent on non-recurring items depends substantially on the extent to which infrastructure is available to some extent and requiring replenishment. In some universities, however, larger amounts might be required if there is inadequate infrastructure. Further, costs of buildings, materials and transportation vary. This would be the case in North-Eastern universities, where materials have generally to the transported over long distances.

In respect of the total non-recurring expenditure, Punjab, Ranchi, Nagpur and Rashtriya Sanskrit Vidyapitham Universities are a few exceptions as they spend more on library, laboratory equipment and other non-recurring expenditure than other universities.

Comparative Picture

Total Income and Expenditure

Table 3.19 gives a comparative picture of the income and expenditure of universities over two points of time viz. 1996-97 and 2001-02. It shows that both income and expenditure of universities have been increasing significantly, at least in absolute terms at current prices; the increase in real terms is however, not so promising. In absolute terms, all the 29 universities had surplus income for both the years. In a few cases, the income of universities has been larger than expenditure. The surpluses have, however, been marginal except in the case of MD University, Bangalore University and Madras University. On the other hand, some universities show large deficits. In quite a few cases, surplus income in 1996-97 has been washed out, with large deficits in 2001-02.

The Central University (AMU) had surplus income of Rs. 364.90 lakh in 1996-97 but after five years i.e. by 2001-02 it started facing the problem of deficit budget, which was Rs. 168.24 lakh. In Deemed to be Universities, the deficit budget was reduced from Rs. 209.34 lakh to 31.73 lakh. Kurukshetra University and Madras University were facing the problem of deficit during 1996-97, but after five years, it converted into surplus income.

Table 3.20 shows position of universities with surplus and deficit budgets during 1996-97 and 2001-02 in terms of their being established before and after independence. During 1996-97, 60 per cent of the universities established before independence had surplus income; the percentage decreased to 20 during 2001-02 indicating that a larger number of universities had deficits. On the other hand, 57 per cent of the universities which were established after independence, had surplus income for both the years. It shows that position of universities established before independence has been deteriorating with regard to total income than universities established after independence.

Income and Expenditure on Hostels

Table 3.21 gives a comparative picture of income and expenditure on hostels of various universities. The income is realized from students in the form of hostel fees and other charges. Most of the universities seem to be subsidizing the expenditure on hostels from other sources. 20 out of 28 universities, which supplied information about this item, only 40 per cent seem to earn more than what they spend on maintenance of hostels during 1996-97. After five years, only 22 per cent of universities had a surplus income from this source. The earning is, however, not very significant. Banasthali Vidhyapeeth (1.26 per cent) had the highest percentage of surplus in 1996-97 in comparison to other universities. But after five years, the percentage decreased to (–) 3.48. The reasons need to be looked into; it may be that maintenance expenditure on hostel services increased or amount of subsidy per boarder has increased.

Table 3.19: Resource allocation and expenditure of Universities

Name of the Universities	*Region*	*Year of Estt.*	*1996-97 (Rs. in Lakh)*		*Surplus/ Deficit*
			Income	*Expenditure*	
Central Unviersity					
AMU, Aligarh		1920	**8220.42**	**7855.52**	**364.9**
Deemed to be Universities					
Banasthali Vidhyapeeth, Rajasthan		1962	496.94	596.63	**-99.69**
Rashtriya Sanskrit Vidyapeethm,Tirupati		1961	107.94	198.26	**-90.32**
Sri Sathya Sai Institute of H.Learning, AP		1981	214.46	233.79	**-19.33**
Total Deemed to be Universities			**819.34**	**1028.68**	**-209.34**
State Universities					
Devi Ahilya University, Indore	**Central**	1964	763.85	979.57	**-215.72**
Dr. Harisingh G.Vishdy. M.P.		1946	1521.56	1289.84	**231.72**
Barkatullah Univ. Bhopal		1970	1516.26	1474.71	**41.55**
Ranchi University, Bihar		1976	42.99	70.40	**-27.41**
Magadh University, Bihar*		1960	4443.12	4345.92	**97.2**
Rani Durgawati University, Jabalpur		1935	805.11	883.59	**-78.48**
Deen Dayal Upad. University, Gorakhpur		1956	1005.45	979.97	**25.48**

(Contd.)

(Contd. Table 3. 19)

Name of the Universities	*Region*	*Year of Estt.*	*2001-02 (Rs in Lakh)*		*Surplus/ Deficit*
			Income	*Expenditure*	
Central Unviersity					
AMU, Aligarh		1920	**15882.01**	**16050.25**	**-168.24**
Deemed to be Universities					
Banasthali Vidhyapeeth, Rajasthan		1962	1398.82	1409.62	**-10.8**
Rashtriya Sanskrit Vidyapeethm, Tirupati		1961	331.49	366.39	**-34.9**
Sri Sathya Sai Institute of H.Learning, AP		1981	454.42	440.45	**13.97**
Total Deemed to be Universities			**2184.73**	**2216.46**	**-31.73**
State Universities					
Devi Ahilya University, Indore	**Central**	1964	3365.22	3544.42	**-179.2**
Dr. Harisingh G.Vishdy. M.P.		1946	2474.29	1631.51	**842.78**
Barkatullah Univ. Bhopal		1970	2282.95	3371.94	**-1088.99**
Ranchi University, Bihar		1976	134.95	166.17	**-31.22**
Magadh University, Bihar*		1960	7307.38	6757.77	**549.61**
Rani Durgawati University, Jabalpur		1935	746.25	1436.51	**-690.26**
Deen Dayal Upad. University, Gorakhpur		1956	2308.58	1792.19	**516.39**

(Contd.)

(Contd. Table 3. 19)

Name of the Universities	*Region*	*Year of Estt.*	*1996-97 (Rs. in Lakh)*		*Surplus/ Deficit*
			Income	*Expenditure*	
Punjab University, Chandigarh	**Northern**	1947	4824.59	4615.33	**209.26**
Kurukshetra University, Haryana		1957	2997.55	3348.67	**-351.12**
M.D. Univ. Rohtak, Haryana		1956	1797.72	2739.22	**-941.5**
Manipur University, Imphal	**North-Eastern**	1980	664.97	577.39	**87.58**
Nagaland University, Kohima		1994	492.38	465.86	**26.52**
Tirpura University, Tipura West		1987	286.80	223.82	**62.98**
Mizoram University		2001	0.00	0.00	**0**
Bhavnagar University	**Western**	1979	418.26	324.23	**94.03**
Swami Rmanand Univ., Nanded		1994	613.45	127.34	**486.11**
Shivaji Univeristy, Kolhapur		1962	2217.15	2040.62	**176.53**
Nagpur University, Nagpur		1923	3166.58	2118.35	**1048.23**

(Contd.)

(Contd.Table 3. 19)

Name of the Universities	*Region*	*Year of Estt.*	*2001-02 (Rs in Lakh)*		*Surplus/ Deficit*
			Income	*Expenditure*	
Punjab University, Chandigarh	**Northern**	1947	8423.19	8021.55	**401.64**
Kurukshetra University, Haryana		1957	7311.71	7295.27	**16.44**
M.D. Univ. Rohtak, Haryana		1956	7688.33	5773.26	**1915.07**
Manipur University, Imphal	**North-Eastern**	1980	1143.44	1199.11	**-55.67**
Nagaland University, Kohima		1994	1394.52	1274.49	**120.03**
Tirpura University, Tipura West		1987	811.11	827.09	**-15.98**
Mizoram University		2001	1534.30	5253.75	**-3719.45**
Bhavnagar University	**Western**	1979	1276.25	644.94	**631.31**
Swami Rmanand Univ., Nanded		1994	568.63	964.30	**-395.67**
Shivaji Univeristy, Kolhapur		1962	3848.97	4043.19	**-194.22**
Nagpur University, Nagpur		1923	5774.01	6258.58	**-484.57**

(Contd.)

(Contd. Table 3. 19)

Name of the Universities	*Region*	*Year of Estt.*	*1996-97 (Rs. in Lakh)*		*Surplus/ Deficit*
			Income	*Expenditure*	
Karnatak Univ. Dharwad	Southern	1950	2746.25	1983.49	**762.76**
Banglore University		1961	3330.29	3336.90	**-6.61**
Mangalore University, Mangalagangothri		1980	1061.93	974.78	**87.15**
Cochin Univ. of Sc. & Tech., Kerala		1986	1484.23	1433.35	**50.88**
University of Kerala, Thiruvanauthapuram		1937	3186.81	3298.46	**-111.65**
Sri Krishnadevaraya Univ., Anantapur		1981	823.69	1123.66	**-299.97**
University of Madras, Chennai		1857	2827.40	3211.32	**-383.92**
Total State Universities			**43038.39**	**41966.79**	**1071.6**
All Universities Total			**52078.15**	**50850.99**	**1227.16**

(Contd.)

(Contd.Table 3. 19)

Name of the Universities	*Region*	*Year of Estt.*	*2001-02 (Rs in Lakh)*		*Surplus/ Deficit*
			Income	*Expenditure*	
Karnatak Univ. Dharwad		1950	4310.17	3911.12	**399.05**
Banglore University		1961	6670.62	5729.64	**940.98**
Mangalore University, Mangalagangothri		1980	1898.98	1779.05	**119.93**
Cochin Univ. of Sc. & Tech., Kerala		1986	2922.59	2899.92	**22.67**
University of Kerala, Thiruvanauthapuram	**Southern**	1937	5561.51	5690.24	**-128.73**
Sri Krishnadevaraya Univ., Anantapur		1981	1192.64	1605.50	**-412.86**
University of Madras, Chennai		1857	8255.25	6996.64	**1258.61**
Total State Universities			**89205.84**	**88868.15**	**337.69**
All Universities Total			**107272.58**	**107134.86**	**137.72**

Note : * = Special assistance during IX plan.

Table 3.20: Distribution of Universities by surplus and deficit budget (established before and after independence)

Sl.No.	1996-97		2001-02	
	Before Independence	*After Independence*	*Before Independence*	*After Independence*
1.	AMU (+)	Banasthali (-)	AMU (-)	Banasthali (-)
2.	Nagpur (+)	Rashtriya Sanskrit (-)	Nagpur (-)	Rashtriya Sanskrit (-)
3.	Dr. Hari Singh Gour (+)	Sri Satya Sai Institute of Higher Learning (-)	Dr. Hari Singh Gour (+)	Sri Satya Sai Institute of Higher Learning (+)
4.	Kerala (-)	Devi Ahilya (-)	Kerala (-)	Devi Ahilya (-)
5.	Rani Durgawati (-)	Barkatullha (+)	Rani Durgawati (-)	Barkatullha (-)
		Ranchi (-)		Ranchi (-)
		Magadh (+)		Magadh (+)
		Denn Dayal Upady. (+)		D. Dayal Upady. (+)

(Contd.)

(Contd. Table 3. 20)

Sl.No.	1996-97		2001-02	
	Before Independence	After Independence	Before Independence	After Independence
		Punjab (+)		Punjab (+)
		Kurukeshtra (-)		Kurukeshtra (+)
		M.D. Rohatak (-)		M.D. Rohatak (+)
		Manipur (+)		Manipur (-)
		Nagaland (+)		Nagaland (+)
		Tripura (+)		Tripura (-)
		Bhavnagar (+)		Bhavnagar (+)

(Contd.)

(Contd.Table 3. 20)

Sl.No.	*1996-97*		*2001-02*	
	Before Independence	*After Independence*	*Before Independence*	*After Independence*
		Swami Rama Nand (+)		Swami Rama Nand (-)
		Shivaji (+)		Shivaji (-)
		Karnataka (+)		Karnataka (+)
		Bangalore (-)		Bangalore (+)
		Mangalore (+)		Mangalore (+)
		Cochin Univ of Sc. & Tech. (+)		Cochin Univ of Sc. & Tech. (+)
		Sri Krishnadev. (-)		Sri Krishnadev. (-)
		Madras (-)		Madras (+)

Note: (+) = Surplus Income, (-) = deficit budget.

Table 3.21: Distribution of University-wise income and expenditure on hostels (in percentage)

Name of the Universities	*Region*	*Year of Estt.*	*1996-97*	
			Income	*Expenditure*
Central University				
AMU, Aligarh		1920	**0.300**	**0.558**
Deemed to be Universities				
Banasthali Vidhypeeth, Rajasthan		1962	35.723	34.464
Rashtriya Sanskrit		1961	0.000	0.000
Sri Sathya Sai Institute of H.Learning,		1981	0.000	0.000
Total Deemed to be Universities			**21.666**	**21.833**
State Universities				
Devi Ahilya University, Indore	**Central**	1964	0.393	1.426
Dr. Harisingh G.Vishdy. M.P.		1946	0.166	0.000
Barkatullah Univ. Bhopal		1970	0.028	0.012
Ranchi University, Bihar		1976	0.089	0.007
Magadh University, Bihar		1960	0.128	0.025
Rani Durgawati University, Jabalpur		1935	0.018	1.586
Deen Dayal Upad. University, Gorakhpur		1956	0.428	1.828
Punjab University, Chandigarh	**Northern**	1947	0.340	0.391
Kurukshetra University, Haryana		1957	0.000	0.000
M.D. Univ. Rohtak, Haryana		1956	0.000	0.000

(Contd.)

(Contd.Table 3. 21)

Name of the Universities	*Region*	*Year of Estt.*	*2001-02*	
			Income	*Expenditure*
Central University				
AMU, Aligarh		1920	**0.258**	**0.519**
Deemed to be Universities				
Banasthali Vidhypeeth, Rajasthan		1962	22.840	26.322
Rashtriya Sanskrit		1961	0.000	0.000
Sri Sathya Sai Institute of H.Learning,		1981	0.000	0.000
Total Deemed to be Universities			**14.624**	**16.961**
State Universities				
Devi Ahilya University, Indore	**Central**	1964	0.208	0.509
Dr. Harisingh G.Vishdy. M.P.		1946	0.187	0.000
Barkatullah Univ. Bhopal		1970	0.230	0.156
Ranchi University, Bihar		1976	0.289	0.010
Magadh University, Bihar		1960	0.324	0.008
Rani Durgawati University, Jabalpur		1935	0.083	1.599
Deen Dayal Upad. University, Gorakhpur		1956	0.388	1.337
Punjab University, Chandigarh	**Northern**	1947	0.334	0.358
Kurukshetra University, Haryana		1957	0.000	0.000
M.D. Univ. Rohtak, Haryana		1956	0.000	0.007

(Contd.)

(Contd.Table 3. 21)

Name of the Universities	*Region*	*Year of Estt.*	*Percentage increase/*	
			1996-97	*2001-02*
Central University				
AMU, Aligarh		1920	**-0.26**	**-0.26**
Deemed to be Universities				
Banasthali Vidhypeeth, Rajasthan		1962	1.26	-3.48
Rashtriya Sanskrit		1961	0.00	0.00
Sri Sathya Sai Institute of H.Learning,		1981	0.00	0.00
Total Deemed to be Universities			**-0.17**	**-2.34**
State Universities				
Devi Ahilya University, Indore	**Central**	1964	-1.03	-0.30
Dr. Harisingh G.Vishdy. M.P.		1946	0.17	0.00
Barkatullah Univ. Bhopal		1970	0.02	0.07
Ranchi University, Bihar		1976	0.08	0.28
Magadh University, Bihar		1960	0.10	0.32
Rani Durgawati University, Jabalpur		1935	-1.57	-1.52
Deen Dayal Upad. University, Gorakhpur		1956	-1.40	-0.95
Punjab University, Chandigarh	**Northern**	1947	-0.05	-0.02
Kurukshetra University, Haryana		1957	0.00	0.00
M.D. Univ. Rohtak, Haryana		1956	0.00	0.00

(Contd.)

(Contd. Table 3. 21)

Name of the Universities	*Region*	*Year of Estt.*	*1996-97 Income*	*1996-97 Expenditure*
Manipur University, Imphal	**North-Eastern**	1980	0.195	1.136
Nagaland University, Kohima		1994	0.122	0.165
Tirpura University, Tipura West		1987	0.704	0.000
Mizoram Univeristy, Aizawl-Mizoram		2001		
Bhavnagar University	**Western**	1979	0.081	0.040
Swami Rmanand Univ., Nanded		1994	0.000	0.000
Shivaji Univeristy, Kolhapur		1962	0.306	0.359
Nagpur University, Nagpur		1923	0.318	1.195
Karnatak Univ. Dharwad		1950	0.432	1.301
Banglore University		1961	0.000	7.089
Mangalore University, Mangalagangothri	**Southern**	1980	0.138	0.000
Cochin Univ. of Sc. & Tech., Kerala		1986	0.016	0.384
University of Kerala,		1937	0.125	0.625
Sri Krishnadevaraya Univ., Anantapur		1981	0.449	3.934
University of Madras, Chennai		1857	0.189	0.023
Total State Universities			**0.175**	**1.228**
All Universities Total			**0.533**	**1.505**

(Contd.)

(Contd.Table 3. 21)

Name of the Universities	*Region*	*Year of Estt.*	*2001-02*	
			Income	*Expenditure*
Manipur University, Imphal	**North-Eastern**	1980	0.090	1.086
Nagaland University, Kohima		1994	0.131	0.525
Tirpura University, Tipura West		1987	0.004	0.005
Mizoram Univeristy, Aizawl-Mizoram		2001	0.012	0.000
Bhavnagar University	**Western**	1979	0.184	0.032
Swami Rmanand Univ., Nanded		1994	0.341	0.000
Shivaji Univeristy, Kolhapur		1962	0.218	0.272
Nagpur University, Nagpur		1923	0.348	0.722
Karnatak Univ. Dharwad	**Southern**	1950	0.573	1.213
Banglore University		1961	0.000	3.292
Mangalore University, Mangalagangothri		1980	0.771	0.000
Cochin Univ. of Sc. & Tech., Kerala		1986	0.215	0.274
University of Kerala,		1937	0.153	0.494
Sri Krishnadevaraya Univ., Anantapur		1981	0.284	5.324
University of Madras, Chennai		1857	0.113	0.024
Total State Universities			**0.213**	**0.784**
All Universities Total			**0.513**	**1.055**

(Contd.)

(Contd.Table 3. 21)

Name of the Universities	*Region*	*Year of Estt.*	*Percentage increase/* 1996-97	2001-02
Manipur University, Imphal	**North-Eastern**	1980	-0.94	-1.00
Nagaland University, Kohima		1994	-0.04	-0.39
Tirpura University, Tipura West		1987	0.70	0.00
Mizoram Univeristy, Aizawl-Mizoram		2001		0.01
Bhavnagar University	**Western**	1979	0.04	0.15
Swami Rmanand Univ., Nanded		1994	0.00	0.34
Shivaji Univeristy, Kolhapur		1962	-0.05	-0.05
Nagpur University, Nagpur		1923	-0.88	-0.37
Karnatak Univ. Dharwad	**Southern**	1950	-0.87	-0.64
Banglore University		1961	-7.09	-3.29
Mangalore University, Mangalagangothri		1980	-	-
Cochin Univ. of Sc. & Tech., Kerala		1986	-0.37	-0.06
University of Kerala,		1937	-0.50	-0.34
Sri Krishnadevaraya Univ., Anantapur		1981	-3.49	-5.04
University of Madras, Chennai		1857	0.17	0.09
Total State Universities			**-1.05**	**-0.57**
All Universities Total			**-0.97**	**-0.54**

(Contd.)

Table 3.22: Percentage distribution of University-wise income and expenditure on Examination in 1996-97 and 2001-02

Name of the Universities	*Region*	*Year of Estt.*	*1996-97*	
			Income from examination charges	*Expenditure on examination*
Central University				
AMU, Aligarh		1920	**0.328**	**1.479**
Deemed Universities				
Banasthali University, Rajasthan		1962	0.706	0.612
Rashtriya Sanskrit Vidyapeethm,Tirupati		1961	3.215	1.957
Sri Sathya Sai Institute of H.Learning, AP		1981	0.000	0.961
Total Deemed Universities			**0.852**	**0.869**
State Universities				
Devi Ahilya University, Indore	**Central**	1964	16.248	15.685
Dr. Harisingh G.Vishdy. M.P.		1946	17.416	9.963
Barkatullah Univ. Bhopal		1970	25.221	12.043
Ranchi University, Bihar		1976	29.734	13.520
Magadh University, Bihar		1960	12.480	10.057
Rani Durgawati University, Jabalpur		1935	4.260	7.964
Deen Dayal Upad. University, Gorakhpur		1956	7.346	8.064

(Contd.)

(Contd.Table 3. 22)

Name of the Universities	*Region*	*Year of Estt.*	*2001-02*	
			Income from examination charges	*Expenditure on examination*
Central University				
AMU, Aligarh		1920	**0.147**	**1.199**
Deemed Universities				
Banasthali University, Rajasthan		1962	0.651	0.728
Rashtriya Sanskrit Vidyapeethm,Tirupati		1961	2.205	0.704
Sri Sathya Sai Institute of H.Learning, AP		1981	0.000	0.734
Total Deemed Universities			**0.751**	**0.725**
State Universities				
Devi Ahilya University, Indore		1964	15.155	14.158
Dr. Harisingh G.Vishdy. M.P.		1946	19.117	7.130
Barkatullah Univ. Bhopal		1970	61.278	66.519
Ranchi University, Bihar	**Central**	1976	63.231	11.120
Magadh University, Bihar		1960	29.865	9.874
Rani Durgawati University, Jabalpur		1935	19.218	6.425
Deen Dayal Upad. University, Gorakhpur		1956	11.268	7.805

(Contd.)

(Contd.Table 3. 22)

Name of the Universities	*Region*	*Year of Estt.*	*Percentage of share of income in relation to expenditure*	
			1996-1997	*2001-2002*
Central University				
AMU, Aligarh		1920	**-1.15**	**-1.05**
Deemed Universities				
Banasthali University, Rajasthan		1962	0.09	-0.08
Rashtriya Sanskrit Vidyapeethm,Tirupati		1961	1.26	1.50
Sri Sathya Sai Institute of H.Learning, AP		1981	-0.96	-0.73
Total Deemed Universities			**-0.02**	**0.03**
State Universities				
Devi Ahilya University, Indore	**Central**	1934	0.56	1.00
Dr. Harisingh G.Vishdy. M.P.		1946	7.45	11.99
Barkatullah Univ. Bhopal		1970	13.18	-5.24
Ranchi University, Bihar		1976	16.21	52.11
Magadh University, Bihar		1960	2.42	19.99
Rani Durgawati University, Jabalpur		1935	-3.70	12.79
Deen Dayal Upad. University, Gorakhpur		1956	-0.72	3.46

(Contd.)

(Contd.Table 3. 22)

Name of the Universities	*Region*	*Year of Estt.*	*1996-97*	
			Income from examination charges	*Expenditure on examination*
Punjab University, Chandigarh	**Northern**	1947	6.546	7.379
Kurukshetra University, Haryana		1957	1.861	2.351
M.D. Univ. Rohtak, Haryana		1956	3.471	0.000
Manipur University, Imphal	**North-eastern**	1980	6.686	8.936
Nagaland University, Kohima		1994	2.650	12.272
Tirpura University, Tipura West		1987	0.007	6.656
Mizoram Univeristy, Aizawl-Mizoram		2001	-	-
Bhavnagar University	**Western**	1979	8.674	8.638
Swami Rmanand Univ., Nanded		1994	17.524	31.373
Shivaji Univeristy, Kolhapur		1962	14.054	13.785
Nagpur University, Nagpur		1923	19.918	19.316

(Contd.)

(Contd.Table 3. 22)

Name of the Universities	Region	Year of Estt.	2001-02	
			Income from examination charges	Expenditure on examination
Punjab University, Chandigarh	Northern	1947	13.099	5.910
Kurukshetra University, Haryana		1957	1.037	1.833
M.D. Univ. Rohtak, Haryana		1956	4.386	1.328
Manipur University, Imphal	North-eastern	1980	8.017	6.581
Nagaland University, Kohima		1994	4.097	6.530
Tirpura University, Tipura West		1987	1.847	8.956
Mizoram Univeristy, Aizawl-Mizoram		2001	1.584	1.617
Bhavnagar University	Western	1979	5.543	8.472
Swami Rmanand Univ., Nanded		1994	4.704	20.761
Shivaji Univeristy, Kolhapur		1962	21.065	11.716
Nagpur University, Nagpur		1923	12.348	10.369

(Contd.)

(Contd. Table 3. 22)

Name of the Universities	*Region*	*Year of Estt.*	*Percentage of share of income in relation to expenditure*	
			1996-1997	*2001-2002*
Punjab University, Chandigarh	**Northern**	1947	-0.83	7.19
Kurukshetra University, Haryana		1957	-0.49	-0.80
M.D. Univ. Rohtak, Haryana		1956	3.47	3.06
Manipur University, Imphal	**North-eastern**	1980	-2.25	1.44
Nagaland University, Kohima		1994	-9.62	-2.43
Tirpura University, Tipura West		1987	-6.65	-7.11
Mizoram Univeristy, Aizawl-Mizoram		2001		-0.03
Bhavnagar University	**Western**	1979	0.04	-2.93
Swami Rmanand Univ., Nanded		1994	-13.85	-16.06
Shivaji Univeristy, Kolhapur		1962	0.27	9.35
Nagpur University, Nagpur		1923	0.60	1.98

(Contd.)

(Contd.Table 3. 22)

Name of the Universities	*Region*	*Year of Estt.*	*1996-97*	
			Income from examination charges	*Expenditure on examination*
Karnatak Univ. Dharwad	**Southern**	1950	23.354	20.436
Banglore University		1961	15.047	21.130
Mangalore University, Mangalagangothri		1980	11.993	19.193
Cochin Univ. of Sc. & Tech., Kerala		1986	1.244	0.181
University of Kerala, Thiruvanauthapuram		1937	9.218	11.439
Sri Krishnadevaraya Univ., Anantapur		1981	16.904	9.274
University of Madras, Chennai		1857	44.796	13.451
Total State Universities			**13.863**	**10.892**
Total All Universities			**11.522**	**9.108**

(Contd.)

(Contd.Table 3. 22)

Name of the Universities	*Region*	*Year of Estt.*	*2001-02*	
			Income from examination charges	*Expenditure on examination*
Karnatak Univ. Dharwad	Southern	1950	11.619	12.357
Banglore University		1961	17.339	7.485
Mangalore University, Mangalagangothri		1980	6.212	8.284
Cochin Univ. of Sc. & Tech., Kerala		1986	4.649	0.210
University of Kerala, Thiruvanauthapuram		1937	5.826	5.003
Sri Krishnadevaraya Univ., Anantapur		1981	15.287	9.535
University of Madras, Chennai		1857	43.998	17.876
Total State Universities			**17.010**	**10.435**
Total All Universities			**14.182**	**8.777**

(Contd.)

(Contd.Table 3. 22)

Name of the Universities	*Region*	*Year of Estt.*	*Percentage of share of income in relation to expenditure*	
			1996-1997	*2001-2002*
Karnatak Univ. Dharwad	Southern	1950	2.92	-0.74
Banglore University		1961	-6.08	9.85
Mangalore University, Mangalagangothri		1980	-7.20	-2.07
Cochin Univ. of Sc. & Tech., Kerala		1986	1.06	4.44
University of Kerala, Thiruvanauthapuram		1937	-2.22	0.82
Sri Krishnadevaraya Univ., Anantapur		1981	7.63	5.75
University of Madras, Chennai		1857	31.35	26.12
Total State Universities			**2.97**	**6.58**
Total All Universities			**2.41**	**5.41**

Income and Expenditure on Examination Fees

Table 3.22 indicates the income accruing to universities from examination fees and the expenditure incurred on conducting them. Analysis indicates substantial variations. Some universities spend more than their income while some are able to generate surplus income. However, except in the case of a few universities, surplus generated is small. For all universities, the surplus was 2.41 per cent in 1997 and 6.41 per cent in 2001-02. The surplus percentage of income from examinations of all universities and total per cent of state universities has shown an increasing trend.

The maximum surplus was in the University of Madras (31.35 per cent in 1996-97) followed by Ranchi University, where surplus percentage of income was very high in 2001-02 (52.11). On the other hand, Swami Ramanand University seemed to be facing the problem of deficit in meeting the expenditure on the conduct of examinations for both the years. During 1996-97, the deficit in the University was 13.85 per cent of income which increased to 16.06 per cent in 2001-02. Universities spending more on examinations are Karukshetra, Rani Durgawati, Swami Ramanand, Bangalore, Punjab, Manipur, Nagaland, Tripura, Kerala and Mangalore for the year 1996-97. Out of these some universities have improved their position; these include Rani Durgawati, Deen Dayal Upadhyay, Punjab, Manipur, Bhavnagar, Bangalore and Kerala.

The variation in the income and expenditure on conduct of examinations in selected universities may be due to variations in student charges and rates of remuneration for examination work like paper setting, evaluation etc.

Comparison of Government and Non-governmental Resources

As mentioned earlier, government support for higher education has been declining in India as well as worldwide and, because of financial constraints, universities are being asked to generate resources from other sources. Many universities are adopting several innovative measures to mobilize resources from non-governmental sources. China has, for instance, shifted its emphasis from traditional higher education to short-cycle programmes, in which enrollment tends to increase rapidly and students are ready to pay for these courses. Hong Kong has a target of increasing non-government resources to 18 per cent through fees in higher education (Tilak 2003).

The comparative picture of government and non-governmental resources of universities in India provides a different scenario (Tables 3.2 and 3.3):

- Aligarh Mulsim (Central University), Ranchi and Magadh (State Universities) received more than 90 per cent grants from government. But none of these universities made any effort to mobilize additional resources between 1996-97 to 2001-02. The share from total fee income of these Universities was meagre. Ranchi University had shown a declining trend as far as income from fees is concerned. The following table explains:

Name of University	*Total Fee Income (%)*	
	1996-97	*2001-02*
AMU (Central University)	3.23	3.33
Ranchi (State University)	6.97	2.66
Magadh (State University)	6.49	7.70

- Karnataka University received 29.34 per cent of its income from government grants during 1996-97 which increased to 37.26 per cent in 2001-02. The university made no effort at mobilization of additional resources from non-government sources. The total fee income, instead of increasing, decreased from 24.32 per cent to 16.47 per cent.
- Madras University's share of government grants was the lowest among the universities, being 8.09 per cent and 9.27 per cent during 1996-97 and 2001-02 respectively. The university, however, made efforts to mobilize additional resources of a sizeable order. The total fee income of the university was 61.65 per cent, which is quite

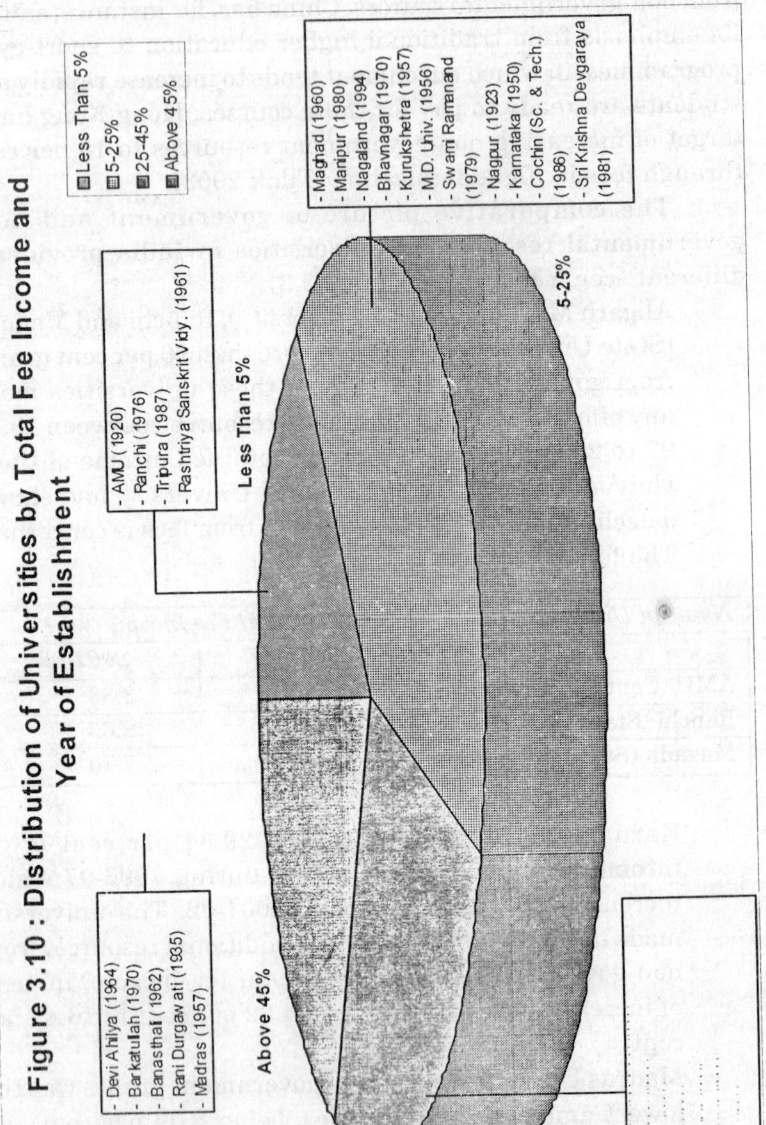

Figure 3.10 : Distribution of Universities by Total Fee Income and Year of Establishment

Table 3.23: Distribution of Universities by fee income – and year of establishment (2001-02)

As Percentage of their Income			
Less than 5	*6-25*	*26-45*	*Above 45*
AMU (1920)	Nagpur (1923)	Kerala (1937)	Rani Durgawati (1956)
Ranchi (1960)	Karnataka (1950)	Dr. Hari Singh Gour (1946)	Madras (1857)
Rashtriya Sanskrit Vidhy. (1961)	M.D. Univ. (1976)	Punjab (1947)	Banasthali (1935)
Tripura (1987)	Kurukshetra (1956)	Gorakhpur (1957)	Davi Ahilya (1964)
	Maghad (1960)	Bangalore (1961)	Barkatullah (1970)
	Bhavnagar (1979)	Shivaji (1962)	
	Swami Ramanand (1994)	Mangalore (1980)	
	Manipur (1980)		
	Sri Krishna Devgaraya (1981)		
	Cochin (Science & Tech.) (1986)		
	Nagaland (1994)		

Note : Figures in the parenthesis are year of establishment of University.

high. it increased to 62.387 per cent between 1996-97 to 2001-02.

Table 3.23 and Figure 3.10 show that there is no relationship between the age of the university and the share of its fee income. Ultimately it depends upon the university's policies and their implementation, which have significance in generating income through other than the governmental sources.

To Conclude

The preceding analysis has brought out the following points about the behaviour of university finances:

University Finances

Pattern of Income

1. The analysis of the income of 29 universities indicates spectacular rise in the total income of the universities between 1996-97 and 2001-02. But a steady decline was observed in the percentage of government grants to Deemed to be Universities and state universities.
2. Other grants that are given through Central government, All India Council for Technical Education (AICTE), other governmental agencies and Local bodies, are very meagre; they too are declining.
3. Government funding for selected universities decreased from 64.99 per cent to 56.72 per cent and income from fees, an important source of funding of universities, increased from 20.06 per cent to 26.10 per cent. It can be assumed that private participation in the university education sector has shown a tendency of enhancing.
4. In 55 per cent of universities, income from tuition fees has shown a declining trend. There is need to start new self-financing courses mainly in innovative and professional subjects and also gradual enhancement of tuition fees.
5. There is no relationship between how old a university is and the share of its fee income. It depends upon the

university's policies and their implementation, which have significance in generating income through other than the governmental sources.

6. Quite a few universities have surplus income from examination fees. However, in 40 per cent of universities, examination fees show a declining trend. The reasons need to be explored so that appropriate action is taken for enabling universities to mobilize additional resources under this head.
7. Income from hostel fees shows a declining trend in more than 50 per cent of universities. There is need for examining the extent to which universities are subsidizing hostellers in meeting such costs as rent, various charges and the amount spent on mess.
8. Wide variation exists in the amount received by universities for projects, sponsored either by government or by non-government organizations. But, project grants are invariably increasing in most of the universities for research projects sponsored by non-governmental organizations.

Pattern of Expenditure

1. It has been noticed that the overall expenditure has substantially increased over the years. Recurring expenditure constitutes the largest proportion of expenditure as against non-recurring expenditure.
2. Though it accounts for very low proportion as compared to recurring expenditure, there has been substantial increase in the proportion of non-recurring expenditure.
3. Universities are incurring most of their non-recurring expenditure on construction of buildings, leaving very little amounts for library, laboratory equipments, furniture, computers etc.
4. Salary expenditure constitutes the largest proportion of university expenditure. The salary expenditure of non-teaching staff has shown an increasing trend in comparison with that of teaching staff in most of the

universities. Considering that primary functions of universities are teaching and research, the increase in non-teaching staff salaries indicates the existence of large number of non-teaching personnel, whose contribution to the realization of the objectives of the institutions might not be significant.

5. It has been noticed that expenditure on hostel facilities has invariably increased over a period of five years i.e. 1996-97 to 2001-02 as compared to income from this source.
6. Universities are spending very meagre amount on student welfare services that consist of hostels, scholarship/ stipends, sports, NCC, NSS, and Cultural activities.
7. It has also been noticed that on scholarships, stipends, games and sports, etc. the share of expenditure has declined for all the universities.
8. With regard to conduct of examinations, only a few universities have shown surplus income.

4

Financing of Higher Education in India: *Role of the University Grants Commission*

The University Grants Commission (UGC) is a statutory organization at the national level charged with the responsibility of coordinating, determining and maintaining standards of university education. It is empowered to take all such steps, in consultation with universities and the government, that it deems necessary to achieve these objectives. Colleges providing higher education also fall within the purview of the UGC. To give effect to its responsibilities, the UGC advises the Central and state Governments and institutions of higher education on the measures necessary for the promotion of higher education. Besides, it also makes such rules and regulations that it considers necessary and are in consonance with its mandate. True to its name, however, one of the major functions of the UGC has been to allocate and disburse grants to universities and colleges for their maintenance and development.

The maintenance (non-plan) grants are provided to eligible universities and colleges to enable them to meet recurring expenditure on salaries, maintenance of laboratories, libraries and buildings and on a host of other recurring items like telephones, utilities, stationery, consumables etc. The central universities, inter-university centres and, until recently, some of the deemed to be universities, being the sole responsibility of the Union Government, have been the major recipients of UGC grants. Development (plan) grants, on the other hand, are provided for developing infrastructure and basic facilities in universities and colleges, for providing teaching and technical manpower, acquiring equipment, books and journals, development of the campus, construction of new buildings and providing amenities to students and staff. While Central Universities, Inter-University Centres and Deemed to be Universities and colleges associated with and affiliated to them are provided development assistance in the form of block grants, state universities are provided such assistance on a matching basis with state governments/ universities providing the prescribed matching share. Often, one time special grants are also given to universities and colleges to meet their specific requirements.

It needs to be stated here that Central Universities, Deemed to be Universities and non-university institutions like Inter University Centres, are a major charge on the funds of the UGC. The support to state universities is relatively small and confined largely to facilitate the procurement of such infrastructural facilities as are not normally available to them from the state governments or other bodies supporting them. Colleges of the Delhi University, Banaras Hindu University and the University College of Medical Sciences are given 90 per cent of the maintenance grant by the UGC. Support to colleges of the state universities is limited to Teachers Awards and Research Support. It needs to be pointed out at the outset that funding of institutions by the UGC is based on the five-year and annual plan allocation that it receives from the central government. In a way, therefore, UGC grants are in the nature of transfers from the source of funding to the recipients. The UGC plays, however, the major role of determining the quantum of assistance that various institutions should receive for their maintenance and further development. Being one of the major instruments for effecting quality improvement of university education, the constraints of financial resources tend to limit UGC's ability to motivate universities, colleges and state Government to take meaningful and consistent action in this regard.

A thematic view of the various types of grants that the UGC allocates to different sectors and different types of institutions is given in Chart 1:

Chart 1: UGC Grants

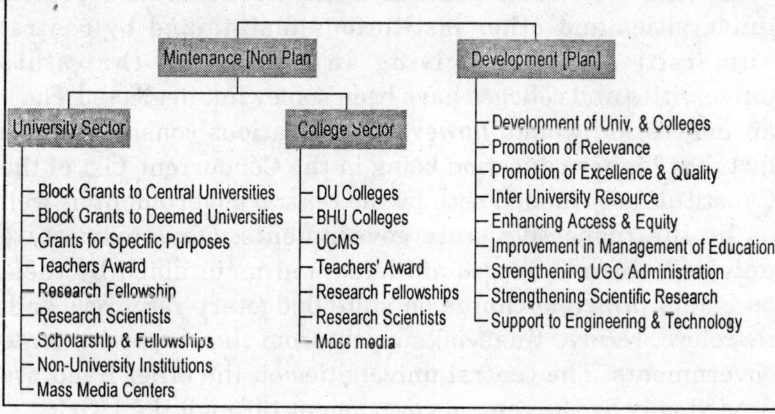

Note: DU-Delhi University, BHU-Banaras Hindu University, UCMS-University College of Medical Sciences.

Ever since its establishment, UGC has been playing an important role in maintenance and development of universities, colleges and other institutions of higher education in the country. This chapter intends to present a detailed analysis of the funding of higher education through the University Grants Commission. The analysis spans over a period of last decade and a half starting from 1991-92 and is based on the data compiled and collated from the Annual Reports of the UGC for each of the years covered under study. The financial data pertaining to UGC are provided at various places in its Annual Reports. Usually, Chapter 1 of the UGC reports contains a few tables, which provide aggregates of non-plan and plan grants received and released by the UGC to different types of institutions. The information is supplemented by detailed institution-wise and state-wise break up, in the form of appendices, of grants released by the UGC through its regional offices as well as the headquarters. The present analysis is largely based on the data available in the reports.

Magnitude of UGC Funding

Analysis of the data reveals that University Grants Commission (UGC) has generally been more generous to central universities and other institutions maintained by central universities; thereby giving an impression that state universities and colleges have been somewhat neglected. Such an impression would, however, be fallacious considering the fact that higher education being in the Concurrent List of the Constitution is funded both by the central government as well as by the respective state governments. Obviously, state universities and colleges affiliated and maintained by them become a principal charge on state budgetary resources and, therefore, receive financial support from the respective state governments. The central universities on the other hand are funded only by the central government through the UGC.

The UGC has been disbursing a substantial amount of its funds as non-plan and plan grants to institutions of higher education; the amount of grants has been increasing year after year. Plan and non-plan grants taken together, amounted to a little over Rs. 430 crore in 1991-92 which has increased to Rs. 2176.11 crore (RE) in 2005-06. As would be expected, a substantial proportion of the UGC funding has been in the form of non-plan grants to central universities as the same, on an average, account for more than 63 per cent of the grants given by it. Importantly, since non-plan grants have been increasing at a rate much faster than plan grants, the proportion of the non-plan grants during the last one decade or so has increased rather steeply Table 4.1 explains.

The Commission does not provide grants only to universities but also to colleges which are declared by it to be

Table 4.1: Total Grants Disbursed by the UGC

Year	Amount (Rs. In Lakh)			Plan as of Total (in %)	Index Number	
	Non Plan	Plan	Total		Non Plan	Plan
1991 – 92	26211.45	16794.89	43006.34	39	100.00	100.00
1992 – 93	30482.08	16203.95	46686.03	35	116.29	96.48
1993 – 94	33125.67	16014.36	49140.03	33	126.38	95.35
1994 – 95	34052.62	22199.88	56252.50	39	129.92	132.18
1995 – 96	42847.63	23905.04	66752.67	36	163.47	142.34
1996 – 97	46336.07	24881.67	71217.74	35	176.78	148.15
1997 – 98	53365.63	38840.38	92206.01	42	203.60	231.26
1998 – 99	97937.46	40067.74	138005.20	29	373.64	238.57
1999 – 00	95818.96	44129.23	139948.19	32	365.56	262.75
2000 – 01	98488.46	46962.47	145450.93	32	375.75	279.62
2001 – 02	98433.00	48297.10	146730.10	33	375.53	287.57
2005 – 06	138981.86	80874.36	219856.22	37	530.23	481.54

Table 4.2: Total Grant Disbursed by the UGC

Years	Amount (Rs in Lakh)			Share of the Universities (in %)	Index Number	
	Universities	Colleges	Total		Universities	Colleges
1991 - 92	34923.45	8082.89	43006.34	81.21	100.00	100.00
1992 - 93	34852.43	11833.60	46686.03	74.65	99.00	146.40
1993 - 94	37877.02	11263.01	49140.03	77.08	108.46	139.34
1994 - 95	42925.88	13326.62	56252.50	76.31	122.91	164.87
1995 - 96	52780.34	13972.33	66752.67	79.07	151.13	172.86
1996 - 97	52356.40	18861.34	71217.74	73.52	149.92	233.35
1997 - 98	67744.58	24461.43	92206.01	73.47	193.98	302.63
1998 - 99	99185.66	38819.54	138005.20	71.87	284.01	480.27
1999 - 00	101794.79	38153.40	139948.19	72.74	291.48	472.03
2000 - 01	105039.25	40411.68	145450.93	72.22	300.77	499.97
2001 - 02	102226.07	43565.77	145791.84	70.12	292.71	538.99
2005 – 06	103998.79	31692.67	135691.46*	76.64	297.79	392.10

Note: *= excludes non-university, establishment and regional centre.

eligible to receive its support. This financial support to colleges is necessary since they cater to bulk of the enrolment at the higher education stage. Any improvement in the quality of higher education depends significantly on the quality of programmes of colleges. It is, however, a fact that universities have over the years been the largest beneficiaries of the UGC funding. They appropriate nearly four-fifths of the total grants disbursed by it. In recent years, however, their share has declined from over 81 per cent in 1991-92 to about 76 per cent in 2005-06. It may be a matter of disquiet and discomfiture for universities that during the past fifteen years, the UGC funding for colleges has increased by about four times as opposed to an increase of about 3 times in flow of funds to the universities. Considering, however, the fact that collegiate sector accounts for nearly 80 per cent of the enrollment in higher education, the trend is a welcome departure (see Table 4.2).

In case of plan grants, the decline has been even more sharp as the share of universities has declined from 86.2 per cent in 1991-92 to a mere 71.4 per cent in 2005 06. The main reason has been the increase in the development assistance to colleges – nearly ten times – during the corresponding period (see Table 4.3).

It may, however, be noted that while plan grants to the universities have recorded a consistent growth, except for the first two years of the analysis, allocations to colleges have generally been fluctuating from year to year. The case of non-plan grants has been slightly different in the sense that the share of universities has been consistent. They still account for about 77 per cent of the maintenance grants disbursed by the UGC (see Table 4.4).

Are universities losing favour with the UGC? Or is it that the needs of colleges are now being recognized as important for improvement of higher education? After all, colleges do account for over 80 per cent of the undergraduate enrolment in higher education. However, it is important to realize that it is the universities that are regarded as the torch-bearers of research and development and are more significant instruments for

Table 4.3: Plan Grants Disbursed by the UGC

Year	Amount (Rs in Lakh)			Share of the Universities (in %)	Index Number	
	Universities	Colleges	Total		Universities	Colleges
1991 - 92	14480.36	2314.53	16794.89	86.22	100.00	100.00
1992 - 93	11363.18	4840.77	16203.95	70.13	78.47	209.15
1993 - 94	12390.03	3624.33	16014.36	77.37	85.56	156.59
1994 - 95	17022.57	5177.31	22199.88	76.68	117.56	223.69
1995 - 96	19202.12	4702.92	23905.04	80.33	132.61	203.19
1996 - 97	16992.70	7888.97	24881.67	68.29	117.35	340.85
1997 - 98	26612.17	12228.21	38840.38	68.52	183.78	528.32
1998 - 99	26239.07	13828.67	40067.74	65.49	181.20	597.47
1999 - 00	31363.24	12765.99	44129.23	71.07	216.59	551.56
2000 - 01	31007.16	15955.31	46962.47	66.03	214.13	689.35
2001 - 02	32576.66	15720.44	48297.10	67.45	224.97	679.21
2005 – 06	57608.43	22912.05	80720.48	71.37	397.84	989.92

Table 4.4: Non Plan Grants Disbursed by the UGC

Year	*Amount (Rs in Lakh)*			*Share of the Universities (in %)*	*Index Number*	
	Universities	*Colleges*	*Total*		*Universities*	*Colleges*
1991 - 92	20443.09	5768.36	26211.45	77.99	100.00	100.00
1992 - 93	23489.25	6992.83	30482.08	77.06	114.90	121.23
1993 - 94	25486.99	7638.68	33125.67	76.94	124.67	132.42
1994 - 95	25903.31	8149.31	34052.62	76.07	126.71	141.28
1995 - 96	33578.22	9269.41	42847.63	78.37	164.25	160.69
1996 - 97	35363.7	10972.37	46336.07	76.32	172.99	190.22
1997 - 98	41132.41	12233.22	53365.63	77.08	201.20	212.07
1998 - 99	72946.59	24990.87	97937.46	74.48	356.83	433.24
1999 - 00	70431.55	25387.41	95818.96	73.50	344.52	440.11
2000 - 01	74032.09	24456.37	98488.46	75.17	362.14	423.97
2001 - 02	70587.67	27845.33	98433.00	71.71	345.29	482.73
2005 – 06	103998.79	31682.67	135681.46	76.65	508.72	549.24

promoting higher education, because of their orientation and focus on postgraduate higher education and research. In the context of constraint of resources, UGC has to make choices, often unpleasant ones.

UGC Support to Central and State Sector

It has often been argued that the principal concern of the University Grants Commission has been central universities and colleges associated/affiliated with them and consequently the central sector is the largest beneficiary of UGC munificence. This section is devoted to ascertaining as to the extent to which this assumption is valid and as to whether there have been changes in the financing pattern over the years.

It has been indicated earlier that the UGC provides financial support both to central as well as state universities. In terms of total grants disbursed by the UGC, the central sector, which comprises the Central Universities, Deemed to be Universities and Inter University Centres, appropriate the lion's share of the UGC resources. This share has been increasing over the years. It may be seen from Table 4.5 that the central sector, which accounted for about 77 per cent of the total grants in 1991-92, rose to an all time high of about 86 per cent in 1998-99 to fall again to about 76 per cent in 2005-06; slightly less than the position in 1991-92. In aggregate terms, financial allocations to state universities have increased only by about 273 per cent as compared to an increase of 316 per cent for the central sector. One would be inclined to conclude that central sector is being financed at the expense of the already impoverished state sector. It should, however, be kept in mind that state universities and colleges are also provided financial support by the respective state governments, whereas the central universities and colleges affiliated and associated with them are dependent solely on the University Grants Commission.

The segregation of the data into plan and non-plan grants presents a different picture. Analysis shows that plan grants to central universities increased from Rs. 72.40 crore in 1991-

Table 4.5: Total Grants Disbursed by the UGC to Universities

Years	*Amount (Rs in Lakh)*			*Share of Central (in %)*	*Index Number*	
	Central	*State*	*Total*		*Central*	*State*
1991 - 92	26956.72	7966.73	34923.45	77.19	100.00	100.00
1992 - 93	28502.3	6350.13	34852.43	81.78	105.73	79.71
1993 - 94	30403.05	7473.97	37877.02	80.27	112.78	93.81
1994 - 95	32410.96	10514.92	42925.88	75.50	120.23	131.99
1995 - 96	43652.12	9128.22	52780.34	82.71	161.93	114.58
1996 - 97	42163.83	10192.57	52356.4	80.53	156.41	127.94
1997 - 98	52809.72	14934.86	67744.58	77.95	195.91	187.47
1998 - 99	85088.26	14097.4	99185.66	85.79	315.65	176.95
1999 - 00	83133.86	18660.93	101794.79	81.67	308.40	234.24
2000 - 01	85271.00	19768.25	105039.25	81.18	316.33	248.14
2001 - 02	80870.16	21355.91	102226.07	79.11	300.00	268.06
2005 – 06	112197.22	29742.28	146939.50	76.36	416.21	373.33

Table 4.6: Plan Grants Disbursed by the UGC to the Universities

Years	*Amount (Rs in Lakh)*			*Share of Central Sector (in %)*	*Index Numbers*	
	Central	*State*	*Total*		*Central*	*State*
1991 - 92	7240.4	7239.96	14480.36	50.00	100.00	100.00
1992 - 93	5683.38	5679.8	11363.18	50.02	78.50	78.45
1993 - 94	5702.02	6688.01	12390.03	46.02	78.75	92.38
1994 - 95	7289.92	9732.65	17022.57	42.83	100.68	134.43
1995 - 96	11556.4	7645.72	19202.12	60.18	159.61	105.60
1996 - 97	8444.16	8548.54	16992.7	49.69	116.63	118.07
1997 - 98	13180.69	13431.48	26612.17	49.53	182.04	185.52
1998 - 99	13653.91	12585.16	26239.07	52.04	188.58	173.83
1999 - 00	14988.39	16374.85	31363.24	47.79	207.01	226.17
2000 - 01	13258.81	17748.35	31007.16	42.76	183.12	245.14
2001 - 02	13152.34	19424.32	32576.66	40.37	181.65	268.29
2005 – 06	22273.07	26633.93	48907.00	45.54	307.62	363.87

92 to Rs. 222.73 Crore in 2005-06. The increase in the these grants was more pronounced during the years 1997-98 through 1999-2000, after which allocations showed a decline once again. This has been the case with plan grants to state universities also; allocations increased from Rs. 72.40 crore in 1991-92 to Rs. 266.34 crore in 2005-06, recording relatively more rapid increase during 1997-98 through 2005-06. What is, however, important to note is the trend that plan grants to state universities did increase more rapidly than those to central universities thereby causing a situation where the share of central universities declined from 50 per cent in 1991-92 to about 46 per cent in 2005-06. It may also be noted that in the 14 year period covered in this study, plan grants to central universities increased at a much slower rate upto 2001-02 than those to state universities (see Table 4.6).

However, in non-plan maintenance grants, central universities are the main beneficiaries. More than 96 per cent of the non-plan allocations and disbursements by the UGC are provided to these universities. Importantly, over the years, not only has the share of central universities remained almost unchanged, the allocations to them have increased at a faster rate than the allocation to state universities. This may be due to the incremental nature of budgetary support for non-plan grants according to which next year's allocation would have to be a little higher than the allocations of the previous years. And this should not cause any surprise. Education, including higher education, is in the Concurrent List. The Central as well as the state governments are both responsible for, and empowered to, promote higher education in the country. While central universities, Inter University Centres and the Deemed to be Universities fall under the direct purview of the Union Government, which provides them financial assistance through the University Grants Commission, state governments are responsible for providing maintenance and development grants to state universities, their associated, constituent and affiliated colleges and other institutions of higher education. UGC does, however, provide development grants to these institutions. The

Table 4.7: Non Plan Grants Disbursed by the UGC to the Universities

Year	*Amount (Rs in Lakh)*			*Share of Central Sector (in %)*	*Index Numbers*	
	Central	*State*	*Total*		*Central*	*State*
1991 - 92	19716.32	726.77	20443.09	96.44	100.00	100.00
1992 - 93	22818.92	670.33	23489.25	97.15	115.74	92.23
1993 - 94	24701.03	785.96	25486.99	96.92	125.28	108.14
1994 - 95	25121.04	782.27	25903.31	96.98	127.41	107.64
1995 - 96	32095.72	1482.5	33578.22	95.58	162.79	203.98
1996 - 97	33719.67	1644.03	35363.7	95.35	171.02	226.21
1997 - 98	39629.03	1503.38	41132.41	96.35	201.00	206.86
1998 - 99	71434.35	1512.24	72946.59	97.93	362.31	208.08
1999 -00	68145.47	2286.08	70431.55	96.75	345.63	314.55
2000 - 01	72012.19	2019.90	74032.09	97.27	365.24	277.93
2001 - 02	68594.32	1993.35	70587.67	97.18	347.91	274.28
2005 – 06	89924.15	3109.35	93033.50	96.65	456.09	427.83

maintenance and recurring expenditure of these institutions is predominantly borne by the respective state governments (see Table 4.7).

UGC Assistance to the Central Sector

So far we have discussed the central sector as a single entity. The discussion would need to take into account the fact that the sector comprises three distinct types of institutions, namely central universities, institutions deemed to be universities and inter-university centres. It would, therefore, be useful to find out as to which of the central institutions appropriate how much of UGC's allocations. Analysis of data in this regard shows that the major share of the UGC's allocation goes to central universities. While interpreting the data presented in Table 4.8, it needs to be kept in mind that the three different types of central institutions are different in terms of their entitlements of financial assistance as well as the nature of their functions. Central universities are nearly totally dependent upon the public exchequer whereas deemed to be universities receive a block grant in lump sum and have the freedom to generate resources to meet their expenses. In contrast, the inter-university-institutions are premier research or regulatory institutions in emerging areas and receive full financial support from the University Grants Commission (see Table 4.8). The freedom to generate resources on their own is also available to central universities, although the effort to do so is not very large. Of late government has allowed some centrally supported institutions, like the Indian Institutes of Technology to create a corpus, which can be used for their programmes. A number of institutions of higher education have trusts with funds for deployment to their activities.

The share of central universities in the UGC's allocation has not only been substantial but has also increased from 78 per cent in 1991-92 to 85 per cent in 2005-06. As against this, the share of non university institutions, which include the Inter-University Centres, has continued to hover between 5 and 6 per cent of the total allocation to the Central sector. A great

Table 4.8: Total Grants Disbursed by the UGC to Universities [Central Sector]

Year	*Amount (Rs in Lakh)*				*Proportionate share of (in %)*		
	Central	*Deemed*	*IUC*	*Total*	*Central*	*Deemed*	*IUC*
1991 - 92	21029.76	4544.77	1382.19	26956.72	78.01	16.86	5.13
1992 - 93	21435.54	5234.09	1832.67	28502.30	75.21	18.36	6.43
1993 - 94	25558.61	2978.54	1865.90	30403.05	84.07	9.80	6.14
1994 - 95	27201.59	3382.14	1827.23	32410.96	83.93	10.44	5.64
1995 - 96	36557.99	4542.68	2551.45	43652.12	83.75	10.41	5.84
1996 - 97	34771.03	4455.04	2937.76	42163.83	82.47	10.57	6.97
1997 - 98	43838.31	5743.80	3227.61	52809.72	83.01	10.88	6.11
1998 - 99	71369.97	8319.38	5398.91	85088.26	83.88	9.78	6.35
1999 - 00	71501.22	7125.14	4507.50	83133.86	86.01	8.57	5.42
2000 - 01	72270.96	8515.75	4484.29	85271.00	84.75	9.99	5.26
2001 - 02	68641.51	8369.94	3959.69	80971.14	84.77	10.34	4.89
2005 – 06	112197.22	11729.63	8078.50	132005.35	84.99	8.88	6.13

Table 4.9: Plan Grants Disbursed by the UGC to Central Universities

Year	*Amount (Rs in Lakh)*				*Proportionate share of (in %)*		
	Central	*Deemed*	*IUC*	*Total*	*Central*	*Deemed*	*IUC*
1991 - 92	4817.36	1071.09	1351.95	7240.40	66.53	14.79	18.62
1992 - 93	2718.53	1170.18	1794.67	5683.38	47.83	20.59	31.58
1993 - 94	3009.81	901.37	1790.84	5702.02	52.78	15.81	31.41
1994 - 95	4441.74	1046.15	1802.03	7289.92	60.93	14.35	24.72
1995 - 96	7815.56	1240.59	2500.25	11556.40	67.63	10.74	21.64
1996 - 97	4333.33	1225.29	2885.54	8444.16	51.32	14.51	34.17
1997 - 98	7994.76	2113.71	3072.22	13180.69	60.66	16.04	23.31
1998 - 99	7626.51	2400.20	3627.20	13653.91	55.86	17.58	26.57
1999 - 00	10909.64	1882.08	2196.67	14988.39	72.79	12.56	14.66
2000 - 01	8531.17	2233.47	2494.17	13258.81	64.34	16.85	18.81
2001 - 02	8796.64	2678.74	1802.24	13277.62	66.25	20.17	13.57
2005 - 06	22273.07	2934.34	5908.50	31115.91	71.58	9.43	18.99

deal of difference in UGC's support to different categories of institutions is accounted for by their different size (for instance in terms of enrolment and faculty), and variety of functions. In sharp contrast, the share of the deemed to be universities, which in 1992-93 was as high as 18 per cent, declined in 2005-06 to about 9 per cent. This has apparently been due to the policy of declaring most deemed to be universities, after 1992, as self-sustaining institutions and restricting the role of the UGC to the extent of providing only development grants. A similar trend, but somewhat less intense, is indicated by the analysis of plan grants to central universities (see Table 4.9).

An interesting point to note, in terms of percentage increase in the allocation of plan grants between 1991-92 to 2005-06, is that the deemed to be universities received more favourable treatment at the hands of the UGC up to 2001-02; thereafter, there was a steep decline.

Since plan allocations do not follow a smooth trend and vary depending upon the year to year allocations to the UGC, allocation to central sector have also fluctuated. What, however, clearly comes out is that central universities have been accounting for around 50 to 72 per cent of the plan allocations whereas the Inter University Centres appropriate between 15 to 18 per cent of the total allocation. Similarly the share of the deemed to be universities ranges between 10 to 20 per cent. Fluctuations in the amounts of allocations apart, the trend clearly indicates that during the past fourteen years, plan allocations to central universities have increased while they have declined in the case of inter university centres and deemed to be universities.

The finding that central universities are the major beneficiaries of the UGC funding of higher education comes out much more sharply in the analysis of non-plan grants; they indicate that the share of the central universities has increased from about 82 per cent in 1992-93 to as high as 89 per cent in 2005-06, and probably at the expense of the deemed to be universities. During the four years, up to 2001-02, however,

Table 4.10: Non Plan Grants Disbursed by the UGC to Central Universities

Year	*Amount (Rs in Lakh)*				*Proportionate share of (in %)*		
	Central	*Deemed*	*IUC*	*Total*	*Central*	*Deemed*	*IUC*
1991 - 92	16212.40	3473.68	30.24	19716.32	82.23	17.62	0.15
1992 93	18717.01	4063.91	38.00	22818.92	82.02	17.81	0.17
1993 - 94	22548.80	2077.17	75.06	24701.03	91.29	8.41	0.30
1994 - 95	22759.85	2335.99	25.20	25121.04	90.60	9.30	0.10
1995 96	28742.43	3302.09	51.20	32095.72	89.55	10.29	0.16
1996 - 97	30437.70	3229.75	52.22	33719.67	90.27	9.58	0.15
1997 - 98	35843.55	3630.09	155.39	39629.03	90.45	9.16	0.39
1998 - 99	63743.46	5919.18	1771.71	71434.35	89.23	8.29	2.48
1999 - 00	60591.58	5243.06	2310.83	68145.47	88.92	7.69	3.39
2000 - 01	63739.79	6282.28	1990.12	72012.19	88.51	8.72	2.76
2001 - 02	59874.37	6567.70	2157.45	68599.52	87.28	9.57	3.14
2005 - 06	89924.15	8795.29	2170.00	106889.44	89.13	8.72	2.15

the allocation to the inter university centres has increased quite significantly; their share increasing from a meagre 0.15 per cent in 1991-92 to over 3 per cent in 2001-02, again to fall to 2.15 per cent in 2005-06. (see Table 4.10).

UGC Assistance to State Universities

Although state universities account for relatively lower proportion of the UGC's financial assistance, in absolute terms, the funds allocated to them are quite substantial. In qualitative terms as well, the development assistance provided by the UGC to state universities is considered quite important for it sets the tone and tenor of development of higher education across the country in a balanced manner and can go a long way in promoting excellence and equity in higher education. From this point of view, it is important to analyze the regional distribution of UGC grants. Table 4.11 indicates that there has been a general increase in the UGC allocation to state universities across all regions of the country. However, funds flowing to different regions have not been uniformly distributed across all regions; the variations in the number of institutions and students in the regions could explain this.

On an average, 33.95 per cent of the total grants allocated by the UGC to state universities have been given to universities in the northern region, followed by the southern region, the grants for which account for 31.59 per cent of the total grants allocated. The Eastern and North Eastern region put together, received an average of about 15 per cent, which is less than what is allocated to universities in the Western Region (see Table 4.12).

The same position emerges in respect of plan grants. Universities in the northern and southern regions have received about 65 per cent of the plan grants from the UGC. In view of fewer universities and colleges, north-eastern region received less than 4 per cent of UGC's plan grants. The western region accounts for about 20 per cent of UGC's assistance (see Table 4.13).

Table 4.11: Total Grants Disbursed by the UGC to the State Universities

Year	*Regions*					
	East	*North*	*North East*	*South*	*West*	*Total*
Amount (Rs in Lakh)						
1991 - 92	973.10	2922.09	263.59	2540.67	1267.28	7966.73
1992 - 93	775.01	2258.36	138.54	2031.96	1146.26	6350.13
1993 - 94	973.92	2522.10	173.05	2539.82	1265.08	7473.97
1994 - 95	1415.39	3918.21	225.33	3130.35	1825.64	10514.92
1995 - 96	1033.41	3388.70	278.06	2879.94	1548.11	9128.22
1996 - 97	1032.80	3617.09	353.41	3444.58	1744.69	10192.57
1997 - 98	1941.06	5265.44	493.60	4667.67	2567.09	14934.86
1998 - 99	1482.00	4475.73	463.37	4845.31	2830.99	14097.40
1999 -00	2583.47	6666.34	656.13	5602.02	3152.97	18660.93
2000 - 01	2255.76	5637.61	517.93	5436.07	5920.88	19768.25
2001 - 02	2257.05	6968.80	711.11	7221.97	4096.00	21254.93

(Contd.)

(Contd. Table 4.11)

Year	*Regions*					*Total*
	East	*North*	*North East*	*South*	*West*	
Percentage						
1991 - 92	12.21	36.68	3.31	31.89	15.91	100.00
1992 - 93	12.20	35.56	2.18	32.00	18.05	100.00
1993 - 94	13.03	33.75	2.32	33.98	16.93	100.00
1994 - 95	13.46	37.26	2.14	29.77	17.36	100.00
1995 - 96	11.32	37.12	3.05	31.55	16.96	100.00
1996 - 97	10.13	35.49	3.47	33.80	17.12	100.00
1997 - 98	13.00	35.26	3.31	31.25	17.19	100.00
1998 - 99	10.51	31.75	3.29	34.37	20.08	100.00
1999 - 00	13.84	35.72	3.52	30.02	16.90	100.00
2000 - 01	11.41	28.52	2.62	27.50	29.95	100.00
2001 - 02	10.62	32.79	3.35	33.98	19.27	100.00
Average	11.92	33.95	3.05	31.59	19.50	100.00

(Contd.)

Table 4.12: Plan Grants Disbursed by the UGC to the State Universities

Year	*Regions*					
	East	*North*	*North East*	*South*	*West*	*Total*
Amount (Rs in Lakh)						
1991 - 92	917.78	2647.48	262.25	2255.99	1156.46	7239.96
1992 - 93	731.85	2036.7	138.39	1816.12	956.74	5679.8
1993 - 94	879.49	2187.99	166.68	2304.26	1149.59	6688.01
1994 - 95	1343.64	3630.85	223.97	2874.86	1659.33	9732.65
1995 - 96	801.85	2693.7	271.73	2508.92	1369.52	7645.72
1996 - 97	797.88	2839.07	348.61	2978.45	1584.53	8548.54
1997 - 98	1694.81	4782.89	488.18	4179.62	2285.98	13431.48
1998 - 99	1326.6	3946.11	457.93	4243.88	2610.64	12585.16
1999 - 00	2198.01	5857.37	639.77	4808.11	2871.59	16374.85
2000 - 01	2140.15	4820.28	515.54	4714.60	5557.78	17748.35
2001 - 02	1937.92	6313.78	675.97	6579.59	3791.78	19299.04

(Contd.)

(Contd. Table 4.12)

Year	Regions					
	East	*North*	*North East*	*South*	*West*	*Total*
Percentage						
1991 - 92	12.68	36.57	3.62	31.16	15.97	100.00
1992 - 93	12.89	35.86	2.44	31.98	16.84	100.00
1993 - 94	13.15	32.72	2.49	34.45	17.19	100.00
1994 - 95	13.81	37.31	2.30	29.54	17.05	100.00
1995 - 96	10.49	35.23	3.55	32.81	17.91	100.00
1996 - 97	9.33	33.21	4.08	34.84	18.54	100.00
1997 - 98	12.62	35.61	3.63	31.12	17.02	100.00
1998 - 99	10.54	31.36	3.64	33.72	20.74	100.00
1999 - 00	13.42	35.77	3.91	29.36	17.54	100.00
2000 - 01	12.06	27.16	2.90	26.56	31.31	100.00
2001 - 02	10.04	32.72	3.50	34.09	19.65	100.00
Average	11.82	33.41	3.35	31.42	20.00	100.00

Table 4.13: Non-Plan Grants Disbursed by the UGC to the State Universities

Year	*Regions*					
	East	*North*	*North East*	*South*	*West*	*Total*
Amount (Rs in Lakh)						
1991 - 92	55.32	274.61	1.34	284.68	110.82	726.77
1992 - 93	43.16	221.66	0.15	215.84	189.52	670.33
1993 - 94	94.43	334.11	6.37	235.56	115.49	785.96
1994 - 95	71.75	287.36	1.36	255.49	166.31	782.27
1995 - 96	231.56	695.00	6.33	371.02	178.59	1482.50
1996 - 97	234.92	778.02	4.80	466.13	160.16	1644.03
1997 - 98	246.25	482.55	5.42	488.05	281.11	1503.38
1998 - 99	155.40	529.62	5.44	601.43	220.35	1512.24
1999 - 00	385.46	808.97	16.36	793.91	281.38	2286.08
2000 - 01	115.61	817.33	2.39	721.47	363.10	2019.90
2001 - 02	319.13	687.28	35.14	642.38	304.22	1988.15

(Contd.)

(Contd. Table 4.13)

Year	Regions					
	East	*North*	*North East*	*South*	*West*	*Total*
Percentage						
1991 - 92	7.61	37.78	0.18	39.17	15.25	100.00
1992 - 93	6.44	33.07	0.02	32.20	28.27	100.00
1993 - 94	12.01	42.51	0.81	29.97	14.69	100.00
1994 - 95	9.17	36.73	0.17	32.66	21.26	100.00
1995 - 96	15.62	46.88	0.43	25.03	12.05	100.00
1996 - 97	14.29	47.32	0.29	28.35	9.74	100.00
1997 - 98	16.38	32.10	0.36	32.46	18.70	100.00
1998 - 99	10.28	35.02	0.36	39.77	14.57	100.00
1999 - 00	16.86	35.39	0.72	34.73	12.31	100.00
2000 - 01	5.72	40.46	0.12	35.72	17.98	100.00
2001 - 02	16.05	34.57	1.77	32.31	15.30	100.00
Average	12.68	38.41	0.55	32.96	15.39	100.00

(Contd.)

The regional variations are accounted for by the number of universities, their enrolment, faculty and the size and variety of operations. The universities in the North-Eastern states are relatively recent and have slightly lower enrolments.

University Grants

It would appear that in terms of percentage of UGC's non-plan grants, the major beneficiaries are the Northern (38.41 per cent) and the Southern regions (32.96 per cent). The North Eastern and Eastern regions have to remain content with about 13 per cent of UGC's assistance. The Western region also accounts for a mere 15 per cent.

In view of the fact that the number of universities varies in different regions, it was, felt appropriate to work out the number of universities receiving financial support in the form of plan and non plan grants so that the per university financial assistance could be worked out to have a realistic picture of financial support to different types of institutions across the country. The number of universities receiving development and maintenance grants from the UGC in each of the years under study was listed. The data is presented in Tables 4.14 and 4.15.

It may be seen from the Table that the number of universities receiving plan grants from the UGC has increased from 148 to 176. As already stated not all universities receive plan grants from the UGC. It is also important to note that the largest concentration of the universities receiving plan grants from the UGC is in the Northern and Southern regions of the country (Table 4.14). Importantly, of the total number, fewer universities receive the non-plan grants from the UGC (Table 4.15).

Since, all universities do not fall within the purview of the UGC in respect of financial allocations, the actual number of universities receiving grants from it is less than the total number of universities in the country. This is as true for India as a whole as in the case of region-by-region and state-by-state

Table 4.14: Number of Universities Benefiting from Plan Grants of UGC

Year	*Central Sector*			*State Universities in Zones*					*Total*
	Central	*Deemed*	*IUC*	*East*	*North*	*North East*	*South*	*West*	
1991 - 92	9	24	4	13	48	4	32	14	148
1992 - 93	10	26	3	11	44	4	28	14	140
1993 - 94	12	27	4	13	46	4	32	14	152
1994 - 95	13	30	6	12	48	4	35	17	165
1995 - 96	14	28	7	13	47	5	33	16	163
1996 - 97	14	33	8	14	49	6	32	20	176
1997 - 98	16	31	7	13	54	6	35	18	180
1998 - 99	16	37	9	12	49	5	32	18	178
1999 - 00	16	39	6	11	48	5	35	19	179
2000 - 01	15	30	7	11	51	5	34	17	170
2001 - 02	20	32	6	12	49	5	35	17	176

Table 4.15: Number of Universities Benefiting from Non Plan Grants of UGC

Year	*Central Sector*			*State Universities in Zones*					*Total*
	Central	*Deemed*	*IUC*	*East*	*North*	*North East*	*South*	*West*	
1991 - 92	9	17	1	9	36	3	27	14	116
1992 - 93	9	17	1	7	35	1	21	10	101
1993 - 94	9	20	2	10	41	4	28	14	128
1994 - 95	10	23	3	10	42	4	24	12	128
1995 - 96	10	25	3	11	45	3	30	13	140
1996 - 97	11	21	3	12	44	6	29	13	139
1997 - 98	13	27	7	9	42	4	25	11	138
1998 - 99	13	31	6	11	41	4	26	12	144
1999 - 00	13	35	9	10	42	4	28	12	153
2000 - 01	13	29	6	8	34	3	24	10	127
2001 - 02	16	25	6	10	35	4	22	12	130

Table 4.16: Per University Total Grants (Rs in Lakh)

Year	*Central Sector*			*State Sector*				
	Central	*Deemed*	*IUC*	*East*	*North*	*North East*	*South*	*West*
1991 - 92	2336.64	221.70	552.88	83.21	69.18	75.26	84.59	78.60
1992 - 93	2256.37	243.45	916.34	75.82	65.82	67.07	80.09	77.68
1993 - 94	2434.15	126.75	621.97	73.05	56.64	39.74	80.44	84.40
1994 - 95	2365.36	127.63	406.05	124.66	82.72	48.78	104.12	106.42
1995 - 96	3046.50	171.42	510.29	80.62	74.90	78.69	93.51	84.26
1996 - 97	2781.68	165.00	534.14	74.13	81.30	67.30	111.32	96.38
1997 - 98	3023.33	198.06	461.09	161.47	119.04	112.20	148.37	174.44
1998 - 99	4922.07	244.69	719.85	120.92	106.02	105.62	171.28	205.41
1999 - 00	4931.12	192.57	601.00	256.50	145.51	141.66	181.45	237.62
2000 - 01	5162.21	288.67	689.89	439.35	1218.86	587.03	715.75	1174.06
2001 – 02	4609.76	293.68	659.95	356.25	1868.31	648.06	989.60	754.10

Table 4.17: Per University Plan Grants (Rs in Lakh)

Year	Central Sector			State Sector				
	Central	Deemed	IUC	East	North	North East	South	West
1991 - 92	535.26	44.63	337.99	66.59	55.56	69.18	70.36	73.00
1992 - 93	271.85	45.01	598.22	59.33	56.40	36.67	63.67	57.07
1993 - 94	250.82	33.38	447.71	60.08	46.89	38.59	69.03	68.69
1994 - 95	341.67	34.87	300.34	108.48	73.24	48.43	82.53	86.16
1995 - 96	558.25	44.31	357.18	57.66	60.34	50.20	77.99	68.47
1996 - 97	309.52	37.13	360.69	54.78	66.60	66.70	91.78	77.08
1997 - 98	499.67	68.18	438.89	120.79	97.27	93.85	115.24	114.39
1998 - 99	476.66	64.87	403.02	104.58	93.33	89.35	143.55	137.35
1999 - 00	681.85	48.26	366.11	200.26	122.86	120.53	139.68	152.51
2000 - 01	568.74	74.45	356.31	354.31	842.59	398.62	531.75	805.84
2001 - 02	603.39	56.32	300.37	283.07	1639.30	582.67	745.59	627.75

Table 4.18: Per University Non Plan Grants (Rs in Lakh)

Year	*Central Sector*			*State Sector*				
	Central	*Deemed*	*IUC*	*East*	*North*	*North East*	*South*	*West*
1991 - 92	1801.38	204.33	30.24	5.42	4.71	0.43	9.50	5.60
1992 - 93	2079.67	239.05	38.00	5.58	5.33	0.15	9.36	14.30
1993 - 94	2505.42	103.86	37.53	7.02	7.22	1.15	7.57	7.73
1994 - 95	2275.99	101.56	8.40	5.66	5.36	0.35	9.61	9.95
1995 - 96	2874.24	132.08	17.07	20.23	13.47	1.53	11.83	10.08
1996 - 97	2767.06	153.80	17.41	13.73	13.27	0.60	16.80	7.78
1997 - 98	2757.20	134.45	22.20	21.94	8.00	1.70	16.94	25.31
1998 - 99	4903.34	190.94	295.29	13.38	9.16	1.73	22.15	16.45
1999 - 00	4660.89	149.80	256.76	30.69	14.35	5.15	28.98	22.16
2000 - 01	4903.06	216.63	331.69	39.60	NA	NA	114.16	NA
2001 - 02	4278.97	262.71	359.58	52.52	151.53	NA	109.24	54.25

situation. Also, invariably, a larger number of universities of different types in different regions receive development grants rather than maintenance grants.

The analysis of grants given to institutions reveals some interesting trends. These seem to somewhat contradict the findings discussed earlier. The analysis of total grants received clearly shows that on an average each of the central universities has been receiving comparatively larger amount year after year. As against this, per university average grants to deemed to be universities have declined significantly particularly during the period 1993-94 to 1999-2000 with the exception of 1998-99. This could have been because of the larger increase that has taken place in the number of deemed to be universities as compared to the increase in the budgetary allocation for this category. In contrast, per institution allocation to the non-university Institutions has increased only marginally (see Table 4.16).

It has been found that while in terms of per university grants, the Northern and North Eastern regions were getting lower allocations in 1991-92, the position underwent a significant change with the Northern region getting the highest per university allocation (Rs. 1868.31 lakh), followed by Southern region (Rs. 989.60 lakhs) and Western (Rs. 754.10 lakhs) in 2001-02. The Eastern region received the lowest per university allocation (Rs. 356.25 lakhs). (see Tables 4.17 and 4.18).

Utilization of Grants Received

As already stated the UGC is primarily a disbursing agency. It does not have any funds of its own. What it receives from the government it disburses among universities and other institutions of higher education. The analysis shows that the UGC has been faring quite well in this regard and it is only rarely that the UGC is not able to utilize the available funds (see Table 4.19).

Scheme wise Distribution of UGC Grants

It would be worthwhile to discuss scheme wise distribution of plan grants sanctioned and released by the UGC as this would

Table 4.19: Utilization of Grants received by the UGC as per Computations from Appendices [Rs in Crores)

Years	Grants Received by the UGC			Grants Released by the UGC			Under Utilization		
	Plan	Non Plan	Total	Plan	Non Plan	Total	Plan	Non Plan	Total
1991-92	170.28	270.00	440.28	167.95	267.14	435.09	(2.33)	(2.86)	(5.19)
1992-93	162.00	311.00	473.00	162.04	310.49	472.53	0.04	(0.51)	(0.47)
1993-94	161.00	336.95	497.95	160.14	338.98	499.12	(0.86)	2.03	1.17
1994-95	257.90	345.59	603.49	222.00	348.55	570.55	(35.90)	2.96	(32.94)
1995-96	234.16	450.82	684.98	239.05	437.57	676.62	4.89	(13.25)	(8.36)
1996-97	223.65	465.00	688.65	248.82	475.90	724.72	25.17	10.90	36.07
1997-98	384.67	545.00	929.67	388.40	548.99	937.39	3.73	3.99	7.72
1998-99	391.20	998.97	1390.17	400.68	999.90	1400.58	9.48	0.93	10.41
1999-00	441.50	975.00	1416.50	441.29	976.33	1417.62	(0.21)	1.33	1.12

Note: Figures in parentheses indicate shortfall in utilization of funds.

indicate the relative priority that it gives to various programmes. Since schemes and their nomenclature have significantly varied over different plan period, our discussion is confined only to the last three plans viz the Eighth, Ninth and the Tenth Plans.

Scheme wise Allocation during the Eighth Plan

Scheme wise distribution of UGC grants during the Eighth Plan is given in the Table 4.20. Importantly, 40 per cent of the total plan grants during the Eighth Plan was given for basic amenities in the universities and colleges. This was followed by the promotion of excellence and research (15 per cent), Inter-university centres (11 per cent) and Innovative courses in emerging areas (10 per cent).

Scheme wise Allocation during the Ninth Plan

The Ninth Plan budget heads are different from those of the Eighth Plan. The analysis of data shows that 51 per cent of the total plan grants was sanctioned for the development of universities and colleges. This was followed by the promotion of excellence and quality (13 per cent), promotion of relevance (10.33 per cent), Inter-university resources (6.37 per cent), scientific research (6.67 per cent), and engineering and technology (6.96 per cent) (see Table 4.21).

Scheme wise Allocation during the Tenth Plan

There has been no consolidated data about the expenditure on various schemes during the 10th plan. The following table, however, indicates the break up of expenditure for various schemes during 2005-06.

From Table 4.22 on p. 250, it would be seen that the largest proportion of expenditure (54.55) was incurred on the development of universities and colleges followed by promotion of quality and excellence. The schemes relating to strengthening of research also got adequate priority (11.00 per cent). Promotion of relevant education, was, however, given lower priority.

Table 4.20: Scheme-wise Allocation of Plan Grants by the UGC during Eighth Plan (Rs. In Lakhs)

Schemes/ Sector	*1992-93*	*1993-94*	*1994-95*	*1995-96*	*1996-97*	*Total*	*Share (in %)*
Basic Amenities	7620	5245	7075	11199	11046	42186	40
Promotion of Excellence & Research	2143	3409	4402	3417	3186	16557	15
Manpower Development	1502	2158	2373	1475	1687	9195	9
Non-Formal Education	309	367	244	516	398	1834	2
Inter University Centre	1748	1844	2088	2652	3047	11379	11
Innovation Courses in Emerging Areas	948	1079	3778	2138	3019	10962	10
International Cooperation	105	86	136	118	98	544	1
Management of UGC	108	122	150	202	220	803	1
Sports & Physical Education	65	73	103	68	15	324	0
Engineering & Technology	1580	1763	2183	2450	2417	10392	10
Total	16129	16147	22534	24234	25132	104175	99
Others	336	235	47	13	168	800	1
Grand Total	16465	16382	22581	24247	25300	104976	100

Source: Compiled from Annual Report of the UGC for relevant Years.

Table 4.21: Scheme-wise Allocation of Plan Grants by the UGC during Ninth Plan

(Rs. In Lakhs)

Schemes/ Sectors	*1997-98*	*1998-99*	*1999-2000*	*2000-01*	*2001-02*	*Total*	*Share*
Development of Universities/Colleges	22460.96	20702.73	25603.06	26715.69	18039.86	113522.30	51.41
Promotion of Relevance	3874.10	4462.59	4034.48	3387.57	7050.40	22809.14	10.33
Promotion of Excellence & Quality	1714.45	4531.24	3823.91	6892.57	12082.00	29044.17	13.15
Inter-university resources for promotion of quality	3392.50	2587.84	2847.65	2998.48	2240.21	14066.68	6.37
Enhancing access and equity	1205.12	1896.82	1657.02	1528 62	1815.02	8102.60	3.67
Improvement in Management of Education	290.26	355.12	466.89	326 92	352.59	1791.78	0.81
Strengthening of UGC Administration	19.52	215.70	211.72	158.97	158.75	764.66	0.35
Programs to strengthen scientific research	2946.34	2760.84	2857.28	2776.68	3376.13	14717.27	6.67
Engineering & Technology	3204.19	2874.48	2894.28	2802.73	3594.63	15370.31	6.96
Total	39107.44	40387.36	44396.29	47588.23	48709.59	220188.91	99.72
Others	136.13	158.49	174.62	65.78	73.48	608.50	0.28
Grand Total	39243.57	40545.85	44570.91	47654.01	48783.07	220797.41	100.00

Source: Compiled from Annual Report of the UGC for relevant Years.

Table 4.22: Scheme-wise allocation of plan grants given by the UGC during 2005-06 (Rs. In Lakhs)

Sl.No.	*Schemes/ Sectors*	*Amount Given*	*Share*
1.	Development of universities and colleges	44121.92	54.55
2.	Enhancing access and equity	7401.93	9.15
3.	Promotion of relevant education	5763.96	7.14
4.	Quality and excellence	14687.33	18.16
5.	Strengthening of research	8899.22	11.00
	Total	80874.36	100.00

Scheme wise Distribution of Non-Plan Grants

Except for some minor variations, the non-plan budgets for different heads have been quite consistent since 1992-93. Presented below is an analysis of the funds allocated to different schemes during 1992-93 to 2005-06. It needs to be noted that over 60 per cent of non-plan funds are allocated to central universities in the form of block maintenance grants. This is followed by grants to the colleges of the central universities (25 per cent) and deemed to be universities (6 per cent) Amounts for scholarship, fellowship, teachers awards and other academic activities and programmes are therefore, very meager (see Table 4.23).

Table 4.23: Scheme-wise Distribution of Non-plan Grants by the UGC

Grants Head	1992-93	1993-94	1994-95	1995-96	1996-97	1997-98
Block Grants to Central Universities	18552.10	22250.10	22293.12	27695.31	29516.37	35005.82
Block Grants to Deemed Universities	3919.76	1813.72	2208.44	3116.25	3118.91	3459.56
Grants for Specific Purposes to Universities	198.58	291.34	316.49	148.10	530.46	311.57
Maintenance grants for Delhi Colleges	6902.67	7543.42	8053.09	9012.23	10717.38	12054.78
Maintenance Grants for BHU Colleges	51.68	54.29	62.72	91.97	120.98	98.57
Maintenance Grants to UCMS				62.77		
Teachers Awards	24.57	38.62	9.11	29.50	27.61	15.07
Research Fellowship	330.89	588.99	562.92	2441.66	1681.04	1469.54
Research Fellowship in Humanities & Sciences						175.62
Scholarship & Fellowship in Engineering & Technology	217.33	232.76	229.13	262.59	269.43	243.29
Reimbursement to Non-University Institutions	20.56	39.83	41.63	2.73	159.53	54.94
Mass Media Centres	284.50	275.11	345.05	348.29	354.03	542.42
Administrative Charges	546.95	732.17	759.21	864.25	1094.49	1478.51
Grants for Specific Purposes	-	-	-	-	-	-
Total	**31049.59**	**33860.35**	**34880.91**	**44075.65**	**47590.23**	**54909.69**

(Contd.)

(Contd.Table 4.23)

Grants Head	1998-99	1999-00	2000-01	2001-02	2005-06
Block Grants to Central Universities	62332.59	59419.36	62169.33	58692.97	87864.66
Block Grants to Deemed Universities	5624.30	4910.79	5940.53	6076.55	8310.98
Grants for Specific Purposes to Universities	2076.27	2474.78	2273.73	2521.14	2435.00
Maintenance grants for Delhi Colleges	24798.12	23576.97	22422.87	26180.47	29112.20
Maintenance Grants for BHU Colleges	111.02	162.04	403.01	180.86	226.40
Maintenance Grants to UCMS		1504.45	1494.96	1337.69	2185.64
Teachers Awards	15.64	28.62	29.03	13.90	-
Research Fellowship	1728.25	2332.43	2128.30	1799.74	2893.909
Research Fellowship in Humanities & Sciences	269.49	257.16	233.02	250.74	304.99
Scholarship & Fellowship in Engineering & Technology	481.70	471.20	738.97	704.39	1448.50
Reimbursement to Non-University Institutions	125.85	262.04	184.46	285.34	674.69
Mass Media Centres	500.08	681.16	657.69	675.33	2815.71
Administrative Charges	1922.22	1552.06	1720.39	1711.88	-
Grants for Specific Purposes	-	-	-	-	**910.00**
Total	**99985.53**	**97633.06**	**100396.29**	**100431.00**	**138981.86**

(Contd.)

(Contd.Table 4.23)

Grants Head	1992-93	1993-94	1994-95	1995-96	1996-97	1997-98
Percentage Distribution						
Block Grants to Central Universities	59.75	65.71	63.91	62.84	62.02	63.75
Block Grants to Deemed Universities	12.62	5.36	6.33	7.07	6.55	6.30
Grants for Specific Purposes	0.64	0.86	0.91	0.34	1.11	0.57
Maintenance grants for Delhi Colleges	22.23	22.28	23.09	20.45	22.52	21.95
Maintenance Grants for BHU Colleges	0.17	0.16	0.18	0.21	0.25	0.18
Maintenance Grants to UCMS	0.00	0.00	0.00	0.14	0.00	0.00
Teachers Awards	0.08	0.11	0.03	0.07	0.06	0.03
Research Fellowship	1.07	1.74	1.61	5.54	3.53	2.68
Research Scientists in Humanities & Sciences	0.00	0.00	0.00	0.00	0.00	0.32
Scholarship & Fellowship in Engineering & Technology	0.70	0.69	0.66	0.60	0.57	0.44
Reimbursement to Non-University Institutions	0.07	0.12	0.12	0.01	0.34	0.10
Mass Media Centres	0.92	0.81	0.99	0.79	0.74	0.99
Administrative Charges	1.76	2.16	2.18	1.96	2.30	2.69
Total	**100.00**	**100.00**	**100.00**	**100.00**	**100.00**	**100.00**

(Contd.)

(Contd. Table 4.23)

Grants Head	1998-99	1999-00	2000-01	2001-02	2005-06
Percentage Distribution					
Block Grants to Central Universities	62.34	60.86	61.92	58.44	**63.17**
Block Grants to Deemed Universities	5.63	5.03	5.92	6.05	**5.97**
Grants for Specific Purposes	2.08	2.53	2.26	2.51	**1.75**
Maintenance grants for Delhi Colleges	24.80	24.15	22.33	26.07	**20.88**
Maintenance Grants for BHU Colleges	0.11	0.17	0.40	0.18	**0.16**
Maintenance Grants to UCMS	0.00	1.54	1.49	1.33	**1.57**
Teachers Awards	0.02	0.03	0.03	0.01	-
Research Fellowship	1.73	2.39	2.12	1.79	**2.08**
Research Scientists in Humanities & Sciences	0.27	0.26	0.23	0.25	**0.22**
Scholarship & Fellowship in Engineering & Technology	0.48	0.48	0.74	0.70	**1.04**
Reimbursement to Non-University Institutions	0.13	0.27	0.18	0.28	**0.49**
Mass Media Centres	0.50	0.70	0.66	0.67	**0.65**
Administrative Charges	1.92	1.59	1.71	1.70	**2.02**
Total	**100.00**	**100.00**	**100.00**	**100.00**	**100.00**

5

Globalization and Higher Education: *A Challenge and An Opportunity*

This chapter has two sections: **Part–I The Challenge:** Multi-dimensional Challenges of Globalization for Education; and **Part–II Response:** Measures for Enhancing the Potentiality of Indian Higher Education to Meet these Challenges.

Part I

The Challenge

India embarked upon deregulation and liberalization of its economy from 1980s. The process received a major thrust from early nineties, when significant changes were introduced by abolishing licensing for domestic manufacturing for all but a few industries and allowing private sector to enter areas hitherto reserved for the public sector. Further, import tariffs were drastically reduced (Parikh et. al., 2002). Internationally, globalization as the on-going process of economic, technological, social and political integration of the world, although reported to have started after the Second World War, has gathered momentum during the last two decades.

Globalization has far-reaching implications for socio-economic development of countries across the globe. It has been defined as "a set of processes by which the world is rapidly being integrated into one economic space via increased international trade, the internationalization of production and financial markets; and the internationalization of a commodity culture promoted by an increasingly networked global telecommunication system" (Graham, 1996).

Globalization transcends socio-economic and political barriers that countries are prone to build around themselves. It is a process not only of "integrating just economy, but also culture, technology and governance. It is giving rise to new markets, foreign exchange and capital markets linked globally, new tools, internet links, cellular phones, media networks, new actors; the World Trade Organization with authority over national governments, the multi-national corporation with more economic power than many states; new rules, multi-national agreements on intellectual property, multi-lateral agreements on trade" (Human Development Report, 1999).

Globalization is expected to have a positive influence on the volume, quality and spread of knowledge through increased interaction among nations. "In a globalized world, as technology becomes its main motor, knowledge assumes a powerful role in production, making its possession essential for nations, if they are successfully to pursue economic growth and competitiveness" (Stromquist, 2000). Education, being the most potent instrument of creation, assimilation and transmission of knowledge, assumes a central role in the process.

In a market oriented competitive world, education has to assume a somewhat different role. It cannot afford to be conventional, rigid and impervious to change. It has to keep abreast of the latest developments in various fields and has to become capable of creating, absorbing and transacting neo-technology and information systems that are sweeping across the countries of the world. There has also to be a paradigm shift in the content of education and the transactional techniques with substantial emphasis on the productivity aspect of the curriculum.

It is, however, necessary to guard against being swept off our feet by the new 'cult of technology', and consequently, 'the diminution of respect for spiritual and cultural values' (Maugey, cited in Namer, 1999). An unfettered and ruthless pursuit of economic goals, without regard to considerations of moral and social values is bound to be retrogressive for the people, and harmful for the society particularly in developing countries. Treading the path of morality could, however, lead to the emergence of a "global culture" and uniform appreciation of diverse cultural perspectives, which are characteristics of countries like India where different kinds of diversities are significant and cherished.

Not An Unmixed Blessing

In spite of the many significant changes brought about in most countries, it would be wrong to consider globalization as a panacea for all economic and social ills. As stated by the Planning Commission: "the accelerated process of liberalization and globalization in the world has increased the opportunities for growth and development, but it has also added new complexities and risks in the management of global interdependence" (Tenth Five Year Plan, Vol. I, p. 97). Some of the complexities identified by the Human Development Report, 2002 are:

(i) Although globalization is forging greater interdependence, yet the world seems more fragmented – between the rich and the poor, between the powerful and the powerless.

(ii) Economically, politically and technologically, the world has never seemed more free and more unjust.

(iii) If the present global progress continues at such a snail's pace, it will take more than 130 years to rid the world of hunger.

(iv) With constrained resource base and inadequate capacities to compete on equal terms, developing countries seem to remain at a disadvantaged position.

(v) Liberalization has not led to transparency in the economic system, particularly of the developing countries, resulting in putting these countries at a disadvantage.

Humane Face of Globalization

It would thus appear that globalization is not an unmixed blessing. It may promote "growth through increased technology and knowledge transfers in developing countries but it could also be sometime a source of instability...." (The Human Development Report in South Asia, UNDP, 1999). It should, therefore, not be construed purely as a faceless economic mechanism but be based on the principles of ethics, equity, inclusion, human security, and development.

Indian Higher Education

A critical study of higher education in India evokes two mutually contradictory perceptions. According to one, the system is a crucial factor for survival, for it provides people an opportunity "to reflect on the critical, social, economic, cultural, moral and spiritual issues facing humanity" (National Policy on Education, 1986). According to the other view, the university system has developed an inbuilt process of metabolic degeneration. The large-scale expansion has, among other things, eroded the quality of university education. Planning Commission, (2002) states: "Although the number of universities has increased and many universities continue to maintain high standards of education, it is a matter of serious concern that, on the whole, the expansion in quantity has been accompanied by a fall in quality..." It has also been contended that the system of education has not been able to provide education relevant to the needs and aspirations of the ever-increasing number of seekers of knowledge, escalating the ranks of the unemployed and unemployable youth in the country. The system has also been castigated as an exclusive preserve of the elitist groups, regardless of their capacity to benefit from higher education.

It is difficult to subscribe fully to either of the extreme views. Like any other system in the world, higher education in India symbolizes a phenomenon of 'lights and shades'. While we have a number of institutions, which can compete favourably with the best in the world, a significant proportion of institutions need to improve their academic standards in order to become a part of a reasonably comparable academic configuration in the global market.

Impact of Globalization on Higher Education

Education, as a service industry is part of globalization process under the umbrella of General Agreement on Trade in Services (GATS). 'Education, in the services sectoral classification of World Trade Organization (WTO) has been mentioned along with five sub-sectors including higher education services. The sub-sector classification is, however, subject to modification in the light of developments in education services negotiations' (Sudhanshu Bhushan, 2004).

The inclusion of education as a component of the services sector under the WTO regime has given rise to quite a few misgivings in the academic world. It has been pointed out that there is a distinct possibility that this might "force countries with quite different academic needs and resources to conform to structures inevitably designed to service the interest of the most powerful academic systems and corporate educational providers... breeding inequality and dependence" (Altbach, 2002). Further: "Globalization... can lead to unregulated and poor quality higher education, with the world wide marketing of fraudulent degrees or other so-called higher education credentials..." (World Bank's Task Force, 2000). It has also been pointed out that India, is likely to turn into "an increasingly attractive market for foreign universities and hence other nations are going to use GATS' provisions to their advantage" (Arun Nigvekar, 2002).

It may be pointed out that any ill-conceived entry into the 'whirl-pool' of globalization would create quite a few problems for Indian education as also its economy. Prudence, therefore, demands that globalization should be *tamed* in such a way that its advantages outweigh the disadvantages for Indian education. It is not too far-fetched to hope that India, with its large and diverse educational system and internationally acclaimed human capabilities, can easily achieve these objectives.

The following aspects of higher education are likely to be specifically impacted by globalization:

(i) It will lead to internationalization of education with all its good and baneful effects;

(ii) It may lay more emphasis on market oriented courses to the relative neglect of courses in humanities and social sciences as also research in basic sciences;

(iii) It may lead to accent on privatization of education, with government reducing its financial support to secondary and university institutions and insisting upon the establishment of self financing institutions/courses; it may also give a boost to unregulated expansion of capitation fee charging institutions, quite a few of which are based on commercial, rather than academic and philanthropic considerations;

(iv) It may lead to de-prioritization of research in basic sciences and humanities, because of their seemingly unrelatedness to the immediate needs of the economy;

(v) An important component of globalization in relation to education is the need for producing high quality scientific and technical manpower, which can successfully face the cut-throat competition in the world market. This would imply selecting the best available human material and giving them education/training of the highest quality. The moot point is: will nurturing of excellence be iniquitous and discriminatory, in that it will deny opportunities to a very large segment of student population who are not so intellectually endowed? Will it not infringe upon the principle of equality of opportunity, which is the mainstay of the democratic polity?

(vi) With competition for entry into institutions of higher education and their dependence on private resources, there would be the danger of poor but meritorious students being denied the opportunity for further education.

We shall discuss some of these issues, in the context of Indian higher education.

Internationalization of Education

Implicit in the system of globalization is the inevitability of internationalization of the educational system, particularly at the higher education stage. This is not peculiar to India. It has become a worldwide phenomenon. As already stated, the entry of the World Trade Organization (WTO) and inclusion of educational services under the General Agreement on Trade in Services (GATS) has given a boost to internationalization of higher education.

The implications of internationalization of education have been discussed in details in a subsequent chapter.

Finance Related Issues

In order to be a part of the global configuration, requirement of funds for education will increase manifold. For this purpose, it will be necessary to augment government funding of education besides the universities generating their own resources. Most developing countries, including India have been facing the problem of paucity of resources. Some half-hearted attempts have been made about mobilization of resources by, among others, involving community and industrial houses in financing and management of educational institutions. Suggestions have also been made about curbing the tendency of de-prioritization of certain sectors of education like higher education. Partial and complete privatization of higher education has also been high on the agenda of the government. We shall discuss these issues briefly in order to assess their relevance in the Indian context. While government funding would be a major source, universities need to mobilize resources from other sources – increase in fees, contribution from alumni, support by NRIs etc.

Down-Sizing Higher Education

Since mid seventies, 'Rate of Return' studies relating to different stages of education showed that higher education was a 'non-merit' good since its private rates of returns exceeded social returns. It was, therefore, suggested that it should attract less public revenues than primary and secondary education. Based on these empirically unconfirmed assumptions, the World Bank also came to the conclusion that its lending strategy should emphasize primary education, relegating higher education to a relatively minor place in its development agenda. The view has been supported by Carnoy (1999). According to him: "Higher education is a high cost level of schooling and basic education is relatively low cost. In addition in many countries, public university education costs are heavily weighted toward non-teaching and non-research expenditures such as student subsidies and administrative costs. The shift of emphasis, it is argued, would enhance opportunities for a larger number of primary school students at the expense of subsidizing a relatively elite group of families that can bear the cost of university education for their wards".

A deeper reflection on this suggestion will bring out its utter shortsightedness. In the first instance, it is wrong to assume that at higher education stage, costs are heavily weighted towards non-teaching and non-research expenditure. Bulk of the expenditure on higher education is on staff salaries including teachers' remuneration (Reference Chapter 3 : University Finances). Moreover, it is academically unjustified to segmentalise education, whose different stages are complementary rather than competitive. For example, if university education is starved of funds, it will be difficult to provide good and competent teachers and administrators for school stage. It must be stressed that education is a continuum in which various stages are complementary rather than competitive. Any attempt at compartmentalizing education in order to deny the requisite funding to a particular sector would be retrogressive and retard the progress of education. As emphasized by Panchamukhi (2002): "at any point of time, weakening of higher education sector would weaken the forces of competitiveness and efficiency in the functioning of different sectors of economy..."

The implementation of this too simplistic a suggestion will also impede the progress of basic research, particularly in frontier areas which have shown promise, among other things, "in upgrading the volume and quality of farm products and greater possibilities of dealing more effectively with morbidities". Further, any scaling down of financial inputs for higher education would result in deterioration of the quality of scientific and technical manpower, which is the mainstay of economic and social development of India.

It is heartening to note that a recent Task Force of the World Bank (2000), while fully supporting continuation of larger investment in primary and secondary education, has rebutted the traditional economic argument, which is based on "limited understanding of what higher education institutions contribute". The Task Force has challenged the notion that public investment in higher education is socially inequitable. It has stated: 'Rate-of-Return Studies treat educated people as valuable only through their higher earnings and the greater tax revenues extracted by society. But educated people clearly have many other effects on society: educated people are well positioned to be economic and social entrepreneurs, having far-reaching impact on the economic and social well being of their communities. Rates of return analysis entirely misses the impact of university based research on the economy - a far reaching social benefit that is at the heart of the argument for developing strong higher education system".

Privatization of Secondary and Higher Education

As a corollary to the suggestions of reducing the public investment in secondary and higher education, a plea has been made to hand over these sectors to private bodies. It has also been suggested that institutions beyond primary and basic education, should increasingly depend upon tuition fees, philanthropy of general public and industrial and commercial organizations, which should be allowed to set up, manage and finance institutions of post elementary education. The problem is multifaceted and has far reaching implications. A detailed discussion of the problem has been made in a subsequent chapter.

Part II

The Response

It may be emphasized that, notwithstanding the problems that might emerge, globalization is a stark reality, which cannot be wished away. It is, therefore, essential that we must take steps to bring about the needed reforms in our system so that our institutions of higher education as also students graduating from these institutions can compete in the world market on equal footing. These reforms will have to be multi-dimensional, necessitating improving/modifying the system from within and from outside. A brief discussion of these reforms follows:

Needed Reforms Within the Educational System

Content of Education

(a) Curriculum Upgradation

Aadvances in information technology have revolutionized, among others, the content of knowledge and the processes of educational transaction. The ever-growing use of electronic media has brought education to the doorsteps of the common man. Information processing technologies provide an efficient framework for storage, management, analysis and application of information. In the process, popular culture and education alike have adopted what may be called 'computational paradigm', the use of computer metaphors, to understand how human beings cognize themselves and the world.

In order to meet the challenges posed by the far reaching changes occurring in the economic, social and technological systems, it is necessary that students are equipped with, besides theoretical knowledge, adequate skills to enable their full participation in the emerging social, economic and cultural environment. Also, universities have to undergo a sea change in their outlook and perspective "leading to fundamental changes in the structure, management and mode of delivery...." (Planning Commission, 2002). The operative part of this paradigm shift is the need for a continuous up-gradation of curriculum in order to introduce the latest developments relating to various disciplines in the curriculum and its transactional technique. Alongside, pruning of existing curriculum would be a necessary condition in order to remove obsolete and irrelevant materials. This process has to be continuous and well conceived.

The fast developing stock of knowledge and the need for its continuous updating has also initiated an era of life-long learning. Education is no longer confined to a particular period of life. It is a continuum with no artificial time barriers restricting the process. Educational institutions need to emphasize the process of learning to learn rather than what can be called 'products' of learning in the sense of a predetermined set of materials and information.

This brings to fore the significance of expanding facilities through non-formal/distance education mode not only to provide an alternate system of education to meet the burgeoning needs of the aspirants of knowledge but also for offering a multiplicity of courses on the 'Cafeteria' basis to meet their varying educational needs.

(b) Productivity Orientation

The basic objective of globalization is to improve the quality of manpower and to make educational system an instrument of preparing students, who can compete in world markets as productive and creative members of the society. To achieve this objective, it is necessary to make skill training as an integral part of the curriculum besides bringing about attitudinal changes so that students do not consider it infra-dig to work with hands.

Our experience of introducing an element of skill training in education, however, has not been very encouraging. The schemes of vocationalisation, both at the school and college stages, have been languishing for want of enthusiastic response on the part of students (and teachers). It has also not received the required social recognition. It may be recalled that the scheme of vocational education at the secondary stage was launched in 1988 as a centrally sponsored programme. Against a target of diverting 10 per cent of students to vocational stream by 1995 and 25 per cent by 2000, only 11 per cent of students have been covered at the plus two stage. At the college stage also where scheme of vocationalisation has been in operation since 1994, it has hardly covered twenty five thousand students out of a total university enrolment of over ten million. Further, there is considerable drop out rate of students from vocational courses, which generally occurs in the mid-session, leading to large waste of facilities.

The reasons for the slow progress of these programmes are many, but the most significant is lack of appreciation – by parents, teachers and students – of need for introducing an element of skill training as a part of the general curriculum. Education is still considered basically as an academic discipline in which intrusion of vocational training is considered unacceptable. Further, the craze for degrees is also an important retarding factor. There is also lack of parity of status between students and teachers of vocational and general streams leading to the former hesitating to join vocational courses. The near absence of facilities for on the job training is also a factor, which slows down the pace of progress.

(c) *Industry/University Linkages*

In order to make university courses productivity oriented, it would be necessary that universities should establish closer links with industry. It must be appreciated that industry is the user agency for manpower trained in the university system. The representatives of industry should, therefore, be actively involved in the preparation of syllabi, organization of skill training, providing supervised on the job training etc. Professionals from industry may be associated with teaching as guest faculty. Further, industrial and commercial houses may be motivated to provide financial assistance to universities by establishing inter-disciplinary chairs for teaching and research.

Vocational education would need to consider the requirement of services of different kinds. These services – paramedical, communicational, travel and tourism, credit and insurance, intelligent use of farm inputs etc. – are required in rural areas also which have so far been denied the knowledge and use of more utilitarian practices.

(d) Research

Indian professionals, particularly in Information Technology and allied fields, are successfully competing in world markets especially in software development, data analysis and outsourcing. This, however, cannot continue for a long time, especially because competition from other developing countries and regulatory mechanisms of industrially developed nation are likely to be very intense in times to come. This underscores the need for emphasizing Research and Development (R & D) in our university institutions particularly in newly emerging areas. As suggested by lyengar (2000): "Our human resource development in the future should be planned such that there are identified areas in which India could compete effectively, and be innovators rather than just followers. These could include areas such as biotechnology, new power sources, education etc. The Government should focus on these areas, and offer incentives to researchers for innovative research in these fields".

(e) Value Education

In order to safeguard against untrammeled competitiveness and use of unethical practices for moving up in the socio-economic ladder, it is necessary that education should lay stress on value education, which emphasizes cooperation rather than competition; sharing of experience rather than personal aggrandizement and learning to live together rather than living in mutually hostile camps. Education should help to engender a new "humanism that contains an essential ethical component and sets considerable store by knowledge of, and respect for, culture and spiritual values of different civilizations, as a much *needed counter weight to a* globalization that would otherwise be seen only in economical or technological terms. The sense of shared values as a common destiny is in fact the basis on which any scheme of international cooperation must be founded" (Delors Commission, 1996).

Improving Human Capital

(a) Student Competencies

There has been considerable expansion of student enrolment at the university stage. From a mere 2 lakh at the time of independence, student enrolment is likely to have reached a figure of more than 10 million. In terms of the relevant age group coverage, however, it is hardly 7 per cent. With the success of the schemes of universalization of elementary education, the pressure on secondary and higher education will further increase. Steps have to be taken to prepare this large student body to face international competition. For this purpose a selective approach of identifying talent and enabling them to procure education of the highest quality will have to be adopted.

It can be argued that nurturing of excellence will be inequitable in that it may deny opportunities to a very large segment of student population, who are not so intellectually endowed, to get into institutions of higher education. It is also feared that the present day techniques of students' assessment are not very reliable tools for measuring the potentiality of students, particularly from rural areas and those belonging to the deprived sections of the society.

It is difficult to deny the force of these arguments. The remedy, however, lies not in denigrating the need for nurturing excellence but in creating opportunities for expanding the *field* of excellence, so as to enable more and more promising students to join institutions of higher learning. This would necessitate qualitative up-gradation of academic and physical infrastructure, reforming teacher education programmes and improving the system of student assessment so that no student with potentiality for benefiting from education is denied that opportunity. It may also require special coaching facilities for the students belonging to the traditionally deprived sections of the society.

(b) Faculty Up-gradation

In spite of very extensive utilization of electronic media and self-study system in the field of education, teacher remains at the centre-stage of education. He/she is a facilitator, inspirer, motivator and guide. His contribution to the students' achievement is, by no means, insignificant. It is therefore necessary that the best available persons should be selected for teaching positions. They should also be exposed to periodic orientation courses to update their academic and professional skills. There should be a system of monitoring and feed back to know about the extent to which the new techniques of knowledge transaction are put into practices in actual class room situations.

Institutional Reforms

(a) Institutional management

There is an urgent need for improving the physical and academic infrastructure of university institutions. Alongside, there is also need for reforming the management and governance systems of universities to better enforce financial and administrative discipline. This, according to the Planning Commission (2002) should include 'decentralization of the university system, greater powers to faculty/department and nomination of students to university bodies on the basis of merit/ excellence.... Further, "the accreditation system will need to be made more transparent and progressively freed from government regulation leading to a situation when the whole procedure would be based on a system of public appraisal/ acceptance".

(b) University Autonomy and Accountability

It needs hardly to be emphasized that universities' role in furtherance of knowledge can be achieved only if they are given unfettered freedom and autonomy to experiment with new ideas and adopt innovative techniques for curriculum transaction. It may, however, be emphasized that autonomy should be tempered with accountability. The society has a formidable stake in the educational system and it has a right to monitor the functioning of the university institutions.

To Conclude

We may conclude by reiterating the inevitability and irreversibility of the structural reforms unleashed by globalization in our socio-economic system. The system of education, particularly higher education all over the world, has to meet the challenges thrown by the entry of global competition by evolving a well-considered policy of dealing with the situation. Further, it is also imperative to bring about modifications in our administrative, academic and financial systems governing the educational institutions. We can no longer afford to live in an exclusive world of our own, regardless of the cataclysmic changes ocurring across the developing and the developed countries. In order to survive in the emerging international scenario in the field of education, as also in other sectors, we have to be much more dynamic, progressive and alive to these changes, so that we are not left behind in the race for socio-economic and educational advancement. We have to ensure that our educational system is adequately responsive to the emerging challenges and take steps to bring about the requisite changes, which would enhance the potentiality of our educational institutions to meet those challenges. Globalization has given us a unique opportunity to face the world squarely, with confidence in our own academic strength. It is hoped that we will not be found wanting in this endeavour.

References

AICTE (1994), *Report of the High Power Committee for Mobilization of Additional Resources for Technical Education*, All India Council for Technical Education, New Delhi.

Altbach, G. Philip and Y. Ogawa (2002), *Higher Education*, 43(1), Introduction Special Issue on Japan: Reform and Change in the Twentyfirst Century.

Amy Stuart Wells et.al. (1998), Globalization and Educational Changes in Andy Hergreaves (ed.) International Hand Book of Educational Change, Vol.5, Kluwer Academic Publishers, London.

Arora, Guljit (2002), Globalization, Federalism and Decentralization, Implications for India, Bookwell.

Arun Nigvekar (2001), GATS and Higher Education, University Grants Commission, (Mimeo).

Azad, J.L. (1975), Financing of Higher Education in India, Sterling.

Azad, J.L. (1986), Government Support for Higher Education and Research, Concept, New Delhi.

Azad, J.L. (1989), State Grants: Patterns, Procedures and Policies in Higher Education, The Institutional Context, published in Amrik Singh et.al. (ed.) Konark.

Azad, J.L. (1993), Higher Education in India: The Deepening Financial Crisis, Radiant.

Azad, J.L. (2003), Financing of Secondary School Education, Aravalli Publications.

Bhushan, Sudhanshu (2004), Measures for Enhancing Competitiveness of Higher Education, NIEPA, New Delhi, (mimeo).

Carnoy, M. (1999), *Globalisation and Educational Reform: What Planners Need to Know*, Report No.63, International Institute of Educational Planning, Paris.

Carnoy, Martin (2000), Globalization and Educational Reforms in Globalization and Education, Nelly P. Stromquist, (ed.) Rowman and Littlefield Publishers.

Government of India (1986), (1992), *Programme of Action on the National Policy on Education*, Ministry of Human Resource Development, New Delhi.

Government of India (1997), *Approach Paper to the Ninth Five-year Plan:1997-2002*, Planning Commission, New Delhi.

Government of India (1997-2002), *Ninth Five-year Plan:1997-2002*, Planning Commission, New Delhi.

Government of India (2000), *Mid-term appraisal of Ninth Five-year Plan:1997-2002*, Planning Commission, New Delhi.

Government of India (2001), *Approach Paper to the Tenth Five-year Plan: 2002-2007*, Planning Commission, New Delhi.

Government of India (2002-2007), *Tenth Five-year Plan: 2002-2007*, Planning Commission, New Delhi.

Hallak, Jacques (1999), Globalization, Human Rights and Education, UNESCO, IIEP. Paris.

Human Development in South Asia (2000), Oxford.

Ilon, L. (1994), Structural Adjustment and Education; Adapting to a Growing. Global Market, *International Journal of Educational Development*, 14(2).

International Association of Universities (2001), Issues in Higher Education, the OECD, Globalization and Educational Policy, Pergamon.

Ministry of Education, (1996). Report of the Education Commission 1964-66, New Delhi.

Panchamukhi, P.R. (2002), Social Sector Development and Economic Reforms: A Focus on Education Sector in Reform and Employment, IAMR.

Parikh, Kirit. S. (Ed.) (2002), India Development Report, Indira Gandhi Institute of Development Research; Oxford.

Ryle, John (ed.) (2002), Globalization, Universities and Issues of Sustainable Development, Edgar and Edgar Publishers Ltd.

Salmi, J. (1992), Perspectives on the Financing of Higher Education, *Higher Education Policy*, 5(2).

Sharma, G.D. (2001), Internationalization of Higher Education, Status and Policy Suggestions, NIEPA, (mimeo).

Sharma, G.D. (2001), Trade in Education Service: An Indian Response, NIEPA, New Delhi, (mimeo).

Stewart, F. (1996), Globalisation and Education, *International Journal of Educational Development*, 16(4).

Stromquist, Nelly. P. et.al. (ed.) (2000), Globalization and Educational Reforms, op.cit.

Tilak, J.B.G. (2000), in Philip G. Altbach, (ed) Private Prometheus, London.

Tilak, J.B.G. (2001a), Education and Globalisation: The Changing Concerns in Economics of Indian Education, Editorial, *Perspectives in Education*,17, Special Issue.

UNDP, Human Development Reports (1999, 2000, 2002 & 2003), Oxford.

UNESCO, (1996). Learning: The Treasure Within, International Commission on Education for the Twenty first Century.

UNESCO, Statistical Year Book, different years.

World Bank (1993), *East Asian Miracle, Economic Growth and Public Policy,* Washington, D.C.

World Bank (2002), *Constructing Knowledge Societies: New Challenges for Tertiary Education*, Washington, D.C.

World Bank (2002), Higher Education in Developing Countries, Peril and Promise, the Report of the Task Force on Education and Society, Washington.

Ziderman, A. and D.Albrecht (1995), *Financing Universities in Developing Countries*, The Stanford Series on Education and Public Policy, The Falmer Press, Washington, D.C.

6

Internationalization of Higher Education

India has been a seat of learning for seekers of knowledge from the hoary past. The ancient universities of Nalanda, Vikramsila and Takshislila attracted students from far off countries like China, Indonesia, Mongolia, Tibet and Korea. (Das, 1986) Indian scholars also travelled to far off lands to spread the message of peace, non-violence and forbearance. This exchange of knowledge and wisdom received a severe jolt, when India was invaded by hordes of marauders from foreign countries who attempted to destroy the fabric of India's civilization and culture and subjected it to prolonged periods of subjugation and servitude. In the process, the *spirit* of India received a devastating set-back.

With the emancipation of India from foreign subjugation, Indian universities attempted to cater to the academic needs of an ever growing number of students. From 26 in 1947, the number of UGC recognised universities has increased to over 300. The enrolment of students also increased from about 2 lakh to over 10 million during the corresponding period (UGC's Annual Reports). The courses of study offered by universities also underwent a sea change in variety, complexion and content.

In the early nineties, India introduced the New Economic Policy with emphasis on liberalisation, privatization and globalisation. The policy has the potential of having far reaching impact on education by providing increasing role for the private sector in the management and financing of educational institutions. The advent of liberalization, privatization and marketisation is changing the shape of education. Implicit in this policy is to give a free play to market forces to determine the scale of expansion, components of curriculum, types of courses and the quantum of cost recoveries from the beneficiaries of higher education.

Borderless Education

It has also given rise to the concept of 'borderless education', particularly in higher education, "which is being shaped by a number of factors including the emergence of the 'Knowledge Economy', pressures for life long learning and advances in the use and nature of information and communication technologies". (Middlehurst, Minerva, 2001-3).

Elaborating the theme, Middlehurst further states that 'coupling, convergence and commoditization' are all emerging as factors in 'borderless' education. "The coupling of corporations with universities and the development of networked interest groups across national boundaries, have created new possibilities as well as greater organisational complexities. Convergence implies greater commonality of structures and processes, for example, across national higher education systems and across business and higher education fed by freely available information and exchange of ideas. Commoditisation is evident both in the packaging of knowledge in different forms and in conception of educational packages as products that can be sold and delivered in 'bitesised' pieces. Competition for higher education has expanded beyond national borders to include international providers and 'for profit' education business".

Further, "the global dimensions of a knowledge economy will drive borderless education...... International activity is not new to universities and many have been international institutions for centuries but 'globalization' has different connotations and is potentially more problematic. "In this era of globalisation, nations are not connected by trade alone; international ties go beyond economic links to those among a variety of institutions. Even a particular educational system whose mandate is to preserve and transmit a nation's unique culture, is affected by interactive and homogenizing trends towards globalisation" [1]

First, it may imply moves toward standardized curricula and modes of delivery. For example, multi-national business that choose to partner with universities are increasingly seeking common curricula that can be delivered by different institutions in different countries. International curriculum development teams are needed alongside integrated delivery systems; these are expensive commodities. Moreover, pressures for international mobility of labour create a need for greater coordination and harmonization of regulatory procedures across national governments to ensure that qualifications and credit are portable and mutually recognised. Finally, if 'global' education brands are established, they may prove more popular than local ones. The role played by national regulatory framework is critical to the encouragement or discouragement of globalisation". (Middlehurst, op. cit.)

Social and Intellectual Change

The most prominent social drives reflected within borderless education are:

- Widening access and participation;
- Rising public expectations of customer service with a strong focus on individual choice and provider accountability;
- Increasing emphasis on self determination and self help for individuals and groups;
- Challenge to traditional notions of educational authority and forms of knowledge; and
- New patterns of interaction and relationship built on networks of all kind.

Whether or not the concept of borderless education encompasses the scope, complexion and methodology of internationalization of education, India is poised to enter the vast arena of international education in order to keep pace with the fast changing scenario of higher education. Besides other catalysts speeding up the country's entry into the global educational market, its international commitments, current and prospective, are also among the potent driving forces. An important factor that is looming large on the Indian economic and legal firmament is the imminent entry of India into the WTO and GATS systems. We shall briefly discuss India's obligations under these international organisations.

WTO Factor[2]

Ever since Adam Smith first described the advantages of international trade in the *Wealth of Nations* in 1776, economists started believing that an expanded world market would contribute to faster economic growth. With the passage of time, nations have started joint ventures including those in the field of education. Education is fast becoming a commodity for sale, which India in past has always denounced. But compelling situations have forced India to become a partner in this process.

The World Trade Organisation (WTO) which came into existence in 1995, negotiated an agreement in 1996 with the objective of progressively liberalising trade in services, so as to provide secure and more open market in-services in similar manner as GATS has done for trade in goods. This agreement in general covers all services including educational services. This is the first multi-lateral agreement, which provides legally enforceable right to trade in all services unless they are provided entirely by the government. However, when services have been provided by either the government, partially or some prices are charged (as happens in education) or provided by the private providers, they shall fall under GATS rule.

GATS in Education Services

GATS rules will apply to services like education in following ways:

(a) Each member country has to give treatment of Most Favoured Nation (MFN) to all member countries;
(b) Each member country will have to make a request offer for a particular service to be a part of the agreement;
(c) Every member country has to eliminate any restraint on competition when requested by another member; and
(d) Every member country has to ensure that all measures are administered in reasonable and impartial manner.

Mode of Trade

The WTO has identified the following four main modes of trade in education:

(a) Cross-Border supplies of a service, which includes any type of course that is provided through distance education or the internet, any testing service and educational material, which can cross national boundaries.
(b) Consumption Abroad, mainly involves the education of foreign students
(c) Commercial Presence i.e., actual presence of foreign investors in the host country i.e., foreign universities setting up courses or institution in another country and
(d) Presence of Natural Persons, which refers to the ability of people to move between countries to provide educational services.

Classification of Education Services

The services include primary, secondary, higher education, adult education and other education not included in the above categories. Thus the entire educational system falls within the purview of the WTO.

Economic Significance of Trade in Education Services

It has been observed that, so far, the main beneficiaries of internationalization of education are the developed countries particularly the UK, the USA, and Canada with developing countries being at the receiving end. For example:

(i) In 2001, there were 27 foreign providers with commercial presence in India, which included 12 from the USA and 10 from the UK. This number rose to 61 in 2004: UK 23, USA 19, Australia 6 and the rest, Canada etc., 13[3].

(ii) While the inflow of foreign students to Indian universities increased from a modest 6,899 (mostly from developing countries) in 2000 to 7738 in 2005, the outflow of Indian students to foreign universities in 2002-03 stood at a formidable figure of 1,03,483 with the USA topping the list with 74,603 followed by the UK: 14,000 (NIEPA, Report, 2004).*

(iii) The USA is the main provider of educational services with 5.83 lakhs students from different countries (2004-05) enrolled in its institutions. It is followed by United Kingdom (2.27 lakhs), Australia (1.80 lakhs) and France (1.39 lakhs);*

(iv) About $27 billion worth higher education is exported to Asia and Pacific by three countries namely USA, UK and Australia; and

(v) A number of countries: USA, France, Canada and Australia - have entered into Twinning/Franchisee/ Distance mode programme with Indian agencies.

(* Source: Global Education Digest, 2005, UNESCO.)

Modes of Internationalization of Higher Education in India

According to some case studies conducted at the National University of Educational Planning and Administration, it was revealed that transnational education or the operations of foreign universities in India is taking place in the following modes:

(i) Consumption Abroad – Information dissemination and recruitment of students through:
   (a) Information Centres of various countries set up by embassies;
   (b) Private Agencies.

(ii) Commercial Presence/Franchisee
(iii) Twining programmes
(iv) Cross Border Supply Universities:
  (a) Campus of A country university in B country;
  (b) Distance Mode of Learning/Virtual university.

It would be seen that Indian education, particularly higher education, falls within the ambit of the WTO and the GATS. We have therefore to accord the Most Favoured Nations' (NFN) status to other countries enabling them to open their university campuses on Indian soil or admit Indian students to their institutions. As a reciprocal measure, Indian universities can open their campuses in other countries and/or admit students belonging to other countries.

Implications of Internationalisation – An Empirical Analysis

Realizing the inevitability of India entering into the global market of education and other countries entering the Indian market, we decided to make a detailed study of various implications of the question of internationalisation of higher education. For this purpose, a detailed questionnaire (See SCH/QUEST/II at the end of the Report as appendix-II) was developed and mailed to University Teachers, Researchers, Educational Administrators and Vice-Chancellors for collecting their views. It may, however, be stated that it is very difficult to strictly compartmentalize the respondents among the four categories indicated above. For example, each educationist does some sort of research, teaching and administration. Further, in some capacity or other, he is also concerned with administration. However, grouping has been done on the basis of their main engagement.

The total number of respondents was 41 (both working and retired). The number in each group and the percentage from the total is given in Table. 6.1 Besides there were representatives from Industries whom we administered Schedule no. SCH/QUEST/III also provided in the report as Appendix-III.

Table 6.1: Category-wise Grouping of Respondents

Sl.No.	*Category*	*Number*	*Percent*
1.	University Teachers	8	19.51
2.	Researchers	8	19.51
3.	Educational Administrators	11	26.83
4.	Vice Chancellors	14	34.15
	Total Respondents	41	100.00

We shall now examine responses of various categories of academics, administrators and industry's representatives in regard to various issues relating to internationalization of higher education. The issues that were posed to the select groups were broadly of the following type:

1. Whether the foreign universities should be allowed to operate on the Indian soil. If so, what should be the mechanism of regulating their activities in India?
2. What are the likely benefits of international academic exchange envisaged under the WTO system?
3. What kind of accreditation/ regulatory system should be introduced to ensure the quality of education of the foreign institutions.

The views, expressed by respondents of various categories, are briefly summarized below:

(A) Allowing Foreign Universities in India

Referring to the 'policy of liberalisation and globalisation under which a number of foreign universities have set up their campuses in India', respondents were asked: (a) whether foreign universities should be allowed to function in India and (b) allowed to function but under strict Government control. The replies of (a) and (b) were to be given in Yes/No. The responses have been tabulated in Table 6.2.

It would appear from the table that out of 41 respondents, 23 (56.10%) said "Yes" meaning thereby that foreign universities may be allowed to function in India but 8 (19.51%) did not favour allowing foreign universities to function and 10 (24.39%) or about 1/4th of the total respondents did not give any reply. However, Industries representatives endorsed the majority view.

Table 6.2: Entry of Foreign Universities in India

Category	*Yes*	*No*	*No Response*
University Teachers	5 (62.50)	1 (12.50)	2 (25.00)
Researchers	3 (37.50)	1 (12.50)	4 (50.00)
Educational Administrators	6 (54.55)	5 (45.45)	0 (0.00)
Vice Chancellors	9 (64.28)	1 (7.14)	4 (28.51)
Total	**23 (56.10)**	**8 (19.51)**	**10 (24.39)**

Note: *N = 41; Figures in brackets are percentages. These are applicable to all future tables.*

It would also be interesting to note that those directly involved in the functioning of universities i.e. Vice Chancellors, University Teachers and Research Scholars – have no objection to the entry of foreign universities in India. On the other hand, a substantial number of Educational Administrators are skeptical about the desirability of this taking place. Considering that the number who responded is small, the above table does not necessarily reflect the dominant view. At best, it indicates the general perception of those concerned with university education.

However, there is one paradox of data in this category. It is true that as a group of 11 Educational Administrators, 54.55 per cent said 'Yes' and 45.45 per cent said 'No', but when we look at the data from the angle that out of total responses of 'No', which was the largest group in the order of saying 'No', it was the Educational Administrators. Out of the total responses of 'No', which were 8 in number, 5 (45.45 per cent) came from the category of educational administrators. This analysis of data has been depicted in Table 6.3.

Table 6.3: Entry of Foreign Universities in India – Category-wise responses

Category	*Yes*	*No*	*No Response*	*Toal*
University Teachers	5 (62.50)	1 (12.50)	2 (25.00)	8 (100.00)
Researchers =	3 (37.50)	1 (12.50)	4 (50.00)	8 (100.00)
Educational Administrators	6 (54.55)	5 (45.45)	0 (0.00)	11 (100.00)
Vice-chancellors	9 (64.28)	1 (7.14)	4 (28.51)	14 (100.00)

(B) The Extent of Government Control

One query in the questionnaire sought response to 'whether universities may be allowed to function but under strict Government control'. To this, out of 41 respondents, a large majority 33 (80.48%) said 'Yes' while 5 (12.20%) did not agree with the suggestion and 3 (7.32%) did not give any response. Table 6.4 explains the position:

Table 6.4: Entry of Foreign Universities in India but under Government Control

Category	*Yes*	*No*	*No Response*	*Total*
University Teachers	8 (100.00)	0 (0.00)	0 (0.00)	**8 (100.00)**
Researchers	8 (100.00)	0 (0.00)	0 (0.00)	**8 (100.00)**
Educational Administrators	7 (63.64)	3 (27.27)	1 (9.09)	**11 (100.00)**
Vice Chancellors	10 (71.42)	2 (14.29)	2 (14.29)	**14 (100.00)**
All Categories	**33 (80.48)**	**5 (12.20)**	**3 (7.32)**	**41 (100.00)**

When we look at the data relating to category wise responses in "Yes" and "No", we find that university teachers and researchers, whose number was 8 each, expressed the view that foreign universities may be allowed to function but under strict government control. However, in the case of vice-chancellors, 10 agreed (71.42%) with this suggestion while 2 (14.29%) did not agree with the view and 2 (14.29%) did not give any response. Out of 11 Educational Administrators, 7 (63.64%) said "Yes" indicating thereby their agreement that universities may be allowed to function under strict government control, 3 (27.27%) did not agree and 1 (9.09%) gave 'No Response'. From the responses it seems evident that a large majority of respondents is in favour of allowing foreign universities to function under strict government control. Industry's representatives also stressed that the entry of foreign universities should be under government control.

(C) Accreditation

To a query: "whether the foreign universities should also conform to accreditation norms laid down by National Assessment and Accreditation Council (NAAC)" respondents as

Table 6.5: Accreditation of Foreign Universities

Category	*Yes*	*No*	*No Response*	*Total*
University Teachers	8 (100.00)	0 (0.00)	0 (0.00)	**8 (100.00)**
Researchers	8 (100.00)	0 (0.00)	0 (0.00)	**8 (100.00)**
Educational Administrators	11 (100.00)	0 (0.00)	0 (0.00)	**11 (100.00)**
Vice Chancellors	10 (71.43)	0 (0.00)	4 (28.57)	**14 (100.00)**
All Categories	**37 (90.24)**	**0 (0.00)**	**4 (9.76)**	**41 (100.00)**

a whole as well category-wise emphasized that accreditation should be done before foreign universities are allowed to operate in this country. The responses to this question have been tabulated in Table 6.5. It will be worth while to mention that throughout the study, it was only one situation where all respondents expressed their total agreement.

Views/Suggestions

Respondents were also requested to give their views/ suggestions on various aspects of internationalisation of higher education. The predominant views/suggestions have been summarised below:

(a) Benefits of Internationalization

Bulk of the respondents felt that following benefits will accrue from internationalisation of higher education:

(i) University education is expected to improve if higher education is internationalized and healthy competition takes place.

(ii) It will provide global opportunities and promote international good will.

(iii) It will encourage exchange of scholars. This can be done with the involvement of reputed scholars in respective countries in curriculum designing.

(iv) Internationalization of higher education is an 'emerging trend'. India should strive to be a provider/exporter of higher education. The time is appropriate for India to take advantage of the opportunity.

(v) The new vision of higher education will depend on:
   (a) Internationalization
   (b) Relevance and
   (c) Quality.

(b) Regulatory Mechanism

About the question: 'what kind of regulatory mechanism should be created to ensure that only genuine foreign universities are allowed to operate in India', a majority of respondents felt that the task should be performed by the University Grants Commission (UGC) and the All India Council for Technical Education (AICTE). Some respondents expressed the view that some sort of a specialized body should be created to examine each case seeking entry.

(c) Modalities of Entry

(1) Foreign universities, which want to set up campuses in India should first have been accredited in their home country. The status of foreign institutions may be further examined in India by the National Assessment and Accreditation Council (NAAC) or National Board of Assessment (NBA)

(2) Pre-entry audit should be done relating to their academic programmes.

(3) A foreign university should sign a formal Memorandum of Understanding (MOU) with the Ministry of Human Resource Development giving the requisite details of their academic activities in India, the number of students to be admitted, their fee structure etc.

(4) There should be a minimum level of investment in academic infrastructure and physical facilities.

(5) Indian embassies should provide information about foreign universities which desire to open campuses in India. The embassies should also give their own assessment of the proposal.

(6) Before a foreign university is allowed to function in India, UGC should assess the standard of the university, course-content and level of infra-structural facilities.

(7) Parliament should pass an act authorizing UGC to assess equivalence of foreign universities and allow them to admit students only in those disciplines of higher education, which are not available in Indian universities.

(d) Element of Reciprocity

The respondents were asked: "what steps should be taken to introduce an element of reciprocity in the university system particularly with regard to Indian universities setting up their campuses in foreign countries". A summary of replies of different respondents is given below:

1. Most respondents feel that setting up of campuses in India should be on a reciprocal basis.
2. Only best Departments of the Indian universities may be allowed to open their campuses in foreign lands. There should be a mutual exchange of faculty.
3. A university wishing to open campus outside the country should:
   (a) submit a detailed proposal to UGC/MHRD,
   (b) justify the demand for its course(s) in a foreign country,
   (c) give details of financial implications,
   (d) obtain permission from the Government of India for opening a campus outside the country and also from the government of the country where the campus is going to be located.
4. Before opening a new campus in a foreign land, the following factors should be taken into account:
   (a) legal provisions with regard to undertaking programmes,
   (b) fee structure,
   (c) employment of local and foreign staff,
   (d) rules regarding repatriation of funds.
5. As far as possible introduction of a course should be a joint venture i.e., the course may be similar but opened on a reciprocal basis by mutual agreement.
6. Profits earned by opening a campus in a foreign land, should be subject to tax(es) as per law of the host country. The same regulation should apply to universities opening campuses in India.
7. Out of the total profits earned by an Indian university from opening a new campus, fifty percent should go to an 'Endowment Fund' and its interest may be used for meeting developmental needs of the institution including awarding of fellowships.

8. Collaborative/partnership programmes where more than one institution is involved will be more successful in comparison to programme offered by individual universities.
9. Some respondents suggested that Indian universities/ deemed to be universities may be given powers under their Acts to pursue internationalization of higher education. The government/UGC, should have no control, but play a positive role.
10. Non-resident Indians help may be taken as and when desired.

To Sum up

The world is slowly, but decisively, moving towards economic, social and cultural liberalization, under which restrictive country – specific economic and legal doctrines are fast becoming obsolete and irrelevant. There is radical transformation of policies and programmes relating to educational planning and development, in so far as emphasis is being laid on globalization of the configuration, content and management of education. Educational systems of various countries are being thrown open to institutions from across the globe, leading to concretization of the concept of 'border less' education. The process of this paradigm shift has been accelerated by various countries agreeing to the provisions of the World Trade Organisation and the GATS.

Internationalization of education, particularly higher education, seem to be a logical corollary of the obligations, which various countries have undertaken under different international agreements – present and prospective. Trade in educational services is already in full swing and some of the advanced countries like the USA, UK, Germany, France and Australia are attracting large number of students from developing countries. In the process, they are also making sizeable profits. Conversely, India which was attracting a few thousand students mostly from countries in its immediate neighbourhood, has suffered a severe set back in this respect in the recent past.

In this not-too-comfortable a position in which India finds itself, there is need for serious consideration of the policy on internationalizing higher education. Further, it is also necessary to lay down a viable regulatory mechanism to control inflow of foreign universities, vying with one another to open their campuses in India or enter into some kind of arrangement with their ever too willing Indian counterparts.

The preceding analysis summarizes responses to issues raised above as also gives the suggestions/ views of a select body of academics, educational administration and other concerned with Indian higher education. Without repeating the reactions of the respondents, it may be stated that:

1. Bulk of the respondents are in agreement with the policy of allowing foreign universities in India because it is seen to have a positive impact on our university institutions by encouraging healthy competition, improving curricular content and promoting exchange of scholars among different countries.
2. Respondents have underlined the need for evolving a well thought out regulatory mechanism so that only genuine institutions are allowed to set up their campuses on Indian soil. For this purpose, a process of accreditation of foreign institutions is favoured.
3. An element of reciprocity should be built into the exchange of institutions between India and other countries. A number of suggestions have been made to concretize this process.
4. Suggestions have also been made about fee structure, employment of local and foreign staff and repatriation of funds generated by various Indian and foreign universities.

Before concluding, it shall be prudent for Indian policy makers to take note of the drawbacks of the multinational education pointed out by Altbach (2000). They include:

(i) "Multinational higher education always has elements of inequality. They are providing 'off the shelf' programmes, which are simply used overseas. The decision about the curriculum, standard, faculty and requirement are always made by the sponsoring institution.

(ii) The motive for establishing institutions is always to make money. British and Australian institutions have been active internationally as a way of making up for budget cuts at home."

It is hoped that India will be able to steer clear of these obvious pitfalls, which can cause serious damage to our rather fragile university system!

References

Arun Nigvekar: GATS and Higher Education, UGC, 2001 (Mimeo).

G.D. Sharma: Trade in Education Services under WTO, NIEPA, 2001 (Mimeo).

Philip G. Altbach: The Crisis in Multinational Higher Education, University News; November 6, 2000.

Robin Middlehurst, University Challenges: Borderless Higher Education Today and Tomorrow. Minerva, Netherlands 2001.

Santosh Kumar Das: The Educational System of the Ascient Hindus, Gian Publishing House, Delhi, 1986.

(Footnotes)

1. International Journal of Educational Development (Special Issue Marketisation & Privatazation to Education, Vol. 20, No. 2, March 2000, p.87)
2. The information contained in this section is based on papers: Trade in Education Service under WTO Regime by Dr. G. D. Sharma and 'GATS and Higher Education: What is at stake for India ' by Prof. Arun Nigvekar (2001). The contributions are gratefully acknowledged.
3. K.B. Powar et.al., 2001 and 2004.

7

Private Participation in Higher Education

Privatisation by definition is a process rather than a state. Generally, it means the process of moving from public ownership, financing and control to private ownership, financing and control of varying degree.

Privatisation is a complex and ambiguous concept. It, however, rests on three focal points: Ownership, Financing and Control. A change in one of these dimensions does not mean changes in all dimensions or any one of them. At the same time it is not always true that privatisation is a planned or a pre-intended activity; indeed privatisation sometimes occurs because of hidden signals from the government; sometimes positive, sometimes negative.

Private Participation in Education

(a) Indian Experience

Pre-Independence Period

The ancient Indian education started as a family concern, both for literary and professional education. As education began to become more complex and exacting, the specialist came into the field in the form of private teacher. *'Guru Griha'* i.e. the abode of the preceptor became the centre of education where the high and mighty of the land, as also those not high up in the socio-economic ladder, flocked to get education and training in literary and vocational skills. During the Buddhist period, corporate educational institutions were established. They were the counterparts of Hindu Gurukuls. The main sources of finances were donations by the royalty and the nobility as also by the community. Tuition fees were conspicuous by their absence. The practice of nobility providing finances for educational institutions continued during the medieval period.

The system of financing of education under the Colonial rule was subjected to strange vicissitudes of time. It took the East India Company more than a century to officially recognise their responsibility for the education of the vast masses of the people, over whose destinies they had the privilege to preside. Even when an inconsequential sum of Rs. One lakh was sought to be given for the education of people, it was subjected to unnecessary legal quibblings and its utilisation was decided, by and large, on extra-educational considerations. Well up to the end of the 19th century, the Government of India fought shy of direct administration of education and insisted upon a policy of gradual withdrawal from education leaving the field to the munificence of private bodies. In the early twentieth century, however, the central and the provincial governments evinced greater interest in the financing of education. The transfer of education to popular ministers under the 'Dyarchy' and later on under the government of India Act, 1935, was expected to improve the financial position of educational institutions but two consecutive economic depressions, which occurred between 1919-24 and 1929-32, forced the provincial governments to economise on educational expenditure. The Second World War (1939-45) added to the financial difficulties and thwarted attempts at running educational institutions on sound lines.

Notwithstanding the financial and administrative problems facing education during the British regime, the period under review witnessed the evolution of some important policies and procedures, which have relevance to the financing of education in the present times. The efforts relating to local resource mobilisation by the provincial governments, the evolution of the system of grant-in-aid for educational institutions and the emphasis on encouragement of private enterprise in education are some of the significant features of history of educational finance, which transcend the barriers of time and can help us in developing policies and procedures of educational finance and management in the present-day India.

Private Participation in the Post-Independent Period

Before we go into the details of private efforts in higher education, it would be worthwhile to know the present position of higher education. Table 7.1 gives the types and number of higher education institutions in India.

Table 7.1: Type and Number of Higher Education Institutions in India, 2005-06

Type	*Number*
Universities	241
Institutions deemed to be universities	101
Institutions of national importance	13
Research institutions	136
Colleges for general education Colleges for professional education (including Teacher Training colleges)	18064

Source: UGC, Annual Report 2005-06.

From the above table, it is clear that in the year 2005-06, there were 355 universities including deemed to be universities and institutions of national importance. Because of state intervention, there was unprecedented growth of higher education in India, which could be seen from Table 7.2.

When access to education becomes easy, the growth in enrolment also occurs. The total enrolment at this stage was

110 million in 2005-06 and the number of teachers stood at 4,88,000. The total enrolment in the relevant age group (Gross Enrolment Ratio), 17-23 years was, however, about 10 per cent.

Table 7.2: Growth of Higher Education in India

	1950-51	*1990-91*	*2005-06*
Universities[1]	30	177	355
Colleges*	750	7346	18,064
Enrolment ('000s)	263	4925	11,028
Teachers ('000s)	24	272	488

Source: UGC Annual Report 2005-06.
** excludes junior colleges.*
Note 1: includes institutions deemed to be universities, as also Institutions of National Importance.

This is less than the corresponding figures for most of the developed and developing countries. The enrolment ratio in higher education is about 100 per cent in Canada, 80 per cent in USA, 50 per cent in france and 30 per cent in U.K. Even in some of the less developed countries like Thailand, Indonesia, Mexico and Brazil, enrolment ratios are higher than that of India.

Table 7.3: Sources of Funds for Higher Education in India (percentages)

Year	*Government*	*Fees*	*Endowments and others sources*	*Total*
1950-51	49.4	36.8	13.8	100.0
1960-61	53.5	34.8	11.7	100.0
1970-71	61.0	25.5	13.5	100.0
1980-81	72.8	16.4	10.8	100.0
1986-87	75.9	12.6	11.5	100.0

Source: Based on Education in India (New Delhi: Ministry of Human Resource Development, various years).

Table 7.4: Number of selected educational institutions by management – 2004-05

Type of Institutions	*No. of Institutions by Management*				*Total*
	Government	*Local Bodies*	*Private Aided*	*Private Unaided*	
1	*2*	*3*	*4*	*5*	*6*
Higher Secondary Schools (10+2 pattern)	18137 (36.08)	550 (1.09)	15603 (31.04)	15982 (31.79)	**50272 (100.0)**
High/Post Basic Schools	32229 (31.66)	11505 (11.30)	29029 (28.52)	29022 (28.52)	**101777 (100.0))**
Middle/Senior Basic School	118026 (42.96)	80327 (29.24)	17616 (6.41)	58762 (21.39)	**274731 (100.0)**
Primary/Junior Basic Schools	332565 (43.33)	359772 (46.87)	19593 (2.55)	55590 (7.25)	**767520 (100.0)**
Pre-Primary/Pre-Basic Schools	34597 (54.40)	18300 (28.88)	4359 (6.86)	6271 (9.86)	**63596 (100.0)**
Total	**535554 (42.57)**	**470454 (37.42)**	**86200 (6.85)**	**165627 (13.16)**	**1257896 (100.00)**

Note: Figures in Parenthesis indicate Percentage to total number of institutions.

Source: Selected Educational Statistics, Ministry of HRD, 2004-05.

Such a sizeable expansion was possible due to public financing of higher education. In 1986-87 the Government share was about 76 per cent (more than 3/4th) while funds from other sources were limited to 24 per cent. The percentage of funding of higher education from various sources is given in Table 7.3.

In a situation where Government funding has increased more than one and a half times from 1950-51 to 1986-87 and fees which are an important source of funding of universities have declined from 36.8 per cent to 12.6 per cent (almost one third of the 1950-51 position), it will be difficult to presume that private participation in the university sector will be enhanced in the near future. Endowment/donations, which have been clubbed with other sources have also been reduced from 13.8 to 11.5 per cent. It is, therefore, obvious that dependence on Government funding is increasing.

The post-independence period witnessed a spurt in private participation in education. While the total number of educational institutions in India increased from 2,79,309 in 1949-50 to 4,72,655 in 1960-61 and 12,57,806 in 2004-05 (signifying an increase of over 300 per cent), the number of institutions under private management also increased from 1,01,678 in 1949-50 to about 2,50,000 in 2005-06, i.e. an increase of over 100 per cent. This shows that the state enterprise has increased much more rapidly than that under private management. This has been primarily because of trend towards nationalisation, particularly at the primary stage of education. In 1949-50, private institutions formed 36.4 per cent of total educational institutions. Now they form an abysmal 26 per cent (2004-05). Bulk of private institutions are at the high and higher secondary school stage. The lowest private participation is in the case of primary schools. Table 7.4 explains:

(b) International Experience

In most countries, private and public sectors co-exist. In some countries like Japan, Republic of Korea, Philippines and Latin American countries mass private and restricted public sectors have developed. However, in South Asian countries including India, Africa, and Western Europe, mixed system prevails. In some countries like the Netherlands and Belgium, both co-exist under public funding. Countries where the role of private sector is limited are Sweden, United Kingdom, France, Spain, Thailand etc. "Asia presents the most varied picture, from non-existence to majority shares. The Philippines (85%), South Korea (77%), Bangladesh (67%) and Indonesia (67%) all show private majorities, with India close, and Turkey and Nepal roughly one fourth private trailed by Malaysia and Papua New Guinea". (The Encyclopaedia of Higher Education, 1992-1184).

Types of Private Universities

Primarily, there are two types of private universities:

(i) Corporate Universities

According to Middlehurst, (2001) there are corporate universities in Europe and parts of the Commonwealth, but most are in the USA, where number has grown from 400 in 1988 to more than 1600 in 1998. They take a variety of forms and are generally linked with some multi-national companies or other large organisations. The driving force behind the corporate universities is the business requirements.

In the first type of corporate university – exemplified by the McDonald's Hamburger University – learning is driven by the need to enhance employee performance and productivity and to ensure consistency of service and the spread of a common culture. Its focus tends to be upon employees, but may extend to suppliers and customers (including small and medium-sized enterprises). In the second type, learning is conceptualised more broadly, to include both individual and organizational development. Features include education and training, but also, perhaps, research, consultancy, best-practice benchmarking and knowledge management (as in the case of the British Aerospace Virtual University).

The UK Report draws out features of corporate universities that appear to be widely shared. These include:

"Professional development activities that are aimed at company and individual needs, specialist in-company departments/ colleges which are staffed by a combination of professional educators/ trainers and practitioners from the businesses and an increasing emphasis on the use of technology for the delivery of education and training. Further notable elements include an emphasis on competency-based training, linked to assessment of outcomes and credit accumulation, with a particular focus on professional/ vocational subjects and training that forms a necessary part of assuring the quality of products and services, for example, through programmes offered to suppliers and customers. Where degrees are offered, there is generally a partnership with existing universities and in all the education and training offered there, a strong emphasis on quality through close attention to curriculum design, staff selection, mandatory teacher training, control of class size and course cohorts, and rigorous evaluation of every process from student admissions to teacher performance and adherence to curricula."(Robin Middlehurst, op cit.)

(ii) 'For-profit' Institutions

Flexibility, convenience and relevance are key features of 'for-profit' education businesses, which include:

(a) Location: Phoenix has set up nearly 80 learning centres in 32 US states on the edge of freeways or in shopping malls in order to minimise student time lost in travelling between work and home;

(b) Access for students: provision and support is often available online (Unexus University, launched recently in New Brunswick, offers access twenty-four hours a day, seven days a week); enrolment times are also convenient – Jones International University enables students to enroll every four weeks; Keller Graduate School of Management runs a five semester year (ten weeks each) and holds all classes in the evenings or on Saturdays;

(c) Length and intensity of study: courses and programmes tend to be shorter (Phoenix has courses of five or six weeks contributing to a two-year programme) with credit accumulated for awards at different levels. Teaching is focused and intensive and classes are small (14-15 students for face-to-face tuition at Phoenix, 8-11 students for online classes);

(d) Credit accumulation and transfer: Sylvan Learning Systems, in an arrangement with Regent's College of New York State, gives credit, and transfers credits from different institutions and gives Regent's examinations in Sylvan's Technology Centres across the US; and

(e) Curriculum: 'Learn tonight, apply tomorrow' is a motto for curriculum relevance, Keller Graduate School of Management offers 'practitioner-led management education' where all faculty are practicing professionals; Phoenix designs and delivers customized programmes for corporations along similar lines.

(c) Private Participation

It may be mentioned that, so far none of the above types of universities has found a place in the Indian educational system. On the basis of the analysis made about India's experience of private participation in higher education, however, it has been found that private organisations have made significant contribution in higher education in India. We shall now examine the various aspects of privatisation in terms of the empirical data collected for the study. We shall also analyse the views/opinions expressed by respondents of various categorises.

(i) Complete Privatisation

A perusal of responses of different categories of respondents reveals that they do not approve of complete privatisation of higher education. Education (at every level whether primary, secondary or higher) is a merit good. It is duty of the state to provide it. For higher education it may give substantial funding. The state funds most continue to be an essential and mandatory requirements for this sector. However, respondent tend to agree to have private participation in this sector. Respondents have expressed the view that total withdrawal of state from higher education is neither possible nor desirable and is also against the spirit of our Constitution. The State should continue to make liberal investments in higher education in order to ensure balanced socio-economic development. Some of the important views given by the different categories of respondents in favour or otherwise of privatisation of higher education are as follows:

University Teachers

(1) If privatisation means complete withdrawal of state from financing and management of higher education, it is not desirable. Government should encourage private efforts and these efforts may also be regulated properly.

(2) Since there are several inequalities in higher education, privatisation would further aggravate the situation. Hence complete privatisation will make the situation worse. Government support to higher education is not charity, but a legitimate responsibility of the State. It is a non-negotiable right of higher education.

(3) It is desirable that private efforts may be encouraged to supplement the state efforts rather than consider it as a substitute. Private participation may, however, improve the quality of higher education.

(4) As privatisation in most cases could lead to profit making, it is not desirable for our country to adopt this path. The poor and meritorious students will never get the chance to acquire higher education.

A microscopic minority in this category advocated privatisation of higher education. Their views are summarise below:

(1) Since the states' capacity to finance education is limited, it is desirable that Government may handle elementary education and higher education sector may be managed by private bodies.

(2) At present there is no accountability in the university system. Privatisation will bring accountability. It is difficult for government to do everything for higher education under the present circumstances.

(3) Privatisation would free higher education from the shackles of government bureaucracy. It will provide opportunities for experimentations/ innovations. It will make higher education more relevant to market and social needs.

Researchers

A number of researchers expressed views more or less similar to those of university teachers. Some of the additional points expressed by them are:

(1) Privatisation of higher education will limit access to higher education for the less affluent students who may be otherwise qualified to enter institutions of higher education.

(2) There should be social commitment of providing education as also higher education, which the Government must fulfil.

Those who were favouring privatisation of education, expressed the following views:

(1) Privatisation is an answer to many of the ills, which higher education system is suffering from. But there should be enough safeguards to ensure access to higher education for:

  (a) meritorious and poor student, and

  (b) students from socially and economically weaker sections.

(2) In view of the need for ensuring high standards in higher education, more resources are required. Since, the government has consistently failed in providing adequate resources, it is perhaps necessary to encourage private participation in higher education.

(3) Industry representatives felt view was that privatisation will build up 'centres of excellence' in various disciplines. It will give congenial atmosphere for work, promote competition and promote excellence.

Educational Administrators

The third category of our respondents was Educational Administrators, whose views are summarised below. It has been noted that in some cases, conditions have been stipulated. Further, alternatives have also been suggested.

(ii) Against Privatisation

(1) Complete privatisation is neither possible nor desirable. What is needed is increasing participation of private sector in higher education in terms not only of provision of adequate resources but also in determining the structure and nature of higher education.

(2) Private sector has a supplementary role to play. It is more like societal participation.

(3) Privatisation should be done in stages. In the first phase, it should be done as a pilot project and if found successful, it may be done for the whole country.

(4) In a mixed economy, privatisation has to play an important part, but a strong government presence is also needed. Considering the poor purchasing power of most of our students, the state's role in providing higher education is desirable.

(iii) For Privatisation

(1) Private managements can contribute to a significant extent in flexibility, efficiency and effectiveness in higher education.

(2) Higher education needs to be opened to private initiative and investment so as to create healthy competitive atmosphere as also to share ever expanding enrolment base. It will also ensure better selectivity in course combinations as per emerging occupational patterns and also contribute to dynamism of the system.

(3) Privatisation is necessary for developing flexible models to achieve excellence, providing more functional autonomy and minimising government interference.

(4) It will meet growing unmet demand, improve access and increase relevance.

Vice Chancellors

The last category of our respondents was university Vice-Chancellors. A perusal of their responses reveals that they have put conditions for the success of privatisation of higher education. It also appears that they are in favour of private participation rather than complete privatisation of university system.

The views expressed by the Vice-Chancellors are summarised below:

(1) Privatisation of higher education is a worldwide phenomena. This phenomena is growing fast in Latin America, parts of Asia and Central and East European Countries. Even the public universities are increasingly becoming responsible for raising their own funds. All these institutions regard students as customers. Privatisation of higher education may have its roots in the following perceptions:

- There is a huge demand for privatisation as private education is qualitatively superior to public education.
- Governments are not in a position to meet the financial burden and therefore it may provide some relief to them by privatising higher education through self-financing schemes.
- Private sector responds more quickly to the market demands on higher education.
- Privatisation of higher education may improve income distribution.

However, the above perceptions may not hold good for the following reasons:

- Privatisation of higher education may have adverse impact on quality control and accreditation.

- The academic profession will be in crisis because many private institutions may prefer appointing only part time faculty in order to save money or cut per student unit costs.
- Whenever market demand changes, the employers may force academicians, without giving much time and money for improving their academic qualifications or diversifying their areas of specialization, to adjust to the new demands/ circumstances or force them to quit the institutions.
- Government institutions of higher education have better infrastructure facilities like buildings, laboratories, qualified teaching staff and research facilities than private institutions. In private sector, there may be only a few institutions which have good staff and infrastructure.
- It is also a fact that the student-teacher ratio, which is a quality indicator of teaching-learning process, of the government institutions is higher than that of private institutions.
- The issues of access and equity, particularly to the disadvantaged groups like economically and geographically weaker sections, women, SC/ST and other backward and minority communities, in the private institutions are often ignored under one pretext or other.
- Accountability will be a problem unless these private institutions are kept under constant regulation by a government authority.

(2) In the interest of the country, there is a need to encourage private participation in higher education.

(3) It is time that government encourages private involvement in higher education. The proposed 6 per cent GNP allocation for education may not provide access to higher education even for 10% of the relevant age group.

(4) Privatisation should be limited to generation of resources, which may make the system effective.

The views of those who favoured privatisation without any conditions are:

(1) Need arises because of shift in government priority. Privatisation will improve the quality of higher education. It will encourage better institution-society interaction.

(2) There is a need for privatisation of higher education. However, the norms, quality, access and non-commercialisation should be kept in mind.

(3) The growth of higher education needs huge requirements of human and material resources, hence privatisation may be considered for higher education.

(i) Privatisation and Its Impact on Higher Education

The respondents were requested to react to certain questions with regard to privatisation of higher education and its expected impact on some of the aspects of higher education. They were asked whether privatisation will lead to improvement in the following areas:

(a) efficiency in the system,

(b) effectiveness of education,

(c) excellence in higher education,

(d) ensuring access to meritorious but economically weaker students,

(e) relevance of education.

The responses in most cases were conditional in nature. Respondents expressed the general view that improvement may become possible if certain conditions are fulfilled as pre-requisites. The replies have been tabulated in Table 7.6.

As could be seen from Table 7.6, the respondents are of the view that privatisation will bring improvement in quite a few areas such as efficiency in system, effectiveness, excellence and relevance of education. But in the case of ensuring access to meritorious but economically weaker students, they expressed their doubts. They also feel that privatisation will make education relevant to the needs of the society. Out of the 41 respondents, 32 (78.05%) said 'yes' to this issue which was followed by improvement in efficiency in system 30 (73.17%), effectiveness of education 28 (68.29%) and excellence in higher education 21 (51.22%).

As already stated, the respondents were doubtful whether privatisation will help in providing access to meritorious but

Table 7.6: Expected Impact of Privatisation on Some Issues of Higher Education

Category	*Improvement in efficiency of system*				*Improvement in effectiveness of education*				*Improvement in excellence of higher education*			
	Yes	*No*	*U/D*	*Total*	*Yes*	*No*	*U/D*	*Total*	*Yes*	*No*	*U/D*	*Total*
University Teachers	4	2	2	**8**	4	2	2	**8**	4	2	2	**8**
	(9.76)	(4.88)	(4.88)	**(19.51)**	(9.76)	(4.88)	(4.88)	**(19.51)**	(9.76)	(4.88)	(4.88)	**(19.51)**
Researchers	6	2	0	**8**	6	2	0	**8**	5	3	0	**8**
	(14.63)	(4.88)	(0.00)	**(19.51)**	(14.63)	(4.88)	(0.00)	**(19.51)**	(12.20)	(7.32)	(0.00)	**(19.51)**
Educational Administrators	9	1	1	**11**	9	1	1	**11**	6	2	3	**11**
	(21.95)	(2.44)	(2.44)	**(26.83)**	(21.95)	(2.44)	(2.44)	**(26.83)**	(14.63)	(4.88)	(7.32)	**(26.83)**
Vice Chancellors	11	2	1	**14**	9	4	1	**14**	6	6	2	**14**
	(26.83)	(4.88)	(2.44)	**(34.15)**	(21.95)	(9.76)	(2.44)	**(34.15)**	(14.63)	(14.63)	(4.88)	**(34.15)**
All Categories	**30**	**7**	**4**	**41**	**28**	**9**	**4**	**41**	**21**	**13**	**7**	**41**
	(73.17)	**(17.07)**	**(9.76)**	**(100.00)**	**(68.29)**	**(21.95)**	**(9.76)**	**(100.00)**	**(51.22)**	**(31.71)**	**(17.07)**	**(100.00)**

(Contd.)

(Contd. Table . 7.6)

Category	Access to meritorious but economically weaker students				Relevance of education			
	Yes	*No*	*U/D*	*Total*	*Yes*	*No*	*U/D*	*Total*
University Teachers	2 (4.88)	4 (9.76)	2 (4.88)	**8** **(19.51)**	5 (12.20)	1 (2.44)	2 (4.88)	**8** **(19.51)**
Researchers	1 (2.44)	6 (14.63)	1 (2.44)	**8** **(19.51)**	6 (14.63)	2 (4.88)	0 (0.00)	**8** **(19.51)**
Educational Administra-tors	5 (12.20)	5 (12.20)	1 (2.44)	**11** **(26.83)**	10 (24.39)	1 (2.44)	0 (0.00)	**11** **(26.83)**
Vice Chancellors	2 (4.88)	11 (26.83)	1 (2.44)	**14** **(34.15)**	11 (26.83)	1 (2.44)	2 (4.88)	**14** **(34.15)**
All Categories	**10** **(24.39)**	**26** **(63.41)**	**5** **(12.20)**	**41** **(100.00)**	**32** **(78.05)**	**5** **(12.20)**	**4** **(9.76)**	**41** **(100.00)**

Abbreviations: U/D: Undecided.

economically weaker students in the sphere of higher education. On this issue, the number of respondents saying 'No' was 26 (63.41%) and those who agreed were 10 (24.39%). The percentage of all categories of respondents saying 'Yes' was higher than those saying 'No'.

Considered category wise, out of the responses about all the issues discussed so far, some interesting results emerge, although some inconsistency is also noticed. Surprisingly, as indicated in table 7.7, out of five major issues (viz. improvement in efficiency, effectiveness, excellence, access and relevance of education) the Educational Administrators reacted most favourably to relevance of education (90.91%) followed by improvement in effectiveness of education and improvement in efficiency in the system (both 81.82%). Excellence in higher education (54.55%) was the least favoured. In the case of 'access to meritorious but economically weaker students', Educational Administrators were equally divided in giving their favourable responses (45.45%) and also expressing their disagreement (45.45%). On this issue 9% of respondents were undecided.

In other categories of respondents, no set pattern of responses has been noticed, as was seen in the case of Educational Administrators. Each category has different views on different issues. It is, therefore, difficult to bring out any recognisable pattern of responses.

(ii) The Policy and Legal Framework

It was interesting to know how the existing legal framework may be modified to promote private sector's active participation in higher education. Majority of respondents suggested framing new acts/ laws and also changing the existing laws so that private participation may be encouraged. The views of respondents given on this aspect are summarised below:

(1) There is an urgent need to bring necessary changes in the acts and statutes of universities so that representation of trade, commerce and industry may become possible on the decision making bodies of the universities like Court, Senate, Executive Council, Syndicate, Academic Council, Faculty Committee, Board of Studies etc. It may also be

Table 7.7: Category-wise responses on some issues of higher education

Category	*Improvement in efficiency in system*				*Improvement in effectiveness of education*				*Improvement in excellence in higher education*			
	Yes	*No*	*U/D*	*Total*	*Yes*	*No*	*U/D*	*Total*	*Yes*	*No*	*U/D*	*Total*
University Teachers	4	2	2	**8**	4	2	2	**8**	4	2	2	**8**
	(50.00)	(25.00)	(25.00)	**(100.00)**	(50.00)	(25.00)	(25.00)	**(100.00)**	(50.00)	(25.00)	(25.00)	**(100.00)**
Researchers	6	2	0	**8**	6	2	0	**8**	5	3	0	**8**
	(75.00)	(25.00)	(0.00)	**(100.00)**	(75.00)	(25.00)	(0.00)	**(100.00)**	(62.50)	(37.50)	(0.00)	**(100.00)**
Educational Administrators	9	1	1	**11**	9	1	1	**11**	6	2	3	**11**
	(81.82)	(9.09)	(9.09)	**(100.00)**	(81.82)	(9.09)	(9.09)	**(100.00)**	(54.55)	(18.18)	(27.27)	**(100.00)**
Vice Chancellors	11	2	1	**14**	9	4	1	**14**	6	6	2	**14**
	(78.57)	(14.29)	(7.14)	**(100.00)**	(64.29)	(28.57)	(7.14)	**(100.00)**	(42.86)	(42.86)	(14.28)	**(100.00)**

(Contd.)

(Contd. Table 7.7)

Category	Access to meritorious but economically weaker students				Relevance of education			
	Yes	*No*	*U/D*	*Total*	*Yes*	*No*	*U/D*	*Total*
University Teachers	2 (25.00)	4 (50.00)	2 (25.00)	**8** **(100.00)**	5 (62.50)	1 (12.50)	2 (25.00)	**8** **(100.00)**
Researchers	1 (12.50)	6 (75.00)	1 (12.50)	**8** **(100.00)**	6 (75.00)	2 (25.00)	0 (0.00)	**8** **(100.00)**
Educational Administrators	5 (45.45)	5 (45.45)	1 (9.10)	**11** **(100.00)**	10 (90.91)	1 (9.09)	0 (0.00)	**11** **(100.00)**
Vice Chancellors	2 (14.29)	11 (78.57)	1 (7.14)	**14** **(100.00)**	11 (78.57)	1 (7.14)	2 (14.29)	**14** **(100.00)**

Abbreviations: U/D: *Undecided.*

provided that industrial houses may establish/ adopt university institutions.

(2) The territorial jurisdiction of universities may be extended so that it may expand its working freely in the country and abroad.

(3) The accountability procedures for academic and administrative staff may be developed and followed strictly. Procedure of term appointments of faculty and staff may be considered. Extension may be given purely on merit/ performance bases.

(4) The monopoly of the state in establishing and managing universities may be done away with so that industrial and corporate houses may consider starting private universities. However, it should be ensured that it does not lead to commercialising of higher education. An act may be passed which may provide for incorporation, monitoring and regulation of universities and colleges under private management.

(5) Private investment in higher education should be made tax-free.

(6) The legal framework should be suitably modified so that private sector may participate in financing and management of universities. For this purpose, Parliament may pass Private Universities Bill, which has been pending for consideration for quite sometime.

(7) An environment may be created by changing the legal framework so that private sector participation may become possible in governance and identification of fields/ subjects, which are in tune with the needs of private parties, in respect of professional and technical manpower.

(8) An act may be passed under which University Grants Commission (UGC), All India Council for Technical Education (AICTE) and other bodies dealing with higher education may come under the purview of a high level body/ umbrella organisation for effective development of higher education and co-ordination of the activities of various agencies concerned with this sector.

Nature and Level of Participation

The views of respondents on some crucial issues like management, curriculum development, admission of student etc. are given below in brief:

(a) Management

The universities should be given complete operational freedom in management. The role of funding agencies and government is to provide guidelines for maintaining the standards and ensuring that the norms laid down by them are adhered to properly. Representation of trade, commerce and industry and the parents' associations should be increased in decision making bodies of universities. They can lend their expertise in strategic planning, organisational management, finance, human resource development and monitoring the progress of various programmes. From this stand point, they need to be represented on Management/ Executive Councils. They may also depute their staff for undertaking these activities. A good number of respondents opined that management should be wholly under private auspices in private managed institutions. While, there should be total autonomy, some Government/ Government bodies may, however, maintain checks and balances.

(b) Curriculum Development

The regulating authority should lay down broad guidelines for the curriculum development. The representation from academic community and public institutions should be invited. The market needs must be kept in mind while developing the curriculum.

(c) Admission of Students

University may invite sponsored students from employers. However, merit may not be neglected altogether. Special courses may be developed to suit the needs of sponsors. The university should be allowed to have some sponsored seats against which candidates fulfilling the requirements for admission may be admitted.

(d) Determining fee structure

The fee structure may be revised but it may not appear as an act of commercialisation or profiteering. The regulating authority can decide differential fee structure but the fee structure should accommodate students from weaker sections and also meritorious students.

(e) Recruitment of Staff

Although procedure for appointments have been laid down for many years, they have not led to improvement in the quality and performance of teachers. Funding agency may provide guidelines and also suggest procedures.

(f) Students Evaluations

Students evaluation may be made on regular basis rather than at the end of the year. They may also be provided freedom to pick and choose the course out of several options available. (Cafetaria Approach)

(iii) Proportionate Contribution from Various Sources in the Event of Privatisation of Higher Education

The respondents were asked to indicate, in the event of privatisation of higher education, the proportionate contribution from various sources to the recurring expenditure on higher education. The responses have been tabulated in Table 7.8.

The items selected for recurring expenditure were 'student fees', 'contribution from industries', 'contribution from trusts and endowments', 'contribution from community' and any 'other important source'. As could be seen from the table, out of total 41 respondents, 9 (21.95%) suggested that in the event of privatisation of higher education, contribution of students fees should be between 20-30 per cent, followed by 8 respondents (19.51%) suggesting it should be between 10-20 per cent. If we add these two groups, the number becomes 17 (about 41% of

Table 7.8: Proportionate Contribution Of Recurring Expenditure In The Event Of Privatisation Of Higher Education

(Responses in Number)

%	*Student Fees*					*Contribution from Industry*				
	UT	*RES*	*EA*	*VC*	*TT*	*UT*	*RES*	*EA*	*VC*	*TT*
0-10	0 (0.00)	0 (0.00)	1 (9.09)	0 (0.00)	**1** (2.44)	0 (0.00)	0 (0.00)	2 (18.18)	2 (14.29)	**4** (9.76)
10-20	3 (37.50)	2 (25.00)	2 (18.18)	1 (7.14)	**8** (19.51)	3 (37.50)	2 (25.00)	0 (0.00)	4 (28.57)	**9** (21.95)
20-30	2 (25.00)	0 (0.00)	2 (18.18)	5 (35.71)	**9** (21.95)	2 (25.00)	1 (12.50)	2 (18.18)	1 (7.14)	**6** (14.63)
30-40	0 (0.00)	1 (12.50)	0 (0.00)	4 (28.57)	**5** (12.20)	2 (25.00)	0 (0.00)	4 (36.36)	2 (14.29)	**8** (19.51)
40-50	1 (12.50)	0 (0.00)	1 (9.09)	0 (0.00)	**2** (4.88)	0 (0.00)	0 (0.00)	0 (0.00)	1 (7.14)	**1** (2.44)
50-60	2 (25.00)	1 (12.50)	0 (0.00)	0 (0.00)	**3** (7.32)	1 (12.50)	2 (25.00)	1 (9.09)	2 (14.29)	**6** (14.63)

(Contd.)

(Contd. Table 7.8)

%	Contribution from Trusts and Endowments					Contribution from Community				
	UT	*RES*	*EA*	*VC*	*TT*	*UT*	*RES*	*EA*	*VC*	*TT*
0-10	0	1	4	3	**8**	2	0	4	4	**10**
	(0.00)	(12.50)	(36.36)	(21.43)	(19.51)	(25.00)	(0.00)	(36.36)	(28.57)	(24.39)
10-20	2	1	2	6	**11**	3	3	2	3	**11**
	(25.00)	(12.50)	(18.18)	(42.86)	(26.83)	(37.50)	(37.50)	(18.18)	(21.43)	(26.83)
20-30	2	1	2	2	**7**	1	0	2	2	**5**
	(25.00)	(12.50)	(18.18)	(14.29)	(17.07)	(12.50)	(0.00)	(18.18)	(14.29)	(12.20)
30-40	0	1	0	1	**2**	0	1	0	1	**2**
	(0.00)	(12.50)	(0.00)	(7.14)	(4.88)	(0.00)	(12.50)	(0.00)	(7.14)	(4.88)
40-50	0	0	0	0	**0**	0	0	0	0	**0**
	(0.00)	(0.00)	(0.00)	(0.00)	(0.00)	(0.00)	(0.00)	(0.00)	(0.00)	(0.00)
50-60	1	0	1	0	**2**	0	0	0	0	**0**
	(12.50)	(0.00)	(9.09)	(0.00)	(4.88)	(0.00)	(0.00)	(0.00)	(0.00)	(0.00)

(Contd.)

(Contd. Table 7.8)

%	Others				
	UT	*RES*	*EA*	*VC*	*TT*
0-10	1	1	0	2	**4**
	(12.50)	(12.50)	(0.00)	(14.29)	(9.76)
10-20	2	0	2	3	**7**
	(25.00)	(0.00)	(18.18)	(21.43)	(17.07)
20-30	1	0	0	1	**2**
	(12.50)	(0.00)	(0.00)	(7.14)	(4.88)
30-40	0	0	0	0	**0**
	(0.00)	(0.00)	(0.00)	(0.00)	(0.00)
40-50	0	0	2	0	**2**
	(0.00)	(0.00)	(18.18)	(0.00)	(4.88)
50-60	0	0	0	0	**0**
	(0.00)	(0.00)	(0.00)	(0.00)	(0.00)

(Contd.)

(*Contd. Table 7.8*)

%	Student Fees					Contribution from Industry				
	UT	*RES*	*EA*	*VC*	*TT*	*UT*	*RES*	*EA*	*VC*	*TT*
60-70	0	0	0	1	**1**	0	0	0	0	**0**
	(0.00)	(0.00)	(0.00)	(7.14)	(2.44)	(0.00)	(0.00)	(0.00)	(0.00)	(0.00)
70-80	0	2	1	1	**4**	0	0	0	1	**1**
	(0.00)	(25.00)	(9.09)	(7.14)	(9.76)	(0.00)	(0.00)	(0.00)	(7.14)	(2.44)
80-90	0	0	1	0	**1**	0	0	0	0	**0**
	(0.00)	(0.00)	(9.09)	(0.00)	(2.44)	(0.00)	(0.00)	(0.00)	(0.00)	(0.00)
90-100	0	0	1	1	**2**	0	0	0	0	**0**
	(0.00)	(0.00)	(9.09)	(7.14)	(4.88)	(0.00)	(0.00)	(0.00)	(0.00)	(0.00)
NR	0	2	2	1	**5**	0	3	2	1	**6**
	(0.00)	(25.00)	(18.18)	(7.14)	(12.20)	(0.00)	(37.50)	(18.18)	(7.14)	(14.63)
Total	**8**	**8**	**11**	**14**	**41**	**8**	**8**	**11**	**14**	**41**
	(100)	**(100)**	**(100)**	**(100)**	**(100)**	**(100)**	**(100)**	**(100)**	**(100)**	**(100)**

(*Contd.*)

(Contd. Table 7.8)

%	Contribution from Trusts and Endowments					Contribution from Community				
	UT	*RES*	*EA*	*VC*	*TT*	*UT*	*RES*	*EA*	*VC*	*TT*
60-70	0	0	0	0	**0**	0	0	0	0	**0**
	(0.00)	(0.00)	(0.00)	(0.00)	(0.00)	(0.00)	(0.00)	(0.00)	(0.00)	(0.00)
70-80	1	0	0	0	**1**	0	0	0	0	**0**
	(12.50)	(0.00)	(0.00)	(0.00)	(2.44)	(0.00)	(0.00)	(0.00)	(0.00)	(0.00)
80-90	0	0	0	0	**0**	0	0	0	0	**0**
	(0.00)	(0.00)	(0.00)	(0.00)	(0.00)	(0.00)	(0.00)	(0.00)	(0.00)	(0.00)
90-100	0	0	0	0	**0**	0	0	0	0	**0**
	(0.00)	(0.00)	(0.00)	(0.00)	(0.00)	(0.00)	(G.00)	(0.00)	(0.00)	(0.00)
NR	2	4	2	2	**10**	2	4	3	4	**13**
	(25.00)	(50.00)	(18.18)	(14.29)	(24.39)	(25.00)	(50.00)	(27.27)	(28.57)	(31.71)
Total	**8**	**8**	**11**	**14**	**41**	**8**	**8**	**11**	**14**	**41**
	(100)	**(100)**	**(100)**	**(100)**	**(100)**	**(100)**	**(100)**	**(100)**	**(100)**	**(100)**

(Contd.)

(Contd. Table 7.8)

%	Others				
	UT	*RES*	*EA*	*VC*	*TT*
60-70	0	0	0	0	**0**
	(0.00)	(0.00)	(0.00)	(0.00)	(0.00)
70-80	0	0	0	0	**0**
	(0.00)	(0.00)	(0.00)	(0.00)	(0.00)
80-90	1	0	0	1	**2**
	(12.50)	(0.00)	(0.00)	(7.14)	(4.88)
90-100	0	0	0	0	**0**
	(0.00)	(0.00)	(0.00)	(0.00)	(0.00)
NR	3	7	7	7	**24**
	(37.50)	(87.50)	(63.64)	(50.00)	(58.54)
Total	**8**	**8**	**11**	**14**	**41**
	(100)	**(100)**	**(100)**	**(100)**	**(100)**

Abbreviations

UT=University Teachers; RES=Researchers; EA=Educational Administrators; VC=Vice-Chancellors; TT=Total; NR=No Response.

Note: Figures in brackets are the percentages to the total.

total respondents) suggesting that student fee should be within the range of 10-30 per cent. Two respondents suggested that students should pay fees to the tune of 90-100 per cent. One among these respondents was in the category of Educational Administrators whose reason for such high percentage was that 'students are primary beneficiaries of higher education, hence, they should pay' such high fees. The other respondent was from the category of Vice-Chancellors, although, his explanation was not clear, probably he was of opinion that students, who belong to the category of NRI/foreign countries, should be charged such high percentage of fees.

There is much talk, that industry may contribute larger amounts for higher education institutions, because the products of these institutions are used by industries. However, our data give a different picture. Nine (22% of total respondents) felt that out of total recurring expenditure, 10-20 per cent may be met from industries' contribution, followed by 8 (19.51%) respondents who suggested that 30-40 per cent contribution should come from industries. The industry's representatives, however, suggested that they may be expected to contribute between 5 to 25 per cent.

It appears that respondents do not give much weightage to the 'contribution from Trusts and Endowments'. Eleven (27%) respondents felt that only 10-20 per cent contribution may come from Trusts and Endowments, followed by 8 respondents (20%) who believed upto 10 per cent contribution will be sufficient for the purpose.

As regards 'Contribution from Community' – 11 respondents (27% of the total respondents) felt that it should be 10-20 per cent followed by 10 respondents (25%) who opined that 0-10 per cent contribution will be adequate in the event of privatisation of higher education. However, respondents expressed the view that community should pay for facilities such as stadium, swimming pool, gymnasium, language laboratories etc.

A majority of respondents strongly felt that even if privatisation of higher education takes place, government should not completely withdraw from the scene. It should continue to contribute directly or through its specialised agencies like UGC and All India Council for Technical Education. It should also over-see the teaching-learning process of privately managed universities. Respondents also suggested that whether it is government or private system of higher education, universities must streamline their cost structure. Students should not be made to pay the cost of corruption and inefficiency that seems to have afflicted some of the university institutions.

(iv) Industry/ University Relationship

An enquiry was made whether industrial establishments should participate in financing and management of higher education. The replies received have been tabulated in Table 7.9.

Table 7.9: Participation of Industrial Establishments in Financing and Management of Higher Education

Category	*Yes*	*No*	*No Response*	*Total*
University Teachers	8	-	-	**8**
Researchers	7	-	1	**8**
Educational Administrators	11	-	-	**11**
Vice Chancellors	14	-	-	**14**
All Categories	**40**	-	**1**	**41**

As is evident from Table 7.9, all respondents (except one who did not respond to this question) said that industrial establishments should participate in financing and management of higher education. It is noteworthy that on this particular issue, there was no difference of opinion within or among different categories of respondents.

Nature of Industries' Participation

The respondents were requested to indicate the kind of partnership that should be established between universities and industrial houses on the following important issues:

(a) Curriculum Development

Majority of respondents opined that curriculum development exercise should be undertaken jointly by the university and the industry. The industry's representatives emphasised that the specific need of the industry should be identified and reflected in the curriculum so that it may become relevant. The issue of relevance should be looked into by a mechanism which is to be built into the system rather than being a 'once a while exercise.' Further, the representatives of industries should be members of Board of Studies, Faculty Committees and Academic Council of the universities. Industries may also provide help in designing the curriculum in those areas where their participation would be meaningful to develop professional courses relevant to market demand. It is expected that industries will make the curriculum more skill oriented; need/ demand based, keeping in view the societal requirements and future occupational mobility. Since the curriculum will be framed jointly, its acceptability will be beyond doubt. However, there was a strong feeling among the respondents that although curriculum exercises may be done jointly, the final decision about the curriculum design may rest with the universities. The partnership should aim at enriching social and academic aspects, incorporating new ideas besides contributing to human resource development, which is very much required for the growth of our country.

(b) Faculty Support

Majority of the respondents were of the view that guest faculty may be invited to support the academic venture. Their inputs in terms of up-to-date knowledge in the field and interaction with the existing staff will make the academic environment more lively and useful. A few respondents suggested that industries may provide finances for the creation of 'endowed chairs' in the universities to augment faculty support. The example of Banks/ Trusts establishing academic chairs was cited in this context. It will not only help the universities in maintaining standards but also enhance the credibility of funding institutions.

(c) Student Admissions

All respondents emphasised that student admissions may be done on the basis of merit. As the demand for higher education is increasing, the number of seats could be increased to accommodate the rush of students seeking entry into university institutions. For this purpose, resources may be provided by the industries and in turn universities may give preferential admission to candidates sponsored by the industry. This will be more true in the case of professional courses, where market demand is high. However, industries may also be asked to share the cost of education of liberal disciplines, which come under the umbrella of Social Sciences and Humanities. It is suggested that a scheme may be developed that for every three sponsored students in professional courses, industry may pay for the education of one student in Social Sciences or Humanities. While this suggestion may be brought to the notice of a wider section of academic community, it should not be construed as charity being extended by the industries to the disciplines of social sciences and humanities.

As regards the admission procedure, the respondents opined that it may not be necessary for universities to involve industries in this exercise. It may be left to the universities, which normally work on the guidelines developed by their respective specialised bodies. A suggestion was also made by respondents that state wise admission policy may be adopted to have a fair representation of all regions of the country. Also suitable tests may be developed to judge the merit of students for admission.

(d) Management

Some respondents suggested that university management should be the joint responsibility of universities and industries. Representation of industries and professional associations may be associated with policy making bodies of universities. It was also emphasised by the respondents that some share may be given to industries in the management of universities. The universities may welcome the financial help given by the industries, but the decisions regarding budgetary allocations should rest with university management.

The other view of some respondents was that university management may be left to the authorities of the concerned university. However, the role of industries may be limited to the extent that some of its members may be on the governing bodies of the universities. Respondents further reiterated that university management and particularly the financial management should be transparent. They also felt that management should be participatory in nature so as to contribute to institutional progress and social credibility in consonance with democratic traditions of the country. Further it may make all possible efforts to rule out the possibility of exploitation of students.

Industries' representatives viewed that their representation should be significant, particularly when they are funding a particular university. They also said that private sector should have adequate control over management in order to ensure compliance with their programme.

(e) Evaluation of Students Performance

The majority view of the respondents was that evaluation of students' performances may be made by the teachers. Teachers may adopt various ways of evaluation, like 'semester-system', 'continuous evaluation' or 'on the job in-built evaluation'. Evaluation function is essentially the concern of teaching community and it should be done by them.

(f) Sponsorships/ Fellowships

Industries should help as much as they can in providing fellowships to deserving but economically weaker students. It could be a joint programme also in which universities and industries may participate jointly. The industry may also develop a scheme of providing fellowships by sponsoring their employees and students enrolled in universities' short-term, week end refresher courses and department sponsored programmes. Industries may institute fellowships to meritorious but economically weaker students. For this purpose, government may allow hundred per cent tax exemption. Industries may also institute fellowship for sponsored research projects.

(g) Research and Development

Industry is generally the major beneficiary of research and development activities. Hence they must give help in setting up laboratories and research facilities in the university campuses. The maximum support from industries is required in the fields where very little work has been done because research work requires huge investments. Some respondents expressed thc viow that, by law, industries may be asked to earmark a portion of their profits for research and development. The representatives of industries also underlined the need for sponsoring/ funding R&D programmes in universities.

v) Corporatisation

The respondents were requested to give their view whether higher education institutions should be corporatised in the sense that a private limited body should be set up to establish, administer and finance higher education. The responses have been tabulated in Table 7.10.

Table 7.10: Views with regard to Corporatisation of (Higher Education

Category	*Yes*	*No*	*No Response*	*Total*
University Teachers	2 (25.00)	5 (62.50)	1 (12.50)	**8 (100.00)**
Researchers	2 (25.00)	5 (62.50)	1 (12.50)	**8 (100.00)**
Educational Administrators	3 (27.27)	8 (72.73)	0 (0.00)	**11 (100.00)**
Vice Chancellors	4 (28.57)	9 (64.29)	1 (7.14)	**14 (100.00)**
All Categories	**11 (26.83)**	**27 (65.85)**	**3 (7.32)**	**41 (100.00)**

As is evident from Table 7.10, out of the 41 respondents, 27 (65.85%) did not agree with the view that higher education should be corporatised. Only 11 (26.83%) respondents agreed to this view. Three respondents (7.32%) did not respond to the question. This means a significant majority does not subscribe to the view that higher education should be corporatised.

Among those who have said 'No' to corporatisation, a very high percentage, 72.73, belongs to was in the category of Educational Administrators, followed by Vice-Chancellors (64.29 per cent). The negative response on the issue was also high in the case of University Teachers and Researchers. Although we did not put any item in the questionnaire to find out reasons for saying 'No' to this particular query, our hunch is that most of the respondents might have felt that making higher education a corporate body in the sense of setting up a private limited company would lead to profiteering, hence they did not agree to the proposal.

About 27 per cent respondents said that higher education may be corporatised as a public limited company. In that case it would be subject to public accountability through transparent mechanism of disclosure and monitoring. A few respondents opined that there is no harm if private parties enter professional education. However some element of scepticism was discernible while replying in the affirmative. They cautioned and suggested some controls. They also said some better mechanism may be developed in order to ensure their accountability.

On the issue of corporatisation of higher education, the respondents were asked to specify advantages and disadvantages of the proposal. It appears that respondents were not very sure in answering this particular query. Out of 41 respondents, 23 (56%) did not give any reply. The break up of the non-respondents is: 4 out of 8 University Teachers (i.e. 50%), 6 out of 8 Researchers, (75%), 6 out of 11 Educational Administrators (54.5%) and 7 out of 14 Vice-Chancellors (50%). However, some important views on advantages and disadvantages are as follows:

Advantages of Corporatisation

(a) Academics and Educational Administrators:

- There will be a greater operational freedom.
- Higher education will be in the hands of professional management and it may become cost effective and result oriented.
- There will be more accountability in the system rather than its following the obsolete procedures.
- It will facilitate public funding.
- It will control the present day ill effects of unions.
- Corporatisation may bring improvement in the curriculum by bringing in flexible, job-oriented and need based courses.
- There will be a greater degree of competitiveness among students and institutions.
- Initiatives and creativity in higher education will be rewarded.
- It will lead to quick growth and development in certain areas.
- After corporatisation, higher education can be brought under the regulation of Companies Act.
- Through corporatisation, higher education can generate bigger capital resources.
- Corporatisation of higher education will bring economy measures in the system.
- More hard work will be done by teachers and students.
- There will be less interference of the Government in management.

(b) Industry Representatives:

- It will provide a better quality of students.
- It will produce better professionally trained students.
- Programmes/ courses will be target oriented.
- Industry may give partial job assurance to students.
- Opportunities will be available for time bound research.

Disadvantages

(a) Academics and Educational Administrators:

- Corporatisation may introduce commercialisation in higher education. It will make universities as business houses rather than making them temples of learning.
- Higher learning has perpetual value; it will be counter productive if seen from the angle of profit only. Universities cannot be managed like profit making agencies.
- Under commercialisation, poor and needy students will suffer.
- In the event of corporatisation, holistic educational and moral development of student may not take place.
- Corporatisation may bring monopolistic behaviour.
- There will be neglect of old values.
- Corporatisation may neglect socially relevant programmes.
- Sanctity of education will be lost, only rich will benefit from education.
- Arts/ Humanities and pure Sciences will get very little attention under corporatisation. They will be neglected because of low market value.
- Equity may be sacrificed if no safe guards are put in place.
- Knowledge discrimination may creep into the system.
- Corporatisation may lead to less accountability to nation.
- Exploitation of faculty members, students and favouritism will prevail.

(b) Industry Representatives:

- There will be less teacher student freedom.
- There will be insecurity among faculty members.
- There will be concern for money. Hence value of education will be reduced.
- It will come in the way of taking risks.
- It may not give opportunities for long term research programmes.

vi) Enacting Private Universities Bill

In response to the query 'should government enact a private universities bill for giving legislative validity to privatisation/ corporatisation of higher education', the responses received have been tabulated in Table 7.11.

Table 7.11: Enacting Private University Bill

Category	*Yes*	*No*	*No Response*	*Total*
University Teachers	5 (62.50)	2 (25.00)	1 (12.50)	**8 (100.00)**
Researchers	4 (50.00)	2 (25.00)	2 (25.00)	**8 (100.00)**
Educational Administrators	8 (72.73)	3 (27.27)	0 (0.00)	**11 (100.00)**
Vice Chancellors	10 (71.43)	2 (14.29)	2 (14.29)	**14 (100.00)**
All Categories	**27 (65.85)**	**9 (21.95)**	**5 (12.20)**	**41 (100.00)**

Out of 41 respondents, 27 (65.85%) were in favour of enacting private universities bill. In other words they feel that private universities may be allowed to function. However, while saying this, the respondents used some riders for giving affirmative response. The riders are that the private university may be permitted to function in the initial stages on experimental basis rather than as a rule even if the institution satisfies all pre-requisite laid down in the bill. Secondly, private universities may experiment with some selected courses rather than introducing all subjects of sciences and social sciences etc. Thirdly, all respondents stressed that this experiment should under no condition be allowed to work for profiteering.

There were 9 (21.95%) respondents who did not agree to the proposal. Their view was that in the present legal framework governing universities, there are adequate provisions to make necessary changes as and when desired. Any fresh legislation will only give rise to controversies and confusion.

5 (12.20%) respondents did not indicate their agreement or otherwise but still gave their views to the question. Two important views emerged from these respondents:

(a) Since the issue under reference is of great importance, it should be widely discussed in the universities to build up consensus.

(b) Government should enact an umbrella legislation for incorporation, operation, management and regulation of universities in the country.

(vii) University as Infrastructure

For the development of any economy both economic and social infrastructures are needed. So far education is considered only as social infrastructure, but development studies have proved that education is one of the basic infrastructure for the economic growth of the country like ports, telecom, highways, banking etc. On the proposition whether university should be regarded as 'infrastructure' service, respondents' views have been given in Table 7.12.

Table 7.12: Universities as Infrastructural Services

Category	*Yes*	*No*	*No Response*	*Total*
University Teachers	5 (62.50)	1 (12.50)	2 (25.00)	**8 (100.00)**
Researchers	2 (25.00)	4 (50.00)	2 (25.00)	**8 (100.00)**
Educational Administrators	4 (36.36)	6 (54.55)	1 (9.09)	**11 (100.00)**
Vice Chancellors	7 (50.00)	6 (42.86)	1 (7.14)	**14 (100.00)**
All Categories	**18 (43.90)**	**17 (41.46)**	**6 (14.63)**	**41 (100.00)**

Out of 41 respondents 18 (43.90) said 'yes' to the question and 17 (41.46) said 'no', hence the difference is not substantial to draw any definite conclusions out of the data. However, it will be interesting to know the views of the respondents who replied in the affirmative. According to them, education is the most important input in the infrastructure development of the country leading to economic growth. Without this input, and its proper harnessing, no development can take place and returns from investment in higher education are sizeable in comparison to returns from physical investments. Hence higher education investment should be given higher status than any other investment. One representative of Industries also said that university may be regarded as infrastructural service.

Those who gave negative response, felt that university is much more than infrastructure service because it provides professional competencies to learners. It also provides value and culture. It is a living storage of our past, present and future. Some respondents said that university should have a higher status than to be considered as infrastructural services only .

(d) Marketisation of Higher Education

It has been suggested that higher education may be given market orientation, so that the curriculum can be job-oriented. In order to find out the reactions, the respondents were requested to indicate advantages and disadvantages of marketisation of higher education. The respondents' views are summarized below:

Advantages

(a) Academics and Educational Administrators:

- It may update the curriculum according to market needs thus making higher education more relevant. It will also avoid wastage of resources and will put higher education on the path of cost reduction. It will inculcate skill oriented education.
- It may put more emphasis on vocationalisation and job oriented courses. There will be a global market for the students.
- Students will be trained for better employment.
- It may lead to increased support from trade, commerce and industry.

- It may keep an eye on the demand and supply factors thus minimizing overproduction of graduates.
- It may remove campus politics.
- There will be a competitive environment which will encourage better performance in higher education.
- A better infrastructure is possible which may provide students better facilities.
- There will be higher flexibility in the teaching-learning activities to match with the changes in the economy.
- It is likely to promote efficiency in the system.

(b) Industry Representatives:

- It will provide increased commercial value of the course.
- It will develop micro-specialised human resources.
- Industry could save time and money in training.
- Quality of education would be improved.
- Global job opportunities would open up for students.
- Market forces will bring competitiveness.

Disadvantages

Respondents also mentioned some disadvantages, which are:

(a) Academics and Educational Administrators:

- There may be possibility of danger of gross commercialization of education. Value based education will be neglected.
- Disciplines belonging to Humanities and Social Sciences and to some extent Pure Sciences may be neglected.
- There might be the debasement of higher education.
- It will come in the way of knowledge accumulation, creativity and depth in basic knowledge.
- Elite class may have upper hand in the admissions. Poor students will suffer.
- It may promote the culture of consumerism and competition.
- Education will be valued according to the marketability of its products.

- The whole system will be motivated by the yardstick of profit rather than service or social relevance.
- Education will be dominated by immediate market needs.
- Generation of knowledge will get a back seat. It will be at a discount.
- Human dignity, development of personality and quality of life will suffer.
- Vested interest will neglect the basic premises of higher education.
- Academic orientation will be lost with quick changes in popularity of subjects. It may lead to some sectors having excess supply as observed in Information Technology sector and earlier in Civil Engineering. Market needs go on changing very fast.
- Demand/ supply imbalance may create unemployment in certain areas, which may look rewarding today but may change after sometime. However, it will be difficult to change whole set-up suddenly with the change in market demand.
- Marketisation may accentuate disparities between affluent and poor students. Education will be costlier and national needs may suffer.

(b) Industry Representatives:

- There is a higher possibility of brain drain.
- Poor meritorious students would be marginalized/ignored.
- Life span of the courses will depend on market behaviour.
- It would neglect general courses.
- If good student do not go for general courses, the future generations would lose good teachers.

There were overwhelming responses on either side with regard to marketisation of higher education, which show the extraordinary concern of educationists and industrialists. However, some respondents observed that higher education in India should be partially market oriented. Higher education should fulfill the aspirations of the country and should be accessible to all those who deserve and are interested in it.

Respondents also suggested that the whole issue of marketisation of higher education may consider two streams of studies:

(1) Higher education related to Fundamental/ Basic disciplines.

(2) Higher education related to Applied/ Application oriented disciplines/ areas.

Although both are necessary for better higher education system, government grant may be given on matching basis so that there may not be any paucity of funds for conducting fundamental/ basic research. In case of Applied/ Application oriented disciplines, the funding may be more from industrial sectors and the government's role may be secondary. Such orientation of marketisation of higher education will lead country on the path of progress. Further, all activities cannot be subjected to market orientation/ development because there are considerable social benefits from higher education and also private benefits.

Academic Issues Related to Marketisation of Higher Education

The respondents were asked how should higher education respond to the demands of market forces on issues like courses/ curriculum, staff appointments, admission procedure, research and development etc. The general view was that in the changing scenario of our economy, it is essential that higher education should respond to the market demands positively and timely. This will not only benefit student population but industry will also improve their production techniques leading to rapid economic development of the nation.

The views about other aspects of marketisation are summarized below:

(a) Course/ Curriculum

1. The courses/ curriculum, should be relevant, need based with skill orientation.
2. At the same time it may keep the essential elements of curriculum development intact.

3. The new curriculum may take care of the findings of researches, needs and demands of industries and business houses.
4. The development of curriculum should be a cooperative exercise by associating representatives of industries.
5. The curriculum should be flexible in nature rather than rigid as happens mostly in the case of conventional courses.
6. Industry view was it should be developed keeping in view the needs of industries also.

(b) Staff Appointments

1. Although staff appointment should be on the basis of merit, there should be flexibility according to needs. Contract appointment may be preferred. No compromise may be made on quality of teachers.
2. Appointed persons should have a sense of commitment to service. They may be made accountable for the job assigned to them.
3. As far as possible staff should have industry exposure. Experienced persons from industries may come on short-term visiting assignments. For selection of staff, joint committees of industry and university may be constituted.
4. The use of community participation in a formal or non-formal manner may be explored. At times, a person in the community without formal degree, can be a better teacher and trainer.
5. Staff appointments will have to be restructured according to the needs of curriculum updating. Industry should be actively involved.

(c) Procedure for student admissions

1. It should be open, transparent and on the basis of merit. At the same time, provision for foreign, NRI and sponsored students on full cost recovery basis may also be made. Scope to accommodate socially and economically disadvantaged groups must not go out of sight.

2. Students' aptitude to serve the community may also be judged while giving admission.
3. Admissions should be on the basis of entrance tests, which should include scholastic and aptitude tests.
4. The number of seats in a particular course may be guided by the demand in the market.
5. The views of industries' representatives was that regional boundaries and domicile restrictions need to be reviewed. In certain courses, sponsored candidates may be encouraged. Industry should be actively involved in these processes.

(d) Research and Development (R&D)

1. Industry should finance Research and Development (R&D). Patents and copyrights should be shared between sponsors, university and researchers.
2. Both basic and applied research needs to be promoted by industry.
3. It is essential to identify and conduct research in 'non-marketable' areas/ subjects. Emphasis should be on collaborative research.
4. Government may impose cess/ levy on industry to provide funds for R&D.
5. R&D should be an integral component of designing course and conducting teaching.
6. R&D activity will be successful if it is undertaken in consultation with production sectors. It will be useful to design and execute projects, which have implications for raising productivity and diversifying occupational patterns of community.
7. R&D should be made more relevant without neglecting traditional subjects. It must keep pace with new challenges and developments.
8. Basic research and short-term market oriented studies should be undertaken. Industry should support both types of researches.

9. An institution, desiring to have a global recognition, will have to function both as a super-conductor, repository and creator of knowledge; a substantial part of which may be used to fulfill market demands.
10. There should be a wider interaction between the teaching community of universities and industry in research and development so that teaching community can understand the practical needs of industry.
11. Excellent R&D centres may be set up overseas to earn revenue for India.

e) Self-Financing Courses

As brought out in a previous chapter, higher education has been gradually down-sized in terms of allocation of resources. This has necessitated the need for generating resources from other than the government agencies. With this end in view, the Eighth Plan advocated involvement of voluntary agencies and private sector in the opening and management of institutions of higher education and encouraging the setting up of self-financing courses with the proviso that this will be subject to proper checks and balances so that quality of education is not compromised at any cost. In view of this suggestion, it was considered necessary to ascertain

Table 7.13: Self-Financing of Courses

Category	*Yes*	*No*	*No Response*	*Total*
University Teachers	7 (87.50)	1 (12.50)	0 (0.00)	**8 (100.00)**
Researchers	6 (75.00)	2 (25.00)	0 (0.00)	**8 (100.00)**
Educational Administrators	11 (100.00)	0 (0.00)	0 (0.00)	**11 (100.00)**
Vice Chancellors	12 (85.71)	0 (0.00)	2 (14.29)	**14 (100.00)**
All Categories	36 (87.80)	3 (7.32)	2 (4.88)	**41 (100.00)**

the views of the academics and other respondents about the suggested policy of self-financing institutions/ courses at the higher education stage.

Table 7.13 sums up the reactions of the respondents about their agreement or otherwise to the proposal of introducing self-financing courses:

Out of 41 respondents, 36 (87.80%) agreed that there should be a system of self-financing/ self-supporting courses in the universities. Only 3 (7.32%) respondents did not agree to this suggestion.

A category-wise data analysis indicates that all Educational Administrators were agreeing to the proposal of self-financing courses. The same was true of Vice-Chancellors (if we ignore two respondents who did not give any response). Further, a larger majority of Researchers (75.00%), agreed to the proposal and 25.00% ($1/4^{th}$ of the total respondents in this category) expressed their disagreement. In the category of University Teachers also, 87.50% were in agreement but 12.50% were not in favour of the proposal.

Course Preferences

As stated earlier, almost all respondents were of the view that some courses of studies should be self-financing/ self-supporting. About the courses, which should be self-financing/ self-supporting, very interesting suggestions were made. The respondents emphasised that courses should be market driven, which may lead to gainful employment. Inspite of variations in phraseology, all were agreeing that job oriented courses are the need of the day. In this background, they suggested various courses, but with one rider that "meritorious students from disadvantaged groups should not suffer". Hence some percentage of seats should be reserved for the meritorious students. It was also suggested that the distribution of seats should be regulated by a statutory body of the Central Government. In this background they suggested Management/ Technical/ Professional Courses, which would be job-oriented.

The respondents suggested a long list of Courses: about 20; but the highest preference given by academics was for Medicine (including Pharmacy) followed by Information Technology (including Computer Education), Management (including Personnel Management) and Engineering and Technology. Some respondents also suggested Bio-Technology, Advertising, Fashion Designing etc. Some other courses suggested were Astrology, Western Music, Electronics etc. The industry's representatives suggested self financing courses like MBA, B.Tech (related to computer and IT), Law and International Trade.

From the above list of preferred courses, it is clear that there was no demand for Social Sciences/ Humanities Courses. This appears to be a disturbing factor and a pointer to the academicians belonging to Social Sciences/ Humanities that some in-built mechanism must be developed to orient these courses according to market demand. In this connection, the scheme initiated by the University Grants Commission of introducing vocational stream as part of, among others, disciplines of social sciences and humanities as also physical sciences in the first degree courses needs to be strengthened.

Possible Neglect of Some Disciplines

The views of respondents were ascertained about the question whether in the event of marketisation of higher education certain disciplines will be relegated to be background. The replies to this question have been tabulated in the Table 7.14.

As is clear from Table 7.14, one of the major shortcomings of the marketisation of higher education is that certain disciplines are bound to be relegated to the background. This is supported by the above table in which a large majority of respondents feel that marketisation of higher education will lead to neglect of certain disciplines. Out of 41 respondents, 34 (82.92%) respondents replied in affirmative; a very small number 4 (9.76%) said in negative and only 3 (7.32%) respondents preferred to give no response.

Table 7.14: Possible Neglect of Courses under Marketisation

Category	*Yes*	*No*	*No Response*	*Total*
University Teachers	8 (100.00)	0 (0.00)	0 (0.00)	**8 (100.00)**
Researchers	6 (75.00)	1 (12.50)	1 (12.50)	**8 (100.00)**
Educational Administrators	7 (63.64)	3 (27.27)	1 (9.09)	**11 (100.00)**
Vice Chancellors	13 (92.86)	0 (0.00)	1 (7.14)	**14 (100.00)**
All Categories	**34 (82.92)**	**4 (9.76)**	**3 (7.32)**	**41 (100.00)**

When asked which disciplines are likely to be relegated, the answers of all the respondents were more or less the same. According to them, disciplines belonging to Social Sciences, Humanities, Languages, Education, Fine Arts, Creative Arts, Performing and Visual Arts, Culture and Civilization and some areas of Agricultural Sciences may suffer most. According to industry's representatives, the traditional engineering disciplines like civil, electrical and mechanical engineering are also likely to be relegated to the background.

In this background, the respondents were requested to indicate the subjects belonging to major faculties, which were likely to be neglected. In Social Sciences, they repeatedly named the subjects: History, Philosophy, Anthropology, Political Science/ Civics, Sociology and Geography; in languages, Classical languages including Sanskrit and theology were mentioned. In Sciences, mathematics was pointed out repeatedly. In a nutshell, the predominant view was that:

(a) all languages and culture based courses, and

(b) all theory based courses like physics, chemistry, mathematics, life sciences, economics, philosophy and commerce are likely to be effected when marketisation of higher education is taken to its logical conclusions.

Measures to Remedy the Situation

What should be done to remedy this situation? Should future citizens (i.e. students) of this country act like tools of different machines or they may be inculcated social and moral values. The views expressed by the respondents are summarized below:

1. Efforts may be made to reorient the contents of sciences and social sciences in such a manner that may become beneficial to industry/ business houses. Examples were cited of the new courses developed in the field of Economics as Business Economics, Trade and Finance, Banking etc.
2. At the same time, it was also suggested that the institutions/ centres which are running courses as per market demand, should also have courses in social sciences to provide the social values among the learners. Example of Engineering Colleges, having the faculty of Humanities and Social Sciences was quoted.
3. It was also suggested that complete marketisation should not be the basic concern of higher education. Excessive emphasis on marketisation of higher education is also not good for the country.
4. A good number of respondents argued that these disciplines should receive hundred per cent government grant for teaching learning activities. In the same way it was also suggested that meritorious students, who are motivated to opt for these courses may be compensated with incentives/ subsidies/ scholarships. For other students, the cost of education for these courses may be reduced.
5. Public opinion may be created in favour of courses like pure sciences, social sciences and languages etc.
6. There should be checks and balances for admission to these courses so that excess supply of students may not be created, which ultimately results in unemployment.
7. Private sector may be motivated to give funds for these disciplines and they may establish trusts/ chairs for higher learning.

8. It was suggested that a few institutions of higher education may be identified and at least one among them may be identified to become promoter of at least one discipline. The students who are really serious to do work in these areas may be admitted. Cost of their education may be fully supported by government or private bodies.

In a nutshell, the universities/funding agencies should not neglect these courses altogether. In order to meet the financial burden, a scheme may be worked out to subsidize the cost of education of these courses. The graduates from the theory disciplines may be given priority for recruitment to teaching positions. All academic programmes should have multi-disciplinary approach for displaying its main characteristics and creating a demand in the market. The inputs from other disciplines may be added to the intrinsic value of above disciplines in terms of their usability, employability and absorbability in wide range of activities, programmes and professions as they would be needed for the all round development of the economy. Industry view was that Government may undertake the responsibility to keep such disciplines alive.

8

Main Findings and Policy Guidelines

(A) Main Findings

The following is a summary of the main findings of the study:

Financing of Higher Education

The behaviour of overall educational finance under central and state governments has been examined. The financing of higher education and institutional efforts to mobilize private resources for educational development have been discussed.

The study reveals substantial increase in expenditure on education both under the central and state governments. From Rs.114 crore in 1950-51, the total expenditure rose to Rs.97,547 crore in 2005-2006. It is however, still far short of being 6 per cent of the National Income as suggested by the Education Commission in 1966. It has also been found that bulk of expenditure is on revenue account - that also on staff salaries - leaving very little for infrastructural development and qualitative improvement of university education.

Most of the state governments are spending between 15 to 25 per cent of their revenue budget on education. Significant correlation between states' per capita expenditure on education and states' per capita Domestic Product (SDP) has been observed.

There have been wide fluctuations in the expenditure on different sectors of education during the five-year plans. Higher education which started with 9 per cent of the total plan outlay in the First Plan rose to about 25 per cent in the Fourth Plan. Thereafter, there has been a steep downslide; with higher education ending up with a lowly outlay of 8 per cent in the Ninth Plan. Correspondingly, elementary education starting with 56 per cent of the outlay in the first plan got a bare 30 per cent in the fourth plan. But, thereafter, it rose to 51 per cent in the Ninth Plan. The same position is discernable in the case of plan and non-plan expenditure of the central and state governments.

An analysis of UGC's allocations of plan grants reveals that bulk of Commission's assistance (40 per cent) was given for improving basic amenities in universities and colleges. Schemes of promotion of excellence and innovative courses got about 15 per cent of the UGC's funding. It has also been noted that bulk of universities' resources are provided through government / UGC grants. There is very little effort to raise community resources. In order to raise the level of cost recoveries from the students, introduction of loan scholarships rather than outright grants and harnessing community resources are of paramount significance. It has also been stressed that wastage of resources in the form of under-utisation of infrastructure, failure of about 50 per cent of students in the university examinations and depletion of trained professional manpower caused by emigration of this category of personnel to foreign lands should be avoided.

University Finances

The various contours of university administration and finances on the basis of data supplied by universities have been examined. The following are the main findings of this analysis:

Pattern of Income

1. The Analysis of the income of 29 Universities indicates spectacular rise in the total income of the universities between 1996-97 and 2001-02. But a steady decline was observed in the percentage of government grants to Deemed to be Universities and State Universities.

2. Other grants that are given through Central government, All India Council for Technical Education (AICTE), other governmental agencies and Local bodies, are very meagre; they too are declining.
3. Government funding for selected universities decreased from 64.99 per cent to 56.72 per cent and income from fees, an important source of funding of universities, increased from 20.06 per cent to 26.10 per cent. It can be assumed that private participation in the university sector has shown a tendency of enhancing.
4. In 55 per cent of universities, income from tuition fees has shown a declining trend. There is need to start new self-financing courses mainly in innovative and professional subjects and also gradual enhancement of tuition fees.
5. There is no relationship between how old a university is and the share of its fee income. It depends upon the university's policies and their implementation, which have significance in generating income through other than the governmental sources.
6. Quite a few universities have surplus income from examination fees. However, in 40 per cent of universities, examination fees show a declining trend. The reasons need to be explored so that appropriate action is taken for enabling universities to mobilize additional resources under this head.
7. Income from hostel fees shows a declining trend in more than 50 per cent of universities. There is need for examining the extent to which universities are subsidizing hostellers in meeting such costs as rent, various other charges and the amount spent on mess.
8. Wide variation exists in the amount received by universities for projects, sponsored either by government or by non-government organizations. But, project grants are invariably increasing in most of the universities for research projects sponsored by non-governmental organizations.

Pattern of Expenditure

1. It has been noticed that the overall expenditure has substantially increased over the years. Recurring expenditure constitutes the largest proportion of expenditure as against non-recurring expenditure.
2. Though it accounts for very low proportion as compared to recurring expenditure, there has been substantial increase in the proportion of non-recurring expenditure.
3. Universities are incurring most of their non-recurring expenditure on construction of buildings, leaving very little amounts for library, laboratory equipments, furniture, computers etc.
4. Salary expenditure constitutes the largest proportion of university expenditure. The salary expenditure of non-teaching staff has shown an increasing trend as compared to that of teaching staff in most of the universities. Considering that primary functions of universities are teaching and research, the increase in non-teaching staff salaries indicates the existence of large number of non-teaching staff whose contribution to the realization of the objectives of the institutions might not be significant.
5. It has been noticed that expenditure on hostel facilities has invariably increased over a period of five years i.e. 1996-97 to 2001-02 as compared to income from this source.
6. Universities are spending very meagre amount on student welfare services that consist of hostels, scholarship/ stipends, sports, NCC, NSS, and Cultural activities.
7. It has also been noticed that on scholarships, stipends, games and sports, etc. the share of expenditure has declined for all the universities.
8. With regard to conduct of examinations, only a few universities have shown surplus income.

Globalisation

Since early nineties, India has embarked upon a process of economic reforms involving fiscal discipline, deregulation and reduction of tariff barriers relating to imports and exports.

Among the reforms envisaged under the new economic policy, it is proposed to encourage private sector to its full capacity. The system of education has also been effected by globalisation.

The impact of globalisation and the consequential stress on liberalization and privatisation has a multi-dimensional impact on the process of education. The following are the areas that have been particularly effected:

(a) Content of Education – Advances in information technology and the ever growing use of electronic media has brought education within the reach of the common man. This has also underlined the need for continuous upgradation of curriculum for incorporating latest developments in the field of education. Further, education has, in reality, become a life long process. The need for making education productivity oriented has been underlined. There is emphasis on research in basic sciences and other disciplines.

(b) Equity Excellence Syndrome – Globalisation has stressed the need for nurturing talent through financial assistance and other incentives. It has been argued that accent on excellence would be inequituous impeding the entry of non-meritorious students to educational institutions. This is, however, a simplistic argument. The remedy lies in expanding the field of excellence so as to enable more and more intellectually endowed persons to enter institutions of higher education. This could be achieved by, among other things, qualitative upgradation of academic and physical infrastructure, reforming teacher education and improving the system of students' assessment. Provision of adequate financial incentives to economically weaker sections of students is also an essential pre-requisite in this regard.

(c) Internationalisation of Education – Globalisation also lays stress on internationalization of the educational system, which will enable institutions of higher education from foreign countries to open their campuses in India. Correspondingly, it will also enable Indian universities to set up their centers in foreign countries.

In response to specific questions about the entry of foreign universities in India as also the vice-versa, the respondents generally supported the proposal because of the assumption that it will have a salutary effect on the quality of Indian higher education. It will also make available global opportunities for exchange of scholars and promote international good will. The respondents, however, did not support an unrestricted entry of foreign universities. They laid stress on regulating the entry of foreign universities through the National Assessment and Accreditation Council and specialized bodies like UGC and AICTE. It was also emphasized that the entry of foreign universities should be on the basis of reciprocity i.e. Indian universities should also be permitted to set up their campuses in foreign countries.

(d) Finance Related Problems – Under globalisation, quite a few finance related problems have cropped up. They relate to deprioritization of certain sectors of education, particularly, higher education and emphasis on privatisation of secondary and higher education. Decentralization of management and financing of education has also been stressed.

It is necessary that each country should decide about the policies and programmes of educational development keeping in view its own priorities, needs and availability of financial resources. There can be no set formula, which would guide action under globalisation. For example, suggestions about down sizing higher education is a remedy worse than the disease. Further, privatisation of education has also to be introduced in a guarded manner. It has to be ensured that privatisation does not lead to commercialization of education and neglect of certain disciplines, which have no ready employment facilities. In sum, each country has to decide about the nature and extent of globalisation in relation to education keeping in view its own national interests and needs. Any thoughtless entry into global education market can end up in harming the vital interests of students for generations to come.

Internationalization of Higher Education

India introduced the New Economic Policy with accent on liberalization, privatisation and globalization. Among other things, this has given rise to 'borderless' education implying internationalization of educational system.

The World Trade Organisation negotiated an international agreement, which provides legally enforceable right to trade in all services unless they are provided entirely by government. Services, which have been charged (as happens in education) or provided by private providers fall under GATS jurisdiction.

According to some case studies conducted at National University of Educational Planning and Administration, transnational education is being provided in the following modes:

(i) Consumption Abroad – Information dissemination and recruitment of students through:
  (a) Information centres of various countries set up by embassies;
  (b) Private Agencies

(ii) Commercial Presence/Franchisee

(iii) Twinning programmes

(iv) Cross Border Supply Universities:
  (a) Campus of A country university in B country
  (b) Distance Mode of Learning/Virtual university.

In the context of the responsibilities stipulated under WTO regulations, the respondents consisting of educationists, administrators and representatives of the industry were requested to give their views about the various aspects of internationalization of higher education. The predominant views of the respondents have been summed up below:

(a) Entry of foreign universities

(i) A large majority of the respondents favoured the entry of foreign universities in India.

(ii) The predominant view was that foreign universities may be allowed to set up campuses in India under strict government control.

(iii) It was also stressed that the foreign institutions wishing to set up their campuses should conform to the accreditation norms laid down by the National Accreditation and Assessment Council.

(iv) Among the benefits of internationalization, mention was made of expected improvement in the system through healthy competition with foreign universities, promotion of international good will, encouraging international exchange of scholars etc.

It was also stressed that regulatory mechanism should be created to ensure that only genuine universities are allowed to operate in India.

(b) Modalities of Entry

It was emphasized that foreign universities wishing to set up campuses in India should be accredited in their own country. Their academic standards, course contents, status in their own country should be examined by the National Assessment and Accreditation Council. Their academic programmes should be subjected to pre-entry audit. They should sign a Memorandum of Understanding with the Ministry of Human Resource Development (MHRD) giving requisite details about their academic activities in India, number of students to be admitted and the amount of fees to be charged. It was also stressed that a minimum level of investment in academic infrastructure and physical facilities should be insisted upon. Further, there should be an element of reciprocity enabling Indian universities to set up their campuses in foreign lands. It was also suggested that Indian universities wishing to set up their campuses should be subjected to rigorous academic audit. Further, profits, earned by Indian universities, should be subject to tax. They should also earmark funds, out of profits, for the development of higher education in the country.

Private Participation in Higher Education

The basic issue of the nature and extent of private participation in the educational system has been subjected to a critical review. It has been pointed out that beginning from the hoary past, private bodies have been contributing to the maintenance and development of educational institutions. The ancient *gurukuls* and the medieval *madrassas* bear testimony to the interest of the community to participate in the process of providing education to the masses. This trend has continued in the post-independence period, though, because of various reasons, community participation, both in financial and physical terms has been substantially reduced leaving the financing of educational institutions primarily to government. The paradigm shifts in the socio-economic systems with emphasis on liberalization, privatisation and globalisation have, however, brought to fore the need for encouraging private participation in education as well as higher education.

The following is a brief summary of views/ suggestions of the respondents relating to various aspects of private participation in higher education.

Privatisation

Complete privatisation of higher education has not been favoured. Instead, private *participation* in the management and financing of higher education has been supported. It has been mentioned that complete privatisation will accentuate inequalities by limiting access of deprived sections of society to institutions of higher education. It may also lead to commercialization of education. Privatisation may also have adverse impact on quality control and accreditation. It may also lead to qualitative deterioration in higher education because private institutions may prefer appointing only part time staff in order to save money.

A few respondents have supported privatisation of higher education on the plea that private managements can contribute to a significant extent in flexibility, efficiency and effectiveness in higher education. It is also expected to engender healthy competitive spirit.

In sum, majority of respondents favour private *participation* rather than complete privatisation of higher education.

Corporatisation

A large majority of respondents did not agree to the view that higher education should be corporatised. About 27 per cent respondents, however, agreed that higher education may be corporatised as a public limited company. In that case, it would be subject to public accountability through transparent mechanism of disclosure and monitoring.

Among the advantages of Corporatisation, mention was made of greater operational freedom for universities. It was also felt that higher education will be in the hands of professional management and it is likely to become cost effective and result oriented. Further, there will be more accountability in the system rather than following the obsolete procedures. It will also facilitate public funding and generation of greater capital resources. Corporatisation may also bring improvement in the curriculum by bringing in flexible, job-oriented and need based courses. Further, it will engender a greater degree of competitiveness among students and institutions.

Among the disadvantages, commercialisation of higher education was perceived as the greatest danger. It was also felt that poor and needy students will suffer. It may also generate monopolistic behaviour. Further, Arts, Humanities and Pure Sciences will get very little attention under corporatisation. They are likely to be neglected because of their low market value.

Impact of Private Participation

The bulk of respondents expressed the view that private participation in higher education will lead to improvement in efficiency and effectiveness of the system. It will promote excellence and relevance of the system. The view that private participation will improve access of meritorious but economically weaker students to institutions of higher education was not accepted.

Private Universities Bill

About two thirds of the respondents favoured the enactment of Private Universities Bill. Some of them suggested that private universities may be set up on experimental basis. They should also experiment with some selected courses rather than all courses.

Policy and Legal Framework

Stress has been laid on framing new acts/ laws as also changing the existing laws so that private participation may be encouraged. It has also been suggested that government may provide legal framework so that private universities may be established on an experimental basis. The need for giving representation to industry, trade and commerce on decision making bodies of the universities has also been emphasized. The monopoly of the state to establish institutions of higher education should be done away with so that individuals and corporate houses may consider establishing private institutions. Care should, however, be taken to ensure that private participation does not lead to commercialization

Nature and Level of Private Participation

The views of the respondents are as follows:

(a) Management

The universities should be given complete operational freedom. The role of funding agencies should be to provide guidelines for maintaining standards. There should be adequate representation for trade, industry and commercial establishments.

(b) Curriculum Development

Representatives of academic community and industrial houses should be associated with programmes of curriculum development. Needs of market should be kept in view.

(c) Admissions

Students sponsored by employers may be admitted subject to their being meritorious.

(d) Fee Structure

While determining fee structure, commercialization of education should be avoided.

(e) Recruitment of Staff

Funding agencies should provide guidelines for recruitment of staff, which should be adhered to.

(f) Student Evaluation

It should be on a continuing basis rather than as one time activity.

Financial Contribution by Private Bodies

Inspite of emphasizing private participation in higher education, it has been stressed that government should continue to provide finances and should not withdraw from higher education. As a consequence, percentage of student fee contribution has been suggested to be within a range of 10 to 30 per cent of the recurring expenditure and industries' contribution has been placed between 10-20 per cent. Similarly, community contribution has also been suggested between 10-20 per cent. Student fees should, however, not be a factor deterring economically weaker students to enter university institutions.

Industry-University Relationship

All respondents emphasized that industrial establishments should participate in the financing and management of higher education. About the related issues, the responses were as follows:

Nature of Industries' Participation

The respondents were requested to indicate the kind of partnership that should be established between universities and industrial houses on the following important issues:

(a) Curriculum Development

Majority of respondents opined that curriculum development exercise should be undertaken jointly by the university and the industry. The representatives of industry should be members of Boards of Studies, Faculty Committees and Academic Councils of the universities. Industry may also provide help in designing the curriculum in those areas where their participation would be meaningful to develop professional courses relevant to market demand. The partnership should aim at enriching social and academic aspects, incorporating new ideas besides contribution to human resource development which is very essential for the development of our country.

(b) Faculty Support

Majority of respondents stressed the involvement of guest faculty to support the academic venture. Their inputs in terms of up-to-date knowledge in the field and interaction with the existing staff will make the academic environment more lively and useful.

(c) Student Admissions

All respondents emphasised that student admissions may be done on the basis of merit. As the demand for higher education is increasing, the number of seats could be increased to accommodate the rush of students seeking entry into university institutions. For this purpose, resources may be provided by the industries and in turn universities may give preferential admission to sponsored candidates. The respondents did not favour the involvement of industries in the process of student admissions. It may be left to the universities, which normally work on the guidelines developed by the institutions themselves.

(d) Management

There was no unanimity about the industries' participating in the management of universities. Some respondents suggested that university management should be joint responsibility of universities and industries and professional associations may be represented on the policy making bodies of the universities. Contrary to this, some respondents suggested that university management should be left entirely to the authorities of the concerned university.

(e) Evaluation of Students Performance

Majority of the respondents emphasised that evaluation function is essentially the concern of teaching community and it should be performed by them.

(f) Sponsorships/ Fellowships

Industries should help in providing fellowships to deserving but economically weaker students. It could be a joint programme also in which universities and industries may participate jointly. Industrial houses may be encouraged to sponsor their employees for short-term, week-end refresher courses and department sponsored programmes. Industries may institute fellowships to meritorious but economically weaker students.

g) Research and Development

Industry is the major beneficiary of research and development activities. Hence they must give help in setting up laboratories and research facilities in the university campuses. Some respondents expressed the views that by law, industries may be asked to earmark a portion of their incomes for research and development.

Marketisation of Higher Education

Among the advantages of giving market orientation to higher education, mention was made of updating the curriculum according to the needs of the employment market, stress on vocationalisation of education, possibility of financial support from industry and trade, help in manpower planning and expected better performance of the universities through the generation of better competitive environment.

Among the disadvantages, the foremost apprehension was that it may give rise to commercialization and neglect of value based education. Further, some of the disciplines like Humanities and Social Sciences may be neglected. It may lead to education being valued according to marketability of its products; generation of knowledge and research taking a back seat.

Self Financing Courses

An overwhelming majority of respondents supported the introduction of self-financing courses. About the courses which should be introduced as self-financing, emphasis was laid on market driven, job-oriented courses. The most important courses suggested by the respondents were Medicine (including Pharmacy), Information Technology (including computer education) and Engineering and Technology. Bio-Technology, Advertising, Fashion Designing etc. A few mentioned Astrology and Western Music. Curiously enough, there was no mention of Social Sciences and Humanities. This needs serious consideration by the government and the academic community.

B. Policy Guidelines

The main findings of the study have been summed up in the preceding Section. Alongside, the suggestions given by the respondents have also been explained. The policy issues emerging out of the study, in the light of the suggestions given by the respondents have also been briefly highlighted. Detailed suggestions/ observations made by the respondents have been given in the relevant chapters.

In this section, it is proposed to discuss a few major issues arising out of the Study keeping in view its main objectives. Effort has been made not to repeat, as far as possible, the points made in the previous Section. In a study of this kind, however, some overlapping is inevitable and, therefore, the indulgence of the reader is earnestly solicited.

(a) Financing Higher Education

1. The incongruities and inconsistencies of financing of education as also of higher education underscore the necessity of streamlining the process and procedures of financing of education as well as higher education. An essential pre-requisite in this direction is increasing the quantum of overall investment in education as also in higher education. This does not necessarily mean spending any specified percentage of GNP on programmes of

educational development. What is required is an objective assessment of needs of education sector from time to time and taking steps to meet those requirements. The resources required for the purpose may not necessarily come from the Government. It is essential to tap community sources besides persuading the industry and trade to open strings of their purse.

2. There is also need to rationalize the investment pattern of University Grants Commission for higher education. It has been noted that in terms of its statutory requirements, UGC has to meet, in full, the financial needs of central universities and their affiliated colleges for their maintenance and development. The fact that the state universities and particularly, the affiliated colleges are not getting adequate financial assistance does not augur well for the integrated development of higher education. The UGC should, therefore, be empowered to give enhanced financial assistance to state universities and the much neglected affiliated colleges.

3. There is a feeling in Government circles that higher education primarily caters to the elitist groups. Further that, under the present dispensation, rates of returns of higher education, are more favourable to individuals rather than the society. It has also been argued that this sector is much more costlier than other sectors of education. As a fall out of this mindset, it is proposed that higher education should be better left to fend for itself or be given over to private bodies.

The fallacy of this argument would be evident from the fact that higher education is concerned with the production of professional and technical manpower of the highest order, so vital for country's development. It also provides teachers and teacher educators for the lower levels of education. It is also intimately concerned with basic research so essential for sustained socio-economic development of the country. In view of these important functions of higher education, any downsizing of higher education, culminating into denial of adequate financial support for this sector would be counter-productive for the entire educational process. It will also retard the process of socio-economic development and cultural regeneration of the country. In fact, education is a continuum and any attempt at segmentalising it will be detrimental to the development of this vital sector of human resource development. We should not lose sight of the fact that India is much lower down in terms of Human Resource Development Index (128 out of 174 countries - Human Development Report 2000, UNDP).

4. It has been noted that the amount spent on student welfare programmes has been on the decline. In this context, the student loan scheme introduced recently needs substantial modifications. The underlying idea of the present loan scheme seems to be to enable Banks to earn profits as they do from other financial ventures like car loans, housing loans etc.

   There is need for a paradigm shift in the basic principles on which the scheme has been formulated. Loan schemes in other countries like the UK, USA and European Countries are not profit oriented. They are genuine efforts to help the needy students to take benefit of the scheme at nil or very nominal rates of interest. Further, repayment is in easy instalments spread over a long period after the student gets employment. There are also remissions in payment in case the student enters into certain specified professions like teaching, army etc. It needs to be emphasised that education is an investment in human capital and any scheme, which facilitates the generation and qualitative upgradation of this capital, has to be on a non-commercial basis.

5. In view of the inability or unwillingness on the part of the Government and its specialized agencies to provide adequate finances for higher education, raising resources through non-government sources assumes paramount importance for the educational system. In this connection two suggestions are offered:

(a) It has been reckoned that there is huge subsidy inbuilt into tuition fees levied on the students. Further, while the cost of education has increased manifold, tuition fees have not been able to keep pace with the rising costs. There is, therefore, need for raising tuition fees keeping in view the cost of service principle. This could also be achieved by introducing a kind of differential fee system under which the quantum of fees could be related to the paying capacity of the students. The meritorious but economically weaker students may, however, be exempted completely or charged at concessional rates.

(b) There is also need for harnessing resources from the community, particularly, the industry, which is a direct beneficiary of higher education in the form of production of highly trained professional manpower as also Research and Development.

6. The educational institutions, particularly universities, are often faced with the problem of inadequacy of resources. In order to meet their immediate requirements, they are forced to contract short term and long term loans from the financial institutions like banks at exorbitant rates of interest.

It is suggested that an Educational Development Bank may be set up in collaboration with the state governments and the NRIs. This Bank will provide soft loans to universities in dire need of finances. It will also operationalise the scheme of loan scholarships for needy students.

It may be recalled that this proposal originally emanated from a Committee appointed by the All India Council for Technical Education under D.Swaminathan, former Member, Planning Commission. Inspite of a favourable response from the government, the proposal has not materialized so far. It is high time that steps should be taken to set up the Bank in order to relieve educational institutions from the stranglehold of ordinary commercial banks.

(b) Globalisation

Globalisation, besides having far reaching influence on the socio-economic systems of the countries of the World, has also the potentiality to usher in far reaching changes in the educational system. It has cast its shadow on the content of education by emphasizing productivity oriented curriculum, accelerating research and development in order to enable the countries to compete in the World market. It has also given rise to finance related problems like de-prioritization of higher education. It has also brought to fore the need for privatization and internationalization of higher education.

What needs to be guarded against is the tendency to enter the global educational market without considering the long term effects of that move. It is recognized that under the present state of World economy, with WTO and GATS entering into the system in a big way, it is difficult to insulate ourselves from the inroads of the global system. The caution that needs to be observed is that the nature and extent of our participation in the World educational market should be keeping in view our own long term interests. We should not be swept off our feet under the dominating pressures of the international organizations, who are out to reap a good harvest under the garb of internationalization of the educational system.

(c) Internationalisation of Higher Education

There are positive benefits accruing from Indian universities entering the international market. It is hoped that it will promote healthy competition among the universities, will encourage exchange of scholars and may promote international good will.

It is, however, necessary that while allowing foreign universities to set up their campuses in India and the vice versa, we should tread with utmost caution. The following steps are necessary in this direction:

(1) Foreign universities should be subject to regulatory mechanism i.e. pre-entry academic audit put in place by the Indian bodies like National Assessment and

Accreditation Council, UGC and other specialized organizations.

(2) The foreign institutions should sign a Memorandum of Understanding with the concerned Ministries in the government of India giving details of their activities in India, their academic infra-structure, fee structure, level of minimum investment etc.

(3) The entry of foreign universities should be on the basis of reciprocity i.e. they should allow Indian universities to set up their campuses in their countries.

(d) Private Participation in Higher Education

The raison-d'etre of this study is, among others, to find out the nature and extent of private contribution in higher education and to suggest measures for encouraging larger partnership of private bodies in higher education without diluting the autonomy of universities and ensuring equity and excellence in the system. An effort has been made to examine the multi-dimensional aspects of private participation including complete privatization of this sector. The policy guidelines emerging out of the analysis are:

(1) Complete privatization, as a policy of future development of higher education, has to be categorically ruled out. Total withdrawal of the state from financing and management of higher education will jeopardize the long term interests of higher education. Complete privatization would accentuate inequities with poor but meritorious students getting little chance of entry into private institutions. It may also lead to commercialization and profit making on the part of private bodies. It is likely to have adverse effect on quality control and accreditation. University system is conceived as a social commitment and a catalyst for accelerating the process of human development. The government should not shy sway from facilitating the achievement of the important task of nation building that the universities have taken upon themselves.

(2) Instead of complete privatization, private participation in the financing and management of higher education should be encouraged. It will bring about efficiency in the system and make it more effective and relevant. It is expected to promote excellence. It will also enable the universities to come out of the stifling confines of academic exclusiveness and become a part of the wider social milieu.

(3) There will be need to bring about changes in the Acts and statutes of universities to enable representatives of industries and trade and other concerned groups to be on the academic and management systems of universities.

(4) Market need should be kept in view while developing the curriculum. The element of productivity orientation should guide the formulation of curriculum framework.

(5) Even when private bodies are encouraged to participate in higher education, student admissions should be solely based on merit. The peculiar needs of the sponsors should, however, be kept in view.

((6) Fee structure should be laid down, without encouraging commercialization and profit making.

(7) Recruitment of staff should be left entirely to university institutions.

(8) Private bodies should contribute substantial amounts for the maintenance and development of university institutions at least to the extent of about 20 per cent of the recurring expenditure. Student fee contribution should be pegged between 20 to 30 per cent. The balance should come from government sources.

(9) A private university Act should be brought on the statute book. This will enable private bodies to set up university institutions under strict government control.

(e) Self Financing Courses

It has been suggested that short of privatization of higher education, it may be advisable to start self financing course. These courses would be market driven, which may help the students to enter into gainful employment. Some of the courses could be in professional subjects like Medicine, Engineering, Business Administration, Bio-Technology etc.

It is, however, feared that undue stress on self financing courses may lead to the possible neglect of courses like Social Sciences and Humanities, Languages, particularly classical languages, Fine Arts, Creative and Performing Arts, History, Philosophy, Anthropology, Archaeology etc. It is, therefore, suggested that effective steps should be taken to prevent the neglect of courses, which may not be job oriented, but which are essential for the social, cultural and moral development of the society. In order to promote these courses, a scheme should be introduced under which special assistance/incentives may be provided for the courses, which are likely to be relegated to the background.

(f) Industry-University Relationship

Industry has a vital stake in higher education. It is not only because of the fact that the institutions of higher education provide trained manpower for jobs in the industry, but also because they, through research and development, open up new vistas of scientific and technological development. It is, therefore, essential that there should be a closer relationship between industry and universities. This relationship could be of the following type:

(1) Industry should be involved in curriculum development particularly in courses, which have integral relationship with industrial processes. In fact, the universities should identify the specific needs of the industry and draw up their curriculum taking that into account.

(2) Industry should also be represented on the decision making bodies of the universities.

(3) Industry should provide faculty support in subject areas, where industry has expertise.

(4) While student admissions should be the sole prerogative of the universities, industry may be consulted about the type of students that would be admitted specially to professional courses.

(5) Industry may provide fellowships and scholarships to meritorious but economically weaker sections of students. They should also finance the establishment of chairs in various disciplines.

(6) Industry should provide financial and material support to universities for Research and Development Programmes. They should also provide facilities for supervised 'Hands on Training' to the university students particularly those pursuing professional courses.

(g) Corporatisation of Higher Education

Corporatisation of higher education is gradually entering into the university system. In quite a few countries, corporate universities have been established. Corporatisation has its advantages like greater operational freedom, availability of professional management, provision of adequate funding of universities etc. Among the disadvantages, mention may be made of the grim possibility of commercialization of higher education, the domination of elitist groups in university admissions, the loss of moral values on which the university system should be based.

On balance, the disadvantages far outweigh the advantages of passing on the university system to corporate sector and hence it is not recommended for introduction in the foreseeable future.

(h) Marketisation of Higher Education

In view of the fact that most of the university courses, particularly, in Humanities and Social Sciences are theoretical and do not enable students to enter professional jobs, it is necessary to give market orientation to university courses. It is expected that this modification will make education more relevant to the needs of society and will enable students to enter employment by developing micro-specialised human resources.

In order to provide market-oriented courses, the curriculum should be relevant, need based and skill orientated. It should be modified in consultation with industry. It should be flexible and should be updated periodically to meet the changing requirements of the economy. For specialized courses, guest faculty may be invited from the industry. Even the regular academic staff should have industry exposure. Patents and copyrights should be shared between sponsors, university and researchers. Industry should also support basic research and short term market-oriented studies. For this purpose, there is need for a wider interaction between the industry and teaching community in research and development.

Appendix -I

SCH/QUEST/I/

Partnership of Private Sector in Financing and Management of Indian Higher Education – An In-depth Study

Information Schedule for Universities

BASIC DATA

1. Name of the University/ Institution: : ______________________

2. Address : ______________________
____
____

Tel. No.: ______________________

Fax. No.: ______________________

E-mail: ______________________

3. Year of Establishment

4. Whether Residential/Affiliating

5. Courses Available

	Regular	**Distance**
(a) Academic		
(b) Professional		

6. Enrolment

2001-2002								
Enrolment	*UG*		*PG*		*Research*		*Total*	
	Regular	Distance	Regular	Distance	Regular	Distance	Regular	Distance
(a) Academic								
(b) Professional								

7. Staff **No.**

(a) Academic

1. Professors
2. Readers
3. Lecturers
4. Others (please specify)

(b) Administrative

(i) Non Teaching Staff
(ii) Karmacharis

FINANCIAL DATA

8. Income

Income from	*Years* 1996-97	2001-02	*Remarks*
	(Rs. in ooo)		
1. Government Grants:			
a. Central Govt.			
b. U.G.C			
c. All India Council for Technical Education			
d. Other Central Govt. Agencies			
e. State Govt.			
f. Local Bodies			
2. Tuition Fees			
3. Examination Fees			
4. Hostel Rent			
5. Other Fees (Please specify)			
6. Consultancy Services			
7. Endowments/Donations from:			
(a) Trust/Management]			
(b) General Public			
(c) Industries			
(d) Corporate Houses			
(e) Others (Please specify)			
8. Sale of Publications			
9. Project Grants:			
(a) Govt. Deptt. sources			
(b) Non Govt. sources			
10. Fellowships			
11. Others (Please specify)			
Total			

9. Expenditure

Expenditure	Years 1996-97	Years 2001-02	Remarks
(a) Recurring	**(Rs. in ooo)**		
1. Salaries of:			
(a) Teaching Staff			
(b) Administrative Staff			
(c) Others			
2. Staff Development (Training and Seminars)			
3. Conduct of Examinations			
4. Libraries (Books and Journals)			
5. Laboratories and workshops (Consumables)			
6. Computers (Software, Maintenance)			
7. Hostel			
8. Stipends, Fellowships / Fee Concessions			
9. Student support / welfare services			
10. Maintenance of Buildings (including Hostels and others)			
11. Electricity charges			
12. Telephone/Fax etc.			
13. Others			
Total (Recurring)			
(b) Non-Recurring			
1. Buildings (including class-rooms, laboratories , workshops etc)			
2. Furniture (including class-room furnitures)			
3. Library (including equipments			

, Almirah, cupboards etc.)
4. Laboratories (including equipments)
5. Others

Total (Non Recurring)
Grand Total (a+b)

10. Has any effort been made to mobilise resources from Industries/Commercial Enterprises/ Community etc.

Yes/No

11. If yes, please indicate the amounts that have been collected in the following years.

Mobilisation of Resources from	*Years*		*Remarks*
	1996-97	*2000-01*	
	(Rs. in ooo)		
1. Industries / Commercial Enterprises (a) Public (b) Private			
2. Financial Institutions			
3. Alumnis/NRIs			
4. Others (Please specify)			
Total			

12. Has the University taken recourse to overdraft/loan from the Banks during the last five years? If so, please give details below:

Sl. No.	*Year*	*Amount of over draft/ loan*	*Bank(s) from which over draft/ loan was taken*	*Remarks*
1.				
2.				
3.				
4.				
5.				
Total				

Appendix-II

SCH/QUEST/II/

Partnership of Private Sector in Financing and Management of Indian Higher Education – An In-depth Study

Interview Schedule/Opinionnarire for Educationists/ Educational Administrators/Policy Planners

1. Name of the Respondent: ____________________

2. Name of the University/ Institution to which attached (if any) : ____________________

3. Address : ____________________

Tel. No.: ____________________

Fax. No.: ____________________

E-mail: ____________________

(A) Privatization of Higher Education

4. Under the new Economic Policy, emphasis has been laid on privatization and liberalisation. In this context, please give your considered views about the need for privatising of higher education.

____

____

____

5. Will privatisation of higher education bring about improvement in:
   - (a) efficiency of the system Yes/No
   - (b) effectiveness of education Yes/No
   - (c) excellence in higher education Yes/No
   - (d) ensuring access to meritorious but economically weaker students Yes/No
   - (e) relevance of education Yes/No
   - (f) any other (please specify) ______________________________

____

(A1) The Policy and Legal framework

6. How should the existing legal framework be modified to promote private sector's active participation in higher education?

____

____

____

(A2) Nature and Level of Private Participation

7. What should be the form of private participation in

(a) Management:

____

____

____

(b) Curriculum development:

____

(c) Admission of students:

(d) Determining fee structure:

(e) Recruitment of staff:

(f) Students evaluation:

(g) Any others (please specify):

8. In the event of privatization of higher education, what should be the proportionate contribution from various sources:

Heads	*Percent of Recurring expenses to be met from*	*Remarks*
1. Student fees		
2. Contribution from industry		
3. Contribution from Trusts and Endowments		
4. Community		
5. Others (please specify)		

(B) Industry/ University Relationship

9. Do you think that industrial establishments should participate in financing and management of higher education? Yes/No

10. If yes, what kind of partnership should be established between universities and industrial houses, particularly in regard to:

    (a) Curriculum development: ____________________

    ____

    (b) Providing faculty support (such as guest faculty):

    ____

    (c) Student Admissions: ____________________

    ____

    (d) Management: ____________________

    ____

    (e) Evaluation of students' performance: ____________________

    ____

    (f) Sponsorships/ Fellowships: ____________________

    ____

    (g) Research and Development:

    ____

    ____

(C) Corporatisation

11. Do you subscribe to the view that higher education should be corporatised in the sense that it should be set up as a private limited body Yes/No

12. If yes, enumerate the advantages and disadvantages:

Advantages	*Disadvantage*
1.	1.
2.	2.
3.	3.
4.	4.
5.	5.

13. What should be the modalities of corporatisation of higher education

____

____

____

14. Should the Government enact a Private Universities Bill for giving legislative validity to privatisation/corporatisation of higher education? Yes/No

15. Do you agree that university should be regarded as 'infrastructural' service (such as ports, telecom, highways etc.)? Yes/No

(D) Marketisation of Higher Education

16. It has been proposed that Indian higher education system should be market oriented. In the light of the above suggestion, please mention below the advantages and disadvantages of the proposal.

Advantages	*Disadvantage*
1.	1.
2.	2.
3.	3.
4.	4.
5.	5.
6.	6.

17. How should higher education respond to the demands of market forces particularly in regard to:

    1. Courses / curriculum :
    2. Staff appointments :
    3. Procedure for student admissions :
    4. Research and Development :
    5. Any other (please specify) :

    ____

18. Do you agree with the view that in the case of marketisation of higher education, certain disciplines will be relegated to the background? Yes/No

19. If yes, please mention those disciplines:

    (a) ______________________________

    (b) ______________________________

    (c) ______________________________

    (d) ______________________________

20. In your views what should be done to prevent this?

    ____

    ____

    ____

(E) Self Financing Courses

21. Do you agree that some courses of studies should be self-financing/self supporting Yes/No

22. If yes, which of the courses should be self-financing/self supporting:

Courses
(i)
(ii)
(iii)
(iv)
(v)

(F) Internationalisation of Higher Education

23. Under the policy of liberalisation and globalisation, a number of foreign universities have started admitting Indian students. Please give your considered views whether Foreign Universities should be:
    (a) allowed to function in India Yes/No
    (b) allowed to function but under strict Government Control Yes/No

24. What kind of regulatory mechanism should be created to ensure that only genuine foreign universities are allowed to operate in India?

____

____

____

____

25. Should these foreign universities also conform to accreditation norms laid down by the National Assessment and Accreditation Council (NAAC)? Yes/No

26. Please mention the steps that should be taken to introduce an element of reciprocity in the university system particularly in regards to Indian universities setting up their campuses in foreign countries.

(i) ____________________

(ii) ____________________

(iii) ____________________

(iv) ____________________

27. Please give below any other view(s)/suggestion(s) with regard to:

(a) Private participation in higher education

____

____

____

(b) Market oriented education

____

____

____

(c) Internationalization of higher education

____

____

____

Appendix-III

SCH/QUEST/III/

Partnership of Private Sector in Financing and Management of Indian Higher Education – An In-depth Study

Interview Schedule/Opinionnarire for Industries/ Business Houses

1. Name of the Respondent and his designation : ____________________

2. Name of the Industry/ Business House to which he belongs : ____________________

3. Address : ____________________
____
____

Tel. No.: ____________________

Fax. No.: ____________________

E-mail: ____________________

(A) Privatization of Higher Education

4. Under the new Economic Policy, emphasis has been laid on privatization and liberalisation. In this context, please give your considered views about the need for privatisation of higher education.

____

____

____

5. Will privatisation of higher education bring about improvement in:

(a) efficiency of the system Yes/No

(b) effectiveness of education Yes/No

(c) excellence in higher education Yes/No

(d) ensuring access to meritorious but economically weaker students Yes/No

(e) relevance of education Yes/No

(f) any other (please specify)

____

____

(A1) The Policy and Legal framework

6. How should the existing legal framework be modified to promote private sector's active participation in higher education?

____

____

____

(A2) Nature and Level of Private Participation

7. What should be the form of private participation in:

(a) Management:

(b) Curriculum development:

(c) Admission of students:

(d) Determining fee structure:

(e) Recruitment of staff:

(f) Students evaluation:

(g) Any others (please specify):

8. In the event of privatization of higher education, what should be the proportionate contribution from various sources:

Heads	*Percent of Recurring expenses to be met from*	*Remarks*
1. Student fees		
2. Contribution from industry		
3. Contribution from Trust and Endowments		
4. Community		
5. Others (please specify)		

(B) Industry/ University Relationship

9. What kind of partnership should be established between universities and industrial houses, particularly in regard to:

(a) Providing financial assistance: ____________________

____

(b) Curriculum development : ____________________

____

(c) Providing faculty support (such as guest faculty):

____

(d) Student Admissions : ____________________

____

(e) Management: ____________________

____

(f) Evaluation of students' performance :

____

(g) Sponsorships/
Fellowship:________________________________

____

(h) Research and Development:

____

____

10. In the last five years, have you extended support to any university/educational Institution Yes/No

11. If yes, please give details:

Year(s)	*University/ Educational Institution*	*Departments/ Courses*	*Amount of Funding*

(C) Corporatisation

12. Do you subscribe to the view that higher education should be corporatised in the sense that if should be set up as a private limited body? Yes/No

13. If yes, enumarate the advantages and disadvantages.

Advantages	*Disadvantage*
1.	1.
2.	2.
3.	3.
4.	4.
5.	5.
6.	6.

14. What should be the modalities of corporatisation of higher education?

____

____

____

____

____

15. Should the Government enact a Private Universities Bill for giving legislative validity to privatisation/corporatisation of higher education? Yes/No

16. Do you agree that university should be regarded as 'infrastructural' service? (such as ports, telecom, highways etc.)? Yes/No

(D) Marketisation of Higher Education

17. It has been proposed that Indian higher education system should be market oriented. In the light of the above suggestion, please mention below the advantages and disadvantages of the proposal:

Advantages	*Disadvantage*
1.	1.
2.	2.
3.	3.
4.	4.
5.	5.
6.	6.

18. How should higher education respond to the demands of market forces particularly in regard to:

    (a) Courses / curriculum : ______________

    (b) Staff appointments : ______________

    (c) Procedure for student admissions : ______________

    (d) Research and Development : ______________

    (e) Any other (please specify) : ______________

19. Has your concern discussed with the neighboring university(ies) about its role in meeting the demand of technical manpower? Yes/No

20. If, yes what was the outcome of this discussion.

    ____

    ____

    ____

21. Do you agree with the view that in the case of marketisation of higher education, certain disciplines, will be relegated to the background? Yes/No

22. If yes, please mention those disciplines:
    (a) ______
    (b) ______
    (c) ______
    (d) ______
    (e) ______

23. In your view, what should be done to prevent this eventuality?
    ______
    ______
    ______

(E) Self Financing Courses

24. Do you agree that some courses of studies should be self-financing/self supporting? Yes/No

25. If yes, which of the courses should be self-financing/self supporting:

Courses

(i)
(ii)
(iii)
(iv)
(v)

(F) Internationalisation of Higher Education

26. Under the policy of liberalisation and globalisation, a number of foreign universities have started admitting Indian

students. Please give your considered views whether foreign universities should be:

(a) allowed to function in India Yes/No

(b) allowed to function but under strict Government Control Yes/No

27. What kind of regulatory mechanism should be created to ensure that only genuine foreign universities are allowed to operate in India?

____

____

____

28. Should these foreign universities also conform to accreditation norms laid down by the National Assessment and Accreditation Council (NAAC)? Yes/No

29. Please mention the steps that should be taken to introduce an element of reciprocity in the university system particularly in regards to Indian universities setting up their campuses in foreign countries.

(i) ______________________________

(ii) ______________________________

(iii) ______________________________

(iv) ______________________________

30. Please give below any other view(s)/suggestion(s) with regard:

(a) Private participation in higher education

____

____

(b) Market oriented education

____

____

(c) Internationalization of higher education

Bibliography

Books

- Altabach, Philip G (Ed.), 1999, Private Prometheus: Private Higher Education and Development in the 21st Century; Centre for International Higher Education Massachusetts U.S.A.
- Altabach, Philip G, Engberg D, 2000, Higher Education: A Worldwide Inventory of Centres and Programmes, Massachusetts U.S.A.
- Ambani, M. and K. Birla (2001), Report on a Policy Framework for Reforms in Education, Government of India, New Delhi.
- Ansari, M.M. (1997). Cost Effectiveness of Higher Education, Concept.
- Azad JL, 1986, Government Support for Higher Education and Research, Concept Publishing Company. Higher Education in India – The Deepening Financial Crisis, Radiant Publishers, 1993.
    - State Grants: Patterns Procedures and Policies in Higher Education, The Institutional Context. (ed. Amrik Singh and GD Sharma) Konark, New Delhi (1989).
    - Criteria Based Funding of Higher Education, Journal of Educational Planning and Administration, 13 (4), 1999.

- Azad, J.L. (1975), Report of the Study of the Patterns, Procedures and Policies of Financing of Higher Education in India, Planning Commission, (mimeo),
- Bikas C. Sanyal, 1995, Innovations in University Management; UNESCO, IIEP, Paris.
- Bray, Mark,1998, Financing Higher Education in Asia: Patterns, Trends and Policies, International Higher Education.
- Carnoy, Martin, 1999, Globalsation and Educational Reforms: What Planners need to know; UNESCO, IIEP, Paris.
- Clark B.R, Neave G, 1992, The Encyclopaedia of Higher Education, England.
- Das S.K.1986, The Educational System of the Ancient Hindus, Gyan Publishing House, Delhi.
- Delanty G, Challenging Knowledge: 2001, The University in the Knowledge Society, SRHE and Open University Press, Buckingham.
- Dhar TN and Azad JL: 1996, Financing of Institutions of Higher Education: An analytical Study of Financing of Central Universities and Deemed to be Universities U.G.C. (Mimeo)
- Douglas A., Adrian Z., 2000: Financing Universities in Developing Countries, The World Bank.
- Five Year Plans: New Delhi, Planning Commission, Government of India
- Garg VP; 1996, *Financing Higher Education: Scope and its Limits*, Radha Publications, New Delhi.
- Hallak, Jacques: 1999, Globalisation, Human Rights and Education, UNESCO, 11E.P. Paris.
- Hirsch WZ, et. al. (Ed.)1999, Challenges Facing Higher Education at the Millennium, IAV Press.
- Huisman J, et. al., 2001, Higher Education and the Nation State; Pergamon, Amsterdam.
- Jamil S. and Adrian M. Verspoor (ed) 1994, Revitalising Higher Education, Pergamon.

- Kaul JN (ed.) 1975, Higher Education: Social, Choice and National Development, Indian Institute of Advanced Study, Shimla.
- Kolhatkar MR,1997, Educational Planning & National Development: Some Crucial Aspects, M.D. Publications, New Delhi.
- Lewin, K. and F. Caillods (2001), *Financing Secondary Education in Developing Countries: Strategies for Sustainable Growth*, UNESCO, International Institute for Educational Planning, France.
- Losco J and Fife B.L, 2000, Higher Education in Transition, Bergin and Garvey, Westport.
- McMullen M.S, et. al. (Ed) 2000, The Emerging Markets and Higher Education, Development and Sustainability; Routledge Falmer, New York.
- Narula, Manju, 2000, Effective Teaching in Higher Education, Commonwealth Publishers, New Delhi.
- NCERT (1999), *Sixth All India Educational Survey*, NCERT, New Delhi
- NSSO (1998), *Attending an Educational Institution in India: Its Level, Nature and Cost*, NSS 52nd Round, July 1995-June 1996, Government of India.
- Powar K.B. (Ed.) 2000, Internationalisation of Indian Higher Education, Association of Indian Universities, New Delhi.
- Radford J, et. al.,1997, Quantity and Quality in Higher Education, Hessica Kingsley, London.
- Rani, Geetha. P. (2002), Financing Higher Education in India during the Post Reform Period: Focus on Access and Equity, *NIEPA Occasional Paper*, No.31, NIEPA, New Delhi, September 2002.
- Reddy K.V., 1990, New Directions in Higher Education in India, Creative Books, New Delhi.
- Singh, Amrik, Philip Altbach (ed.) (1974). The Higher Learning in India, Vikas, New Delhi.
- Srivastava, D.K. and Tapas, K. Sen (1997), *Government Subsidies in India*, National Institute of Public Finance and Policy, New Delhi.

- Sulochana M. (1991). Financial Management of higher Education in India, Chugh.
- Sulochana M,1991, Financial Management of Higher Education in India, Chuglr Publications, Allahabad.
- Tilak JBG, Journal of Higher Education, Vol. 16 (2), 1993.
- Tilak JBG and Geetha Rani, University Finances in India: A Profile, NIEPA, 2000.
- Tilak, J.B.G. (1989), Education and its Relation to Economic Growth, Poverty and Income Distribution: Past Evidence and Further Analysis, World Bank Discussion Paper No.3, World Bank, Washington, D.C.
- Tilak, J.B.G. (1997), *Lessons from Cost Recovery in Education, in Marketising Education and Health in Developing Countries: Miracle or Mirage?* (ed). C. Colclough), Oxford: Clarendon Press.
- Tilak, J.B.G. (2001b), *Building Human Capital: What Others Can Learn*, World Bank Institute Working Paper, World Bank, Washington, D.C.
- Tilak, J.B.G. and G. Rani (2000), University Finances in India: A Profile, National Institute of Educational Planning and Administration, *Mimeo*, New Delhi.
- Tilak, J.B.G. and N.V. Varghese (1985), *Discriminatory Pricing in Education*, NIEPA Occasional Paper No.8, NIEPA, New Delhi.
- Uberoi NK, 1995, Some Current Developments in India's Higher Education, International Higher Education, U.G.C., New Delhi.
- UGC (1993), *UGC Funding of Institutions of Higher Education, Report of Justice Dr. K. Punnayya Committee*, 1992-93, University Grants Commission, New Delhi.
- UGC (1996-97, 1997-98), *Annual Reports*, University Grants Commission, New Delhi.
- UGC (1997), *Report of the Pylee Committee on the Recommendations of the Punnayya Committee Relating to Unit Cost of Higher Education and Other Issues*, University Grants Commission, New Delhi.

- UGC (1999), *Report of the Expert Committee Appointed by the University Grants Commission to Review the Maintenance Grants Norms for Delhi Colleges,* University Grants Commission, New Delhi.
- UGC (2000), *Report of the Committee Constituted by UGC for 'Formulation of Revised Fee Structure in the Central and Deemed to be Universities in India',* University Grants Commission, New Delhi.
- *UNESCO (1998), Higher education in the Twenty-first Century: Vision and Action, Final Report, World Conference on Higher Education, UNESCO, Paris.*
- UNESCO, 1996, Learning: The Treasure Within; International Commission on Education for the Twenty first Century.
- UNESCO, Statistical Year Book, 1999; 2000.
- World Bank, 1994, Higher Education: The lessons from Experience, Washington DC.
- Woodhall, M. (1991), *Student Loans in Higher Education: No.2, Asia,* International Institute of Educational Planning, Paris.
- World Bank (1994), *Higher Education: Lessons from Experience,* Washington, D.C.
- World Bank Country Study (1999), India, Reducing Poverty, Accelerating Development, Oxford.

Journals

- Levy, Deniel C, Problems of Privatisation in Higher Education, Journal of Educational Planning and Administration. Vol. VII (3), 1933, NIEPA.
- Marks C, Paying for Education: Leave Higher Learning to the Market and Primary Education to the State, *India Today*(1997).
- Philip G. Altbach:
- Higher Education and the WTO, University News, September, 2001.
- The Crisis in Multinational Higher Education, University News, November, Vol. 38 No. 45, 2000

- The Rise of the Pseudo Universities; International Higher Education, The Boston College for International Higher Education, No. 25, Fall, 2001.
- Raghunathan V, Financing Education; Capital Talk, The Economic Times online, February, 29, 2001.
- Robin Middlehurst: Challenge to Universities from Borderless Education; Minerva, Vol. XXXIX, No. 1, Netherlands, 2001.

Reports

- AICTE, Report of the High Powered Committee for Mobilization of Additional Resources for Technical Education, New Delhi (1994).
- Nigvekar Arun: GATS and Higher Education, University Grants Commission, 2001 (Mimeo).
- Challenge of Education; Ministry of Education, 1985.
- Financing Education: Issues and Options, Seminar and Conference on Private Initiative in Indian Higher Education, 2001.
- Higher Education in Developing Countries, Peril and Promise. Report of the Task Force; The World Bank, 2000.
- Human Development in South Asia, 1999-2000 Oxford University Press, 2000
- Human Development Report, 1999/2000 UNDP, Oxford University Press; 2000.
- Iyengar, P.K.: Information Innovation and Development for a Knowledge Society; Paper Submitted to a Workshop on Knowledge Based Society, convened by the Planning Commission, 2000 (Mimeo).
- National Policy on Education, 1986/ 1992, Government of India, Ministry of HRD, 1992.
- Report of the Education Commission 1964-66, Ministry of Education, 1966.
- University Grants Commission, New Delhi, Annual Reports for various years.

- University Grants Commission, UGC Funding of Institutions of Higher Education, Report of Justice K. Punnayya Committee, 1992-93.
- Sharma GD, AIU-ICSSR, National Seminar on University and College Finance, New Delhi, (1978).
- Internationalization of Higher Education; Status and Policy Suggestions, NIEPA.
- Trade in Education Service; An Indian Response, NIEPA, New Delhi, 2001 (Mimeo)
- Singh Amrik, The Fallacy of More Funds, in Profile of Indian Education, Parle, Tilak Vidyalaya, Golden Jubilee Committee, Bombay (1971).

Index